The financial services sourcebook

A guide to sources of information on banking, insurance and other financial services

By **Robert Cunnew**

BA FLA; Librarian, Chartered Insurance Institute

with **Alison Scammell**

BA, MA

Published by Aslib-IMI

ISBN 0 85142 448 1

Information Management International (IMI) is a trading name of Aslib.

Aslib-IMI provides consultancy and information services, professional development training, conferences, specialist recruitment, Internet products, publishes journals (in hard copy and electronic formats), books and directories and provides outsourcing revises to the information community.

Aslib-IMI, founded in 1924, is a world class corporate membership organisation with over 2000 members in some 70 countries. Aslib actively promotes best practice in the management of information resources. It lobbies on all aspects of the management of, and legislation concerning, information at local, national and international levels.

Further information is available from:

Aslib-IMI
Staple Hall
Stone House Court
London EC3A 7PB
Tel: +44 (0) 20 7903 0000
Fax: +44 (0) 20 7903 0011
Email: *aslib@aslib.com*
WWW: *http://www.aslib.com*

Printed by Bell & Bain Ltd., Glasgow

Contents

Contents in depth

Acknowledgements

Many thanks to the Chartered Insurance Institute for providing access to most of the resources described in chapters 1, 3, 4 and 5; to the library staff at the Chartered Institute of Bankers and the City Business Library; and to Howard Picton and his colleagues at the Bank of England Library and Simon Rex and Charles Knight at the Library of the Building Societies Association/Council of Mortgage Lenders.

Introduction

Why this book?

This book is an attempt to map the area where two of the more significant legacies of the 20th century combine. The second industrial revolution ushered in the service economy, in which people sat around producing nothing at all – or at least nothing that you could eat, or keep warm in – and the most abstract service of all was the financial services industry, the whole basis of which was an abstraction called money. As the service economy developed it became clear that a second abstraction – information, or knowledge – was the fuel on which it ran, and this led to the idea of the knowledge economy.

There have been notable attempts to provide financial services without information. There is the Lloyd's underwriter who ignored newspaper articles about the newly discovered perils of a substance called asbestos. There is the nurse who unwittingly transferred her occupational scheme to a new product called a personal pension. There is the product supplier that had to recall its entire sales force because they were inadequately trained. The case for more, and better, information has surely been proved – and a large number of information suppliers have waded in to meet this need. But naturally they have done so in an uncoordinated way: they have dabbled in a wide array of different media, and like all product suppliers they would prefer to dazzle than inform their customers about their wares. Hence the need for a map – a guide for all who need published information about financial services, whether product providers, intermediaries, consumers, students, researchers or information specialists, and regardless of the form that information might take.

Defining financial services

But what is this thing we call financial services? Is it the same as finance? Or is it any service that is financial? And if so, is the Royal Mint a financial service? Or the National Lottery? And what about taxation?

There are two common definitions of the term in use, a broader and a narrower one. The broader definition concerns itself with all industries whose main function is to provide a service that is essentially financial in nature. It thus includes as mainstays banking and insurance. It also includes institutions and products that exist either to lend you money (for instance mortgages) or to take your money and make it grow (for instance unit trusts). Insofar as pensions are provided by insurance companies and comparable institutions this is also a financial service. It is questionable whether a wholly self-administered pension scheme run by your employer can be described as part of the financial services industry, but for convenience pensions as a whole tends to be included within this broader definition. The National Lottery, the pools and your local church raffle are services and they are financial, but by established usage they are not financial services. Similarly, schemes run solely by the state, like the national 'insurance' system, tend to be excluded.

All of these areas are *retail* financial services: products that are sold directly to the consumer (whether personal or corporate). Their wholesale equivalents are the financial or capital markets: stock exchanges, money markets, commodity markets and so on. These markets do not sell directly to the consumer, who must approach a financial institution like a bank in order to access them. But they remain financial services in the broader sense.

This leaves a large, fuzzy area called 'finance' and including – as well as all the areas already considered – possible candidates for inclusion such as taxation, international finance, and the entire contents of the *Financial Times*. These areas do not form part of financial services, although they may *include* financial services. Note that the Financial Times group has a section called FT Finance, which implies the other sections do something else.

The narrower definition of financial services is difficult to pin down. If you go into a high street bank you may see a notice that says 'Financial Services'. At this counter you can buy stocks and shares and arrange insurance on your house. So everything else the bank does – its traditional, core business – is something else. But ask an insurance broker about financial services and you will be told about investment and banking. The broker's core business is something else. Another variant of this narrow definition of financial services dates from the Financial Services Act 1986. As is common with legislation, this act deals with a much smaller area than its title suggests. Apart from one or two minor measures thrown in to the act because it happened to be passing through Parliament at the right time, it concerns itself almost entirely with 'investment business', and to many people financial services now means just that. This act led to the 'polarisation' of investment advice and the 'independent financial adviser', and perhaps by extension the most popular form of this narrower definition of financial services describes the concerns of the IFA: retail investment business (including life assurance and personal pensions), mortgage broking and other forms of lending – as well as tax and general financial planning.

For the purposes of this book we have steered a middle course between the broad and the narrow definitions, taking all included in the broader with the exception of the wholesale financial markets. These would require another book the size of this one. Background areas like taxation are only covered where they apply expressly to financial services, such as the taxation of insurance policies, or where a source is clearly targeted at the financial services industry. Thus a newsletter ostensibly on space insurance may concentrate on news of satellite launches and so on, with little reference to insurance cover. But if it is called *Space Insurance Weekly* then it's in.

Selection and organisation

It would be unhelpful to list everything published on financial services and the following principles have been followed in selecting entries:

1. Sources must be reasonably substantial, both physically and with respect to content.

2. Sources must not be too narrow in their subject focus. You will find works on pensions and works on personal pensions, but you will not find works dealing exclusively with the taxation of small self-administered pensions for expatriate directors. However, prolific sources of such works are highlighted where appropriate.

3. Sources describing conditions or practice peculiar to a particular region outside the United Kingdom are not generally included – but this doesn't mean that a US work on investment will necessarily be excluded and certainly doesn't exclude works that are international in coverage, many of which adopt a useful country by country approach.

4. Sources published in the UK are preferred to those that are not, but this is not a blanket exclusion.

5. Currency is vital and works are not included for their historical interest. There can be no single cut-off date as currency is affected differently by developments in a particular area, for instance legislation.

6. Works of transitory interest are not generally accorded separate entries and priority has been given to serial publications and to monographs regularly published in new editions. Thus individual market research reports – important as they may be – tend to have a limited shelf life and the entries under 'Market research' are mostly

restricted to publications in serial form. Introductory notes will indicate the most important producers of reports etc, with examples of their recent output.

7. Sources should be generally available: they shouldn't be out of print (but may become so!) or available only to members of a certain organisation or to clients of a particular firm. But if a source is important enough it might be worth joining an organisation to get it, and if membership is fairly open such sources may be included.

The breakdown into chapters follows established practice rather than any theoretical agenda. A chapter addressing the most general sources is followed by chapters on the two biggest services: banking and insurance. A short chapter covers certain investment products like unit trusts, which fall into neither of the previous two chapters; a further chapter covers a particular application for investment products – pensions. You will find contact details for publishers in a separate chapter at the end, together with a chapter on libraries and indexes by subject, form, author and title.

Within each chapter the sections represent the principal divisions of the subject, although some standard headings – such as law and management – appear in most chapters. Each section is divided into standard subsections according to type of source, for instance periodicals and web sites.

Classification is a crude and dangerous tool and there will be overlaps between chapters, sections and subsections. As a general rule, where more than one section or subsection is appropriate to an item the one appearing later is preferred. Thus you will find company research in the subsection 'Company research' but these will be printed sources and you may also find company research in the later subsections 'CD-ROMs', 'Web sites' and so on. It is hoped that the arrangement followed will facilitate browsing, but a work such as this is necessarily one-dimensional and use of the indexes will be essential if you are to see the subject in 3D.

Wherever possible entries are based on the latest information available, but – as publishing seemingly defies the current trend towards a low-inflation economy – prices in particular are subject to change and the figures given here should be regarded as indicative only. In general prices are given only where this information is readily available and reasonably straightforward. Where several prices apply to a particular item – UK or overseas, with or without a discount, and so on – we have generally given the undiscounted price for delivery within the United Kingdom.

This book is aimed at subject experts with little knowledge of information sources, at information specialists with little knowledge of the subject and at those with little knowledge of either. So many readers will find some things explained that they don't need to be told about. Just skip it – we know you know, but others might not.

The sources

The following notes are presented in terms of the standard subsection headings employed throughout the book.

Consumer guides

These are cheap and there is often a choice available, but you will find much consumer information available free of charge on the Web or in the form of factsheets and information packs from trade associations and even regulators.

Textbooks

This term is used in a broad sense to refer to any comprehensive book on a subject intended for study, but not necessarily a student work. However, many of the coursebooks produced by professional associations and other bodies can be useful as general works of reference, particularly if they are regularly updated.

Manuals

This term is used to refer to looseleaf and similar works of reference. The looseleaf is the most unwieldy and in many ways unsatisfactory form of print and there is a marked trend to issue such works additionally on CD-ROM. Before you opt for the looseleaf think about who is going to update it every month or quarter. Inserting looseleaf amendments in ring binders is tedious and time-consuming work, and the CD also offers advantages in quick access – it is faster and more effective than most printed indexes. Of course the publisher will have factored this in to a cost differential, and may even deprive you of the choice by bundling manual and disk into a single package.

Source materials

The primary sources in financial services are chiefly legislation, case law and contract wordings. You will find UK Acts of Parliament from 1996 on the Web at [http://www.hmso.gov.uk/acts.htm] and statutory instruments from 1997 at [http://www.hmso.gov.uk/stat.htm], but the added value of some of the commercially published sources lies in the annotations provided by the publishers, which can save a lot of head-scratching. You are unlikely to find most contract wordings on the Web, but in addition to the compilations listed here you can always approach individual firms for sample contracts, although product providers may be reluctant to make these documents available. It is helpful to know to what extent standard wordings are used for a particular class of product; in some areas of insurance, for example, there is a high degree of uniformity in policy wordings. In such cases you only have to obtain one document, or set of documents. Some summary information on contract wordings will also be found in the standard subsection 'Product research'.

Technical reports

This material is often available free and it can be profitable to get your name on the mailing lists of some of the important suppliers. However, as the material is free there may be no mailing list. Some corporate web sites are worth checking regularly for news of recent publications.

Market research

Market research as defined in this book is aggregate data concerning market conditions generally, without reference to particular companies. It is frequently statistical in nature. The suppliers include government agencies, trade associations and private firms. Depending on which of these sources it comes from market research could be free, modestly priced or with a price tag in three or four figures. If it is the latter you may well find there are discounts for multiple purchases and you may find it fruitful to haggle. In assessing such sources there are several things to look out for. To start with, look for number of pages. Buying market research isn't like buying potatoes but if you are paying £500 or more for a report it makes a difference if what you get is a fat binder containing several hundred pages or a slim pamphlet with double spacing and lots of pictures. Publishers rarely give this information in publicity. Look also for where the research comes from. Is it desk or field research? At one extreme a report could consist entirely of reprocessed data taken from published sources, many of these available free. You may still find such a report worthwhile for the way it brings everything together and summarises it for you, but it is worth knowing that this is what you are getting. At the other extreme a report will consist entirely of original research, based on field or telephone surveys. In such cases you may want to know the size of the sample and – for postal surveys – the size of the response rate.

Company research

This heading relates to in-depth company-by-company studies, usually of a statistical nature. This material can be very expensive and it is worthwhile looking at how comprehensive the data is, where it comes from, what added value is supplied by the publisher and how up to date it is. Regarding comprehensiveness a clear distinction needs to be made between United Kingdom only and international, but if it is international how much of the world does it cover? It is useful to know the actual size of the total company population being addressed, although you need to bear in mind that many listed companies are just brass name plates. The main sources for published company information are the annual shareholder reports and in certain cases (such as UK insurance companies) the fuller official returns required by statute. In some cases the source may be individual interviews or questionnaires but if so then coverage is likely to be patchy. Added value can range from simply saving you the legwork to the addition of commentary, ratings, ratios and other statistical analysis. When looking at currency you need to bear in mind that reporting periods will vary, and the wider the coverage and the more the added value the less up to date a source may be.

Product research

This heading generally relates to product-by-product studies, typically including but not limited to comparative tables. It is useful to know how comprehensive such works are, as much of their value lies in the overview they give of a complete product range. Such sources can supply different kinds of information: product features, contact details, ratings and performance. Product features may include contract wordings and prices as well as comparative tables with rows of Ys and Ns. Ratings tend to be rare outside the pages of *Which?*. There is quite a lot of this kind of information on the Web, although it may not be free. The Financial Services Authority is also taking a close interest in such material, with the suggestion that it may play some part itself in ensuring easy access to product comparisons. It is currently unclear how this will affect the publishing market.

Directories

As with company research it is useful to establish how comprehensive a directory is with regard to its stated area of coverage. Does an entry depend on a questionnaire successfully returned, or (worse) a fee paid to the publisher? Publishers appreciate the need for comprehensiveness and a typical pattern is a basic entry for as many firms as possible, with extra details if a questionnaire was returned and a display advertisement or logo if it was returned with a cheque. And how much information is given for each firm? Is it just name and address or does it include senior executives, class of business, and so on? What kind of indexes are included? One of the commonest uses for directories in financial services is for the building up of mailing lists. Most directories are produced from databases and you can often buy a mailing list in electronic form or on labels direct from the publisher, or they may publish a CD-ROM version with some kind of charging mechanism for downloads. If there is a CD-ROM it may be preferable for other reasons. If you just want to look up the odd company by name a printed volume may be fine (and cheaper) but if you are interested in searching by place or class of business a CD-ROM may have the edge, even if the printed version has appropriate indexes. The CD-ROM may also be published more frequently.

Dictionaries

You need to ask two questions about the kind of specialist dictionary listed in this book. Is it a translating (e.g. French–English, English–French) or a defining (e.g. English–English) dictionary? If the latter does it just define or does it also explain, like an encyclopaedia?

Bibliographies

In addition to the bibliographies listed in this book there is an increasing number of library catalogues available over the Web, the most comprehensive in the United Kingdom being the British Library catalogue, available free at http://blpc.bl.uk. If you can indentify the primary publishers in your area it can also be useful to ask for their catalogues and get on to their mailing lists.

Periodicals

This heading covers a wide range of printed publications, ranging from slim newsletters to glossy magazines and hefty academic journals. Prices cover a similar range. Some magazines are free, or free to certain categories of firm, on completion of a registration card. Some newsletters are free to clients, some can be £800 or more a year. They may or may not be worth this – to you. Increasingly, periodical subscriptions buy you a package, which could include a password for a related web site, an email news service, ad hoc printed supplements or a free enquiry line. Some magazine publishers make all or part of their printed products available free on the Web to all.

Newspapers

The difference between a newspaper and a periodical is a fine one, and most periodicals include some news while most newspapers carry some articles. Those newspapers listed in this book tend to be weeklies of which a major function is to carry recruitment advertising. For this reason you can often get them free. As with periodicals, there may also be free supplements bundled in, and a web site.

CD-ROMs

All of the headings listed above are for printed publications and any of the kinds of information covered could also be available in electronic form, in particular those involving some kind of systematic presentation of data. The electronic format can offer several advantages, in particular compactness, enhanced searching capabilities and the means to produce customised reports and other documents. For textbooks, periodicals and market research it is less satisfactory. Publishers are well aware of the advantages (and the glamour) of the CD-ROM format and tend to price it well above printed equivalents. If you want to network a disk it will become still more expensive. You also need to consider limitations on use imposed by licence agreements (which may, for example, prohibit you from supplying data to clients) or by technical means (which may require you to pay for separate units before you can print or download). If you are not using a PC running Windows 95 or higher you may have to go for the book anyway.

Web sites

It isn't always clear why so much apparently high quality information is available free of charge over the Internet. The answer may be philanthropy, advertising, or foolishness, but it could be that less information is freely available than seems the case at first. What you get may be a taster only, or you may get a free trial after which you need to pay a subscription. Often the drawback is that a site is American and has scant relevance to users outside the United States, or a site may be provided by a particular product supplier and be chiefly geared towards generating sales. However, in terms of the overall range of what is available, much that applies to CD-ROMs also applies here. Even where charged the web site medium often scores over CD-ROMs because it is more up to date and you don't have to carry out any installation. But the web can be slower, and if you have a choice your decision may depend on the quality of your Internet connection.

It can be difficult to assess web sites. They can be deceptive; you cannot quickly flick through them to gain an understanding of what they contain. A surprisingly large number of sites include little or no original content, being made up largely of different kinds of links to other sites. You can start with an attractive looking news page, which on closer examination turns out to consist of links to stories posted elsewhere. Or the news might be syndicated – comprising the same news you can find on several other sites. You can then follow up a promising link to a supposedly comprehensive guide, which turns out to be classified links to external sites. And that imposing archive of apparently original information resources can turn out to consist of more links to pages on other sites. This is not to decry the value of a good web guide, but it is useful to understand exactly what it really is.

Online services

This heading describes database hosting services available by subscription or pay-as-you-go via a remote connection – originally a private, dial-up connection but increasingly via the Internet. Online services can be very expensive and before subscribing it is worth finding out exactly what alternatives are available free over the Net. But if these sources exactly match your requirements a free web site is unlikely to fit the bill.

The publishers

For many years there were a number of small, well-established specialist firms focusing on financial services or a cosy niche within it. In the late 1990s this situation rapidly began to change. Thus in insurance the publishers Lloyd's of London Press – responsible for one of the oldest newspapers in the world, *Lloyd's List* – was sold by the Corporation of Lloyd's in a management buyout and relaunched as LLP, which shortly after this took over the small DYP Group and its stable of insurance and related newsletters, then two or three years later merged with IBC to become the Informa Group, which went on to buy Emap Finance and its range of trade magazines, and many newsletters and other publications from FT Business. Meanwhile the US ratings agency Standard & Poor's took over the tiny UK-based Thesys, which had specialised in the analysis of insurance company returns; S&P's rival Moody's acquired Syndicate Underwriting Research, another small firm specialising in an even smaller niche; and the US insurance giant A M Best took over Financial Intelligence & Research, also dedicated to the analysis of UK insurance returns.

One effect of these movements may be to reduce the range of sources available as new owners close down or merge loss-making or overlapping products. But in a parallel development it is becoming easier and easier to be a publisher. Anyone with a PC and a printer can produce a newsletter; add a free Internet connection and they can also set up their own web site. So as long-established niche firms are swallowed up by a small number of publishing giants new firms spring up overnight, and every firm of solicitors, accountants or management consultants with a serious interest in financial services will be producing its own client newsletters and briefings, some surprisingly good and easy to get hold of. The only clear trend that can be identified is change itself – and lots of it.

Chapter 1

Financial services in general

1.00 General sources

1.00.01 Consumer guides

Be your own financial adviser. Lowe, Jonquil. [New ed]. London: Which?, 1998. 352 p. (Which? consumer guides) £9.99.
Subtitled on the cover 'how to work out your financial standing and take steps to improve it'. Commissioned and researched by the Consumers' Association; distributed by the Penguin Group.

The Daily Telegraph guide to lump sum investment. Walkington, Liz. 11th ed. London: Kogan Page, 1999. x, 318 p. £10.00.
Describes the various possibilities for short and long-term investment of lump sums, including fixed-capital investments, gilts, equities, unit trusts, individual savings accounts, life assurance and pension plans.

Saving and investing: how to achieve financial security and make your money grow. Whitely, John. Oxford: How to Books, 1999. 128 p. £9.99.

The Sunday Times personal finance guide to tax free savings: how to make your money work harder for you. Gilchrist, Christopher. 2nd ed. London: HarperCollins, 1998. 175 p. £12.99.

Which? way to save and invest 2001. London: Consumers' Association, 2000. 416 p. £14.99.
Includes investment in property, national savings, building societies, pensions, shares, unit trusts, insurance, annuities, commodities, wine and diamonds.

Your taxes and savings 2000–2001: a guide for older people. West, Sally. London: Age Concern Books, 2000. 176 p. £5.99.
A straightforward approach to tax-efficient savings for the mature consumer.

1.00.02 Career guides

Getting into financial services. London: CIB Publishing, 1998. 200 p. £7.99.
Practical advice and information for those contemplating a career in banks or other financial institutions.

1.00.03 Textbooks

The financial planning examinations of the **Chartered Insurance Institute** are taken by a majority of UK financial advisers and the supporting textbooks produced by the Institute collectively constitute a useful corpus of technical information whether you are taking the examinations or not. All the books are in looseleaf format, between 250 and 500 pages long and typically updated annually. The titles for the Financial Planning Certificate are *Financial services and their regulation* (FP1), *Protection, savings and investment products* (FP2) and *Identifying and satisfying client needs* (FP3). These are £20 to CII members, £25 to others. The titles for the higher level Advanced Financial Planning Certificate (mostly produced in association with **Taxbriefs**) are *Taxation and trusts* (G10), *Personal investment planning* (G20), *Business financial planning* (G30), *Pensions* (G60), *Investment portfolio management* (G70), *Long-term care, life and health protection* (G80), *Supervision and sales management* (H15) and *Holistic financial planning* (H25). These are £45 each. There are also single textbooks to support the standalone Mortgage Advice Qualification (MAQ) and International Certificate for Financial Advisers (ICFA) and two coursebooks have been published to support CPD (continuing professional development) requirements: *Financial services developments* (FSD1) and *Planning for a flexible retirement: a guide to pension fund withdrawal and other retirement options* (PFW1). These additional titles are £20 or £25 with the exception of the ICFA coursebook, which is only available as part of a complete examination package. Some collections of case studies have also been published (in association with **Taxbriefs**) to support some of the financial planning subjects. **BPP** also publishes textbooks for the Financial Planning Certificate.

An alternative set of qualifications for financial advisers is offered by the **Chartered Institute of Bankers**. The textbooks for the advanced Professional Investment Certificate are useful as general guides to the subject; they are *Business investment planning and advice, Offshore investment planning, Operating in a regulated environment, Pensions* and *Personal investment planning*. Some of the textbooks for the Certificate in Financial Services Practice (for counter and customer contact staff) and Diploma in Financial Services Management are also useful as general guides; these include *Personal financial literacy, Business financial literacy* and *The financial services environment*. The textbooks for the CIB associateship naturally focus on banking but include the more general titles *The monetary and financial system* and *Financial services*. Most of these textbooks are priced at £30.

Finance and financial markets. Pilbeam, Keith. Basingstoke, Hampshire: Macmillan, 1998. xxii, 390 p. £50.
Describes the operations of financial institutions, markets and instruments worldwide. Aimed at students of economics and finance at both

undergraduate and postgraduate or MBA levels. Coverage includes the role of intermediaries, interest rate determination, the domestic and international money and capital markets, equities, foreign exchange and derivatives.

Financial products: a survival guide. Collinson, Fiona, Giddings, Michael and Sullivan, Malcolm. London: Euromoney, 1996. vi, 209 p. £69.95.
Concentrates on corporate and wholesale products, with a short section on the consumer market. Clearly laid out, with a few pages on each product. Includes tables, diagrams etc.

The Financial Times guide to using the financial pages. Vaitilingam, Romesh. 3rd ed. London: Financial Times Pitman, 1996. xv, 368 p. £16.99.
Explains 'how to make the best use of the comprehensive range of financial and economic statistics available'.

How the City of London works: an introduction to its financial markets. Clarke, William M. 5th ed. London: Sweet and Maxwell, 1999. 150 p. £11.
Long-established introduction to the City's financial markets and institutions. Now includes sections on regulation and the euro.

An introduction to global financial markets. Valdez, Stephen. 3rd ed. Basingstoke, Hampshire: Macmillan, 2000. xviii, 386 p. £21.99.
An 'introduction to the world's principal financial markets and institutions'. With a glossary.

The money machine: how the City works. Coggan, Philip. 4th ed. London: Penguin, 1999. xiv, 194 p. £8.99.
A journalist explains 'the nuts and bolts of the financial system' – an overview of how banks, building societies, insurance companies and other institutions fit in to the financial structures that make up the City.

Success in investment. Winfield, R. G. and Curry, S. J. 5th ed. London: John Murray, 1994. 461 p. £10.50.
Intended to support professional studies including the examinations of the Chartered Institute of Bankers, the Securities Institute and the Chartered Insurance Institute. Covers all forms of investment including securities, investment funds and life assurance. Also has chapters on investor protection, taxation etc.

1.00.05 Manuals

The financial adviser's factbook. Wicks, David, ed. London: Gee. 1 vol. (looseleaf).
Includes sections on different kinds of investment and protection products, mortgages, regulation, taxation and marketing. Very much a reference work, with a lot of tables and lists. Around 500 pages, updated by looseleaf amendments (twice yearly) and a quarterly *Financial adviser's newsletter*.

Moneyguide: the handbook of personal finance. Hanson, D. G. London: Sweet & Maxwell. 1 vol. (looseleaf). £135.
Wide-ranging manual, including savings, investment, insurance, pensions and banking, as well as background subjects like taxation, travel and 'family finance'. Comprises around 500 pages, updated by looseleaf amendments.

Personal financial planning manual. London: Butterworths. £39.95.
Sections on insurance, retirement planning, investments, tax planning and 'the life cycle'. Each annual replacement issue comprises some 400 pages. Annual.

The professional adviser's factfile. London: Taxbriefs. £26 per issue.
Contains sections on investments, house purchase, life assurance, pensions and taxation. Two issues a year. Each issue replaces the last, in a ring binder.

Professional Briefing: [briefing pack]. Sheffield: Professional Briefing. £350 per year.
Conceived as a comprehensive updating service for financial advisers. Comprises several separate series of monthly publications in ring binders. Briefing notes deal with individual topics like 'Fixed interest gilts' and 'Remortgages for clients', including some on particular legal cases. An *Adviser guide* covers a single subject each month in more detail. There is also a newsletter, and a *Newsfile* providing an in-depth round-up of recent news on a particular topic, e.g. 'Stakeholder pensions'. The same text is available online (to subscribers only) at http://www.probrief.com, together with a *Web file*: a series of links to individual press releases, announcements from regulators, trade associations and so on in financial services.

1.00.07 Source materials

Taxbriefs report planner. London: Taxbriefs. £167.
Collection of over 2,000 standard paragraphs, arranged by subject, from which the adviser can quickly produce tailored client reports and 'reason why' letters. Also available on disk (Windows 3.11 or higher). Annual updates.

1.00.08 Technical reports

FSA occasional paper. London: Financial Services Authority.
Series of pamphlets from the main UK regulator, concentrating on financial regulation and related subjects. Recent titles include *Household saving and wealth accumulation* (no. 5) and *Some aspects of regulatory capital* (no. 7).

1.00.12 Market research

FT Finance has published a wide range of management reports on financial services, including several broadly focused on the retail area, e.g. *Call centres: strategies for survival* (£595) and *Branding in retail financial services* (£795). As from 2000 these reports are available from **Informa**. The parent organisation **FT Business** has recently teamed up with the **CII Society of Fellows** and the **Society of Financial Advisers** to produce *Financial services today: provider perceptions vs consumer needs*, a title in its new FT Market Trends Series (£1,500).

Market Assessment International publishes widely in this area, with recent titles including *Individual savings accounts 1999, Customer services in financial organisations 1999* and *Niche marketing in the financial services industry 1999*. Prices are around £650 for one report; some are published under the **Key Note** imprint. **Datamonitor** is also very active in financial services. Its more broadly focused titles have included *UK direct sales forces and tied agents 1999* (£1,495) and *Worksite marketing in UK financial services 1999* (£1,495). In conjunction with **Reuters** it has published many titles under the Reuters Business Insight imprint, including *UK financial services on the Internet, The high-tech retail financial services revolution* and *The impact of the FSA on wholesale financial services* (£495 each).

The reports published by **Mintel** also include many on financial services. Recent titles include *Telephone and postal distribution, Internet distribution* and *Branch distribution*. These reports are also available to subscribers on the Mintel web site. The Dublin-based firm **Lafferty** produces a steady stream of market research on financial services, often focused on the whole European market. Recent reports include *Mergers and acquisitions in financial services, The future of retail financial services* and *Growing brand loyalty*. Prices are typically £999 for one report. Finally, the **Millennium Group** has published several management reports in the series Creating Value In The New Financial Services Marketplace, e.g. *Customer lifestyles, loyalty and lifetime value* (£445).

The 'City' table. London: British Invisibles. Free.
Statistics showing overseas earnings of the UK financial sector over 11 years. Annual.

Consumer research. London: Financial Services Authority.
Extending its remit beyond that of the pure regulator the Financial Services Authority has launched this occasional series of consumer research to inform its core activities. Titles published to date are *Better informed consumers: assessing the implications for consumer education of research by BMRB, Stakeholder pensions decision trees: a stage-by-stage guide to the development of a stakeholder pension decision tree* and *In or out?: financial exclusion: a literature and research review.*

The financial services pocket book. Henley on Thames: NTC.
Handy compilation of statistics from various published sources, plus the NOP's Financial Research Survey. Covers personal financial markets, with sections on the economic and demographic background as well as a wide range of individual services including life and general insurance, mortgages and banking. Formerly published as *The financial consumer* and the emphasis is squarely on the buyer of financial services. Published in association with NOP Financial. Issued every two years.

Financial services survey. London: PricewaterhouseCoopers. £325 per year.
Reports on a regular survey of the 'health, perceptions and plans of the financial services industry', including banks, the insurance industry, fund managers, and so on. Published in association with the CBI and modelled on its long-running Industrial Trends Survey. Arranged by sector. Quarterly.

Household saving in the UK. Banks, James and Tanner, Sarah. London: Institute for Fiscal Studies, 1999. 110p. £25.
A review of the economics of household saving, the taxation of financial assets in the United Kingdom and official sources of information on savings and wealth. Topics include economic theories of saving behaviour, the taxation of saving, official sources of information on saving and wealth, and trends in asset ownership since 1978.

International financial markets in the UK. London: British Invisibles.
Aims to set out 'the position of UK financial services in international financial markets as well as highlighting their wider contribution to the UK economy'. Statistics plus commentary. Annual.

1.00.18 Product research

IFA contact: the official yearbook of the IFA magazine. London: IFA Association. £20.
Compendium aimed at the UK independent financial adviser, with tabulated product comparisons, directories of product suppliers and some short articles.

Life & pensions & unit trusts moneyfacts: the monthly manual of life, pensions and collective investments. Norwich: Moneyfacts.
Tabulated guide to rates and plan details, with a regular 'Fund performance' supplement. Monthly.

The savings market. Stokenchurch, Bucks: Research Department. £110 per year.
Tabulated guide to investment products (including bank and building society accounts), life and health insurance policies and individual pension plans. Three issues a year.

Statspack. Macclesfield, Cheshire: Lipper.
Series of reports on investment products consisting chiefly of tabulated
performance statistics. Comprises separate volumes on insurance funds,
managed funds, pension funds, and so on. Monthly. Also available on
CD-ROM.

1.00.21 Directories

Crawford's directory of City connections. London: AP Information Services. £295.
Provides contact and other information on major UK companies and the
advisers who act for them – including stockbrokers, financial advisers,
auditors, solicitors, insurance advisers, financial public relations consultants and pensions consultants. Annual.

Who's who in the City: incorporating Beckett's directory. London:
Macmillan, 1997. xiii, 1,116 p. £125.
Lists 16,317 key individuals operating within the City or with strong City
connections. Modelled on the general *Who's who*, giving career details,
education etc. Includes an index by firm, with full contact details.

1.00.24 Dictionaries

An A–Z of finance: a jargon-free guide to investment and the City. Becket,
Michael. London: Kogan Page, [1999]. vi, 199 p. £12.99.
An informal, journalistic guide for the layman, which takes the form of a
dictionary. Published in association with the Daily Telegraph.

A dictionary of finance and banking. 2nd ed. Oxford: Oxford University
Press, 1997. 378 p. £7.99.
Aimed at students, practitioners and investors. Contains over 4,000 en-
tries covering all aspects of finance and banking.

**Lamont's glossary: the definitive plain English money and investment
dictionary for the finance professional and money-minded consumer**.
Lamont, Barclay W. London: Advanced Media Group, 1997. 310 p.
Defines over 3,500 terms. Includes a CD-ROM containing the full text of
the dictionary in a searchable format – or you can buy a cheaper version
with browsable diskette. System requirements: PC, Windows 3.11 or higher.

1.00.31 Periodicals

Bloomberg money. London: City Financial Communications. £24.50 per
year.
Consumer magazine on investment and other aspects of personal finance.
Includes news and features, with regular details of savings rates. There's
a related web site; see section 1.00.75. Monthly.

Financial timesaver: the essential monthly newsletter for the busy financial adviser. London: Taxbriefs. £128 per year.
Technical digest with short features on recent developments. Lots of lists and bullets.

The IFA magazine: the official magazine of the IFA Association. London: IFA Association. Free to qualifying readers (registration required).
Short articles on aspects of financial services aimed at the independent adviser, together with some material on the IFA Association itself.

IFA review: the magazine for the professional adviser. London: Mitre House. £48 for two years.
Short articles aimed at the UK adviser. The subscription includes issues of *Investment management*. Six issues a year, some combined with other titles.

Journal of financial services research. Boston, USA; London: Kluwer Academic. NLG880 per year (students), NLG440 per year (institutions).
Describes itself as 'a comprehensive forum for rigorous theoretical and applied microeconomic analysis of financial service institutions, instruments and markets'. Long articles, chiefly from the United States. Three issues a year.

Money management: the professional's independent adviser. London: Financial Times Business. £65 per year.
Glossy trade magazine aimed at the UK financial adviser and focusing on personal finance, especially retail investment business, life assurance, pensions products and mortgages. Fairly substantial articles with an emphasis on products, often including comparative tables. Plus news, regular product statistics, the quarterly supplement *Corporate solutions* and other ad hoc supplements. Monthly.

Money marketing focus: the professional adviser's guide. London: Money Marketing. £4.95 per issue.
A series of product surveys on personal finance, principally retail investment, life and health insurance and pensions. Each issue focuses on a particular area, e.g. 'With-profits and unit-linked survey', 'Healthcare survey', with a lot of comparative tables. 10 issues a year.

Money observer. London: Guardian Magazines. £33 per year.
Personal finance magazine for consumers, with an emphasis on investment and savings. News and short articles, regular performance statistics and occasional supplements. Monthly.

Moneywise: Britain's best-selling personal finance magazine. London: RD Publications. £35.40 per year.
Consumer magazine on personal finance from the Reader's Digest group.

News and short articles, product listings and statistics. There's also a web site: see section 1.00.75. Monthly.

Planned savings: the business magazine for financial advisers. London: Informa. £62 per year.
Close rival to *Money management* (see above). News and fairly substantial articles on personal finance, especially retail investment, life assurance, pension products, mortgages. An emphasis on products, with lots of comparative tables. There's also a regular statistical 'Investment monitor' at the back and some shorter columns (e.g. 'Business briefing', 'Technical briefing'). Monthly.

Prospect: for the professional financial adviser. Crawley, West Sussex: Harrington. £3.50 per issue.
Published for the Life Insurance Association – or the LIA as it tends to call itself now, underlining the change in its membership over several decades from life assurance salesmen to financial advisers. In addition to LIA news includes short articles on life assurance, other investment business and organisational matters (such as how to manage your time better, how to sell more business). Monthly.

The review of financial studies. Cary [North Carolina]: Oxford University Press.
Academic journal publishing 'significant new research in financial economics, striving to establish a balance between theoretical and empirical studies'. Articles are long and often include algebra. Subscriptions are equally complex, ranging from £7 per year for students to £200 per year for institutions (UK).

Technical adviser: the technical newsletter of the Society of Financial Advisers. London: Society of Financial Advisers. £5 per issue (free to SOFA members).
Quite substantial articles of a technical but practical nature aimed at financial advisers, e.g. 'Tax planning after the Finance Bill', 'Offshore trusts: the current position'. There's also a regular section 'SOFA news'. Recent articles are on the SOFA web site, see section 1.00.75. Quarterly.

1.00.36 Newspapers

Financial adviser. London: Financial Times Business. £90 per year (free to qualifying readers).
Tabloid-format weekly paper containing news and short articles aimed at the financial adviser together with regular product directories and product statistics. Includes the monthly supplements *FA investment extra*, *FA mortgage extra*, *FA careers extra*, *FA protection extra* and *FA pensions extra*, together with other supplements, among these a regular survey of direct sales.

Investment week: the premier publication for professional advisers. London: City Financial Communications. £90 per year.
Weekly tabloid-format newspaper aimed at financial advisers. Carries news and some short articles. Tends to concentrate on retail investment products. Includes product reviews and a monthly supplement *Fundstats*, providing more detailed statistical analysis.

Money marketing: first for the professional financial adviser. London: Money Marketing. £75 per year.
The first UK financial weekly, originally appearing in 1985 (before financial advisers were invented) with the subtitle 'the news weekly for the personal investment intermediary'. News, short articles, a regular product directory and some product statistics. Also includes occasional supplements, the quarterly *New product review* and a regular CD-ROM containing demonstration versions of electronic products for the financial adviser.

1.00.72 CD-ROMs

To support the financial planning examinations of the **Chartered Insurance Institute** the **Unicorn Training Partnership** produces two CD-ROMs in its CII Training Technology range, in association with the Institute. These products are also appropriate for more general training needs. The same range includes an *ISA assessment system* and the *Cascade competency assessment system*.

Financial journals index. London: Sweet & Maxwell.
Indexes and briefly abstracts articles from over 85 financial services journals, including many titles on pensions, insurance and banking. Available as part of the *Current legal information* service, either on CD-ROM or via the Web (http://www.smlawpub.co.uk). Prices start at £1,575 per year.

Hindsight. [UK]: Lipper.
Windows-based financial analysis and presentation program incorporating a database of price and performance data on a wide range of funds, including UK unit trusts, life and pensions funds, broker managed funds, investment trusts, equities and savings accounts, together with offshore funds. Allows comparison of fund performance against benchmarks, sector indices and other funds. You can export data to spreadsheets for further manipulation. Updated daily, weekly or monthly.

IFAresearcher. London: Money Marketing. £47 per month plus VAT (IFAs only).
Integrated tool that enables the IFA to search the market, rank appropriate products and create tailored 'reason why' letters and product comparison reports. Includes product data on UK life assurance, pensions and investment.

Micropal workstation. London: Standard & Poor's Micropal.
Comprehensive system for the analysis and presentation of investment
fund data, with a core database of information on stock markets, indices
and foreign exchange rates, plus one or more modules carrying fund data.
Allows you to create reports, charts and other documents. The range of
data available includes UK unit trusts, investment trusts, pension funds,
linked life funds and equities, with an extensive international database.
Can be updated daily or weekly via diskette or modem. An in-depth analysis module is available separately as *TAP*.

Standard & Poor's Micropal fund expert. London: Standard & Poor's
Micropal.
Range of services giving comparative data for individual investment prod-
ucts allowing you to produce customised fact sheets, graphs, charts,
rankings and databases. The modules available are UK Unit Trusts, UK
Linked Life Assurance Funds, UK Unit Linked Personal Pensions and
UK Investment Trusts. Monthly.

1.00.75 Web sites

In addition to the sources of technical and market information listed below there are many web sites from individual product providers and
from the larger firms of intermediaries. Some of the directories described
below list these. There are also web sites providing useful background
information, e.g. on taxation or inflation rates, but these are outside the
scope of this book. Most of the sites listed here are aimed at consumers.
Most of them are free, but it seems unlikely there is enough advertising
and other forms of sponsorship to support such a wide profusion of free
information indefinitely. A few sites are aimed at IFAs. See also *CII Library
online*, section 3.00.75.

Blay's Guides savings & finance. [UK?]: Blay's Guides Limited. http://
www.blays.co.uk. Free.
Detailed consumer guidance on a wide range of financial services from a
firm with 19 years of providing such information to newspapers and
financial institutions. Includes calculators.

Bloomberg.co.uk. [US?]: Bloomberg. http://www.bloomberg.com/uk/
ukhome.html. Free.
UK section of the broader Bloomberg site. Offers financial news, market
prices and an online version of the magazine *Bloomberg money* (1.00.31)
as well as a (non-financial) section on sports news. Aimed at the consumer.

The City handbook. 3rd ed. London: Bank of England. http://
www.bankofengland.co.uk/cityhandbook. Free.
A very useful list of over 150 City-related organisations listed in alpha-

betical order and by function with a list of abbreviations and links to their web sites. Only available on the Internet: there is no printed version.

Financewise. [London]: Financial Engineering Ltd. http://www.financewise.com. Free (some sections require registration).
Portal-type site focusing on financial information with a particular emphasis on capital markets, financial risk management, investment and banking. Combines a specialist search engine with an annotated directory of financial web sites. Also offers news from Reuters and other external suppliers, special reports and a job searching facility.

Financial planning horizons: a free service provided by Financial Services Education for Consumers Limited. [UK]: Financial Services Education for Consumers Limited. http://www.financial-planning.uk.com. Free.
Consumer guidance on financial planning, including sections for different age groups and small businesses, fact find forms, a quiz and competitions. There are also useful addresses, news and a glossary.

Find: financial information net directory: the leading Internet directory for UK financial services. [UK]: Omnium Communications Limited. http://www.find.co.uk. Free.
Classified web directory dedicated to financial services. Links are annotated and there are helpful introductions to each section. Includes a useful section listing online calculators.

FT Quicken: UK personal finance. [London?]: [Financial Times Limited?]. http://www.ftquicken.co.uk. Free.
Personal finance site aimed at consumers and featuring news, articles, financial indicators, calculators and so on from Financial Times and Intuit, the developers of the Quicken personal financial management software.

IFA online. London: City Financial Communications. http://www.ifaonline.co.uk. Free to authorised advisers (registration required).
A site for IFAs including news, product information, a discussion forum and links to other financial services sites. There's a detailed product database that allows you to build your own tables comparing different companies feature by feature.

InMarkets. [UK?]: InMarkets Limited. http://www.inmarkets.com. Fee-based, with some free services.
Describes itself as 'a dedicated learning portal for finance professionals and sophisticated investors', offering over 100 online self-study courses on aspects of financial services together with tailored instructor-led programs. Oriented towards securities, derivatives and corporate finance, but a section on personal finance is promised. Also includes a glossary in English, French, Spanish and German and a web directory covering over 10,000 listed companies.

Interactive IFA. [London]: Interactive Investor International. http://www.ifa.co.uk. Free (some sections require registration).
Aimed at IFAs and sharing some features with the consumer-oriented site from the same stable (see *Interactive investor*). Includes current news, a browsable news archive, articles, financial indicators, performance data and links to fund management and life companies. Also some online tools, for instance, you can build and monitor investment portfolios online.

Interactive investor. [London]: Interactive Investor International. http://www.iii.co.uk. Free (some sections require registration).
An extensive site aimed primarily at the UK consumer (with links to III's South African and Asian sites). Includes articles on financial services, financial indicators, financial news, discussion forums and in-depth sections on home banking, savings, mortgages, ISAs, insurance and new issues. There's also a web directory of investment management companies, an online bookshop and online forms you can use to request III newsletters by email or advice from a panel of IFAs.

L1 money. [UK?]: LineOne. http://www.lineone.net/money. Free.
Part of the broader LineOne site; features news and information on all aspects of personal finance, aimed at consumers.

Maxmoney. [UK?]: Hollinger Digital. http://ukmax.com/maxmoney. Free.
Part of the UKmax portal site, containing news, guidance and other information on personal finance aimed at consumers. Includes a personalised portfolio service, a directory of UK financial services web sites and a search engine for finding an independent financial adviser by location or company.

Money marketing on-line. [UK]: Money Marketing. http://www.moneymarketing.co.uk. Free to authorised advisers (registration required).
News, articles, product data and other information from the weekly newspaper *Money marketing* (section 1.00.36). Access to non-advisers is on application.

Money money money .co.uk. [UK?]: S2 New Media Ltd. http://www.moneymoneymoney.co.uk. Free.
'The place to visit before you buy a financial product.' Includes news, articles and guidance.

The money shop. [UK?]: Net Services International Limited. http://www.moneyshop.co.uk. Free.
Classified links to product providers, with helpful introductory text. Includes a separate directory aimed at professionals, with full contact details of more specialist service providers.

Moneyextra. [UK]: The Exchange. http://www.moneyextra.com. Free. Provided in association with Microsoft Money, a personal finance site aimed at consumers. Includes news, guidance, financial indicators and a search engine you can use to find an independent financial adviser.

Moneyweb. Dickson, Ian. [UK?]: Ian Dickson. http://www.moneyweb.co.uk. Free.
Long-established one-man site maintained by an ex-IFA. Articles on different aspects of personal finance aimed at consumers but with a section for 'industry professionals'. Includes a currency converter and a database of IFAs searchable by postcode, giving both contact details and (where appropriate) links.

Moneywise personal finance. [UK?]: RD Publications Ltd. http://www.readersdigest.co.uk/finance.htm. Free.
Online equivalent of the printed magazine *Moneywise* (1.00.31). Current news and features on personal finance, with an archive of older items. Includes online insurance quotes and share prices.

Moneyworld. London: Moneyworld UK Ltd. http://www.moneyworld.co.uk. Free.
Personal finance site aimed at consumers. Includes recent news, stockmarket reports, product guides, performance statistics, financial indicators, rate tables, a glossary and a directory of finance-related sites. With some interactive features, e.g. online insurance quotes and a comparative mortgage cost calculator.

The motley fool UK. [UK?]: The Motley Fool. http://www.fool.co.uk. Free.
UK version of a US web site on personal finance, aimed at consumers. Includes news, articles, online quotes, a portfolio facility and financial indicators. Registration provides additional access to bulletin boards and other facilities.

The Society of Financial Advisers. [London]: Society of Financial Advisers. http://www.sofa.org. Free (some sections members only).
Includes the full text of recent articles from the journal *Technical adviser* (see section 1.00.31), consumer guides to financial products and a 'find an adviser' facility. This enables you to search the SOFA database of professionally qualified financial advisers by category of business, location, name and charging method. Some of the site is open to members only, e.g. the more recent journal articles.

Sort. [UK?]: Sort Ltd. http://www.sort.co.uk.
Registered members can access 300 pages of free information on personal finances, including mortgage and pension calculators, step-by-step guides and a question-and-answer forum. An additional advisory service is offered online for a fee.

This is money: your personal financial adviser: from the Daily Mail, Mail on Sunday, & Evening Standard. [London?]: Associated New Media. http://www.thisismoney.co.uk. Free.
News, articles, calculators, a portfolio builder, financial indicators and other information from the publishers of three UK newspapers.

Times-money. [London]: Times Newspapers Ltd. http://www.times-money.co.uk. Free.
Personal finance site including daily news updates, share prices and articles.

UK directory. Finance. [UK]: UKdirectory Ltd. http://www.ukdirectory.co.uk/fin. Free.
Section of wide-ranging UK-oriented web directory with subsections on banks, insurance, offshore, the stock market etc.

Web-train. [Brighton]: Financial Services Training College. http://www.fstcollege.co.uk/webtrain.htm. £25 per month plus VAT.
Interactive site designed to provide structured CPD for financial advisers.

Yahoo! UK & Ireland finance. [US?]: Yahoo! http://www.uk.yahoo.com. Free.
Portal-type site with financial news and indicators and links to other Yahoo! sites. The news is mostly American.

Yahoo! UK & Ireland. Finance and investment. London: Yahoo! UK Ltd. http://uk.dir.yahoo.com/BusinessandEconomy/FinanceandInvestment. Free.
Section of well-known web directory covering UK and other financial sites. You can limit by topic or region. Links are annotated.

1.00.78 Online services

The broad-based online service *Lexis-Nexis* (http://www.lexis-nexis.co.uk) is a major provider of full-text legal and business information. There is a US emphasis, but after the recent purchase of the FT Profile service Lexis-Nexis can also boast a good range of UK financial services sources. These include *Insurance day*, *Money marketing*, *Post magazine* and *Reinsurance*. Legal coverage includes reported and unreported UK cases, UK legislation, legal journals, EU law, European Convention on Human Rights, Commonwealth law, US federal and state case law, international law and worldwide legal sources.

Reuters business briefing (http://www.factiva.com) is another broad-based online service strong in financial services. Coverage includes Reuters and Dow Jones news and other selected daily wire services, press releases and stock exchange announcements; an archive of business databases with access to national and international news wires and newspapers, trade journals, research reports; company share prices and indexes; currency rates; financial company background data on over 30,000 companies and links to web sites. There are 294 trade publications, magazines and journals covering the financial services sector providing full-text articles from key journals around the world, although again with a mainly US bias. See also *Reuters insurance briefing*, section 3.00.78.

The *Datastar* and *Dialog* services from the Dialog Corporation (http://www.dialog.com) together comprise the largest online database host with hundreds of databases containing financial data, full-text news, full-text market research and other company information. The *Profound* service concentrates on business information.

Daily adviser. London: Financial Times Business.
A real-time news service targeted at IFAs, including product details and analysis. Available free to subscribers to the EDI service the Common Trading Platform.

1.02 General sources (international)

Financial services in the narrower sense tends to change at national borders, on account of its close relationship with taxation. For this reason this section concentrates on sources dealing with the much broader and more global area of international finance, and also with 'offshore finance', i.e. financial services that exploit tax havens.

1.02.24 Dictionaries

The handbook of international financial terms. Moles, Peter and Terry, Nicholas. Oxford: Oxford University Press, 1999. lxxix, 605 p. £25.
Aims for a 'clear explanation of the use of terms and instruments in different markets and different countries'. Over 14,000 entries, often quite detailed.

International dictionary of banking and finance. Clark, John. Chicago; London: Glenlake, 1999. 352 p. £45.
Wide-ranging dictionary giving short definitions of the specialist terms of banking and general finance, aimed at both students and professionals as well as consumers. A companion to *Dictionary of insurance and finance terms* (section 3.00.24), with which it shares many entries. Published in association with the Chartered Institute of Bankers.

International dictionary of finance. Bannock, Graham and Manser, William. [New ed]. London: Profile Books, 1999. vi, 289 p. £25.
Short definitions of over 2,000 terms used in financial markets world-

wide. Includes vocabulary relating to domestic as well as international finance, particularly those from the United States and United Kingdom.

1.02.31 Periodicals

Journal of European financial services. [Warsaw]: [University of Insurance & Banking]. £50 per year.
Substantial articles, mostly by academics. First published in 1998 and to date most contributions focus on the United Kingdom, Poland or the European Union in general, although a broader range is clearly anticipated later. Two issues a year.

1.02.75 Web sites

Global adviser.com. London: City Financial Communications. http://www.globaladviser.com. Free to authorised advisers (registration required). Internationally oriented site from the same stable as *IFA online* (section 1.00.75), with which it shares many features. Includes news, product information, links to other sites and an interactive portfolio system.

Micropal.com. London: Standard & Poor's Micropal. http://www.micropal.com. Free.
As well as information about Standard & Poor's Micropal products this site includes free information analysing funds from major markets worldwide. Coverage includes UK unit trusts, pensions and life assurance funds.

1.07 Quantitative methods

Actuaries were traditionally life assurance mathematicians but have gradually extended their expertise into general insurance, for instance, constructing rating models for motor insurance, and from there into investment business and even beyond financial services to the calculation of damages awards. Hence the inclusion in this chapter rather than chapter 3 of actuarial works. The literature of actuarial science tends to make extensive use of mathematical formulae, rendering it somewhat opaque to the outsider. But amid the algebra there is some surprisingly practical information. The principal publishers in this area are the two UK actuarial institutes, the **Institute of Actuaries** and the Scottish **Faculty of Actuaries**. Notwithstanding constitutional moves in the opposite direction these two organisations are increasingly acting as one.

1.07.02 Career guides

The inside careers guide to actuaries. London: Cambridge Market Intelligence. (Inside Careers) £16.50.
Includes a directory of consulting actuaries and insurance company actuarial departments and articles on education and training and the

actuarial profession generally. Published in association with the Institute of Actuaries and the Faculty of Actuaries. Annual.

1.07.03 Textbooks

An introduction to actuarial studies. Atkinson, M. E. and Dickson, C. M. Cheltenham: Edward Elgar, 2000. xiv, 172 p. £39.95.
Scope includes compound interest calculations, demographic theory and techniques and the pricing of life assurance policies. With many worked examples.

1.07.08 Technical reports

The two actuarial bodies, the **Institute of Actuaries** and the **Faculty of Actuaries**, produce a stream of discussion papers although many of these eventually find their way into the *British actuarial journal* (section 1.07.31). You can subscribe directly to the discussion papers.

Actuarial research paper. London: City University, Department of Actuarial Science.
Irregular series of highly mathematical reports on actuarial aspects of insurance, pensions and investment. Recent titles include no. 114, *Contribution and solvency risk in a defined benefit pension scheme* and no. 115, *Controlling solvency and maximising policyholders' returns*.

1.07.31 Periodicals

See also the somewhat more narrowly focused *Insurance: mathematics & economics* (section 3.07.31)

The actuary. London: Staple Inn Actuarial Society. £30 per year.
The publisher was originally known as the Institute of Actuaries' Students Society but its remit now extends beyond the actuarial student and this magazine usefully supplements the length and austerity of the senior *British actuarial journal* (q.v.). Contains professional news and short articles – sometimes summaries of longer presentations that might find their way into the longer journal. With a large situations vacant section. Monthly.

The ASTIN bulletin: the journal of the ASTIN and AFIR sections of the International Actuarial Association. Leuven, Belgium: Ceuterick. BEF2,500 per year.
The two acronyms neatly define the subject content of this journal: Actuarial Studies in Non-life (ASTIN) and Actuarial Approach to Financial Risks (AFIR). This was a ground-breaking journal in extending actuarial methods to areas such as motor insurance. The AFIR section goes further, focusing on investment and the management of the asset–liability risk of financial institutions. The articles are long, with lots of mathematics.

Many are theoretical but some apply quantitative methods to real-life problems. Two issues a year.

British actuarial journal: incorporating Journal of the Institute of Actuaries and Transactions of the Faculty of Actuaries. London: Institute of Actuaries. £95 per year (free to members of the Institute and Faculty of Actuaries).
Solid professional journal; a typical issue runs to 150 pages with four or five long articles. These are usually discussion papers presented to the Institute or Faculty, with or without an abstract of the actual discussion (see section 1.07.12). Articles are frequently accompanied by actuarial notation but the overall tone of the journal is not excessively theoretical and some articles are surprisingly factual and of interest to a wider audience than actuaries, e.g. 'The likely financial effects on individuals, industry and commerce of the use of genetic information' (in vol. 3, part 5, and algebra-free). Five issues a year.

The Geneva papers on risk and insurance theory. Boston, USA; London: Kluwer Academic. $149 (institutional), $40 (individual).
Slimmer half of the original *Geneva papers on risk and insurance*, which split in 1990 (see also *The Geneva papers on risk and insurance, issues and practice*, section 3.00.31). The articles are very theoretical. Published for the Association Internationale pour l'Etude de l'Economie de l'Assurance, also known as the Geneva Association. Two issues a year.

1.07.75 Web sites

Balducci's actuarial preprint service. Scollnik, David P. M. [Calgary, Canada?]: David P. M. Scollnik. http://balducci.math.ucalgary.ca/aps.html. Free.
A series of links to actuarial research and working papers available on the Web (including some on this site), arranged by author. Formats vary and some papers are available from more than one source.

1.10 Law and regulation

Financial institutions such as banks and insurance companies have been regulated in the United Kingdom for a very long time but traditionally it has been the *security* of such organisations that has been monitored, with less attention paid to their marketing activities and to the giving of financial advice generally. There was thus little common ground between the regulatory regimes applying to different kinds of financial institution and consequently little call for works addressing the whole of the financial services area from a legal or regulatory viewpoint. But with the introduction of the Financial Services Act in 1986 the beginnings emerged of an across-the-board, comprehensive approach to financial services regulation. However, this Act concerned itself primarily with investment business (defined to include the giving of investment advice as such, investment management, all forms of life assurance except term assurance and the activities of financial markets like the London Stock Exchange) and many of the works listed in this section retain that limitation.

The 1986 Act introduced a devolved approach to regulation, with a bewildering number of 'self-regulatory organisations' and 'recognised professional bodies' policing their own patch on behalf of the main regulator, the Securities and Investments Board (SIB). Each of these organisations produced its own swathe of consultative documents, regulatory bulletins, rule books and so on, to the delight of legal publishers but to the confusion of most others. A clear need was felt for a more integrated approach and this began with the transformation of SIB into the **Financial Services Authority** (FSA) in 1997. The FSA is gradually taking over the powers of the subordinate regulators and has extended its remit beyond investment business by taking over the supervision of banks from the Bank of England and the supervision of insurance companies and friendly societies from the Treasury. It looks as though the regulation of mortgage business and general insurance distribution will be on a voluntary basis outside the full remit of the FSA, but the whole situation will not be fully resolved until the implementation of the Financial Services and Markets Bill. Until then the FSA is a new organisation operating under old powers, and works on financial services regulation – unless regularly updated – are shots at a moving target.

1.10.07 Source materials

Encyclopedia of financial services law. Lomnicka, Eva Z. and Powell, John L., eds. London: Sweet & Maxwell. 4 vols (looseleaf). £690.
Contains the annotated text of UK statutes and statutory instruments together with the rules of the Financial Services Authority and other regulatory bodies, EU directives and related material. Concentrates on the regulation of investment business. Updated by amendments.

Financial services and EC law: materials and cases. Empel, Martijn van and Pearson, Patrick, eds. The Hague; London: Kluwer Law International. 4 vols (looseleaf). (Amsterdam Financial Series) £262.50.
Collection of EU legislation and draft legislation relating to capital movements, banking, insurance and securities trading, together with EU case law and decisions of the European Commission. Updated by looseleaf amendments.

Financial services law and practice. Whittaker, Andrew, ed. London: Butterworths. 4 vols (looseleaf). £475.
Contains annotated statutes and statutory instruments, the rules of the

Financial Services Authority and other regulators, EU directives and other materials. Focuses on investment business. Updated by replacement pages and bulletins.

1.10.21 Directories

How countries supervise their banks, insurers and securities markets. Courtis, Neil, ed. London: Central Banking, 1999. xxviii, 188 p. £110. Guide to financial regulation internationally and the agencies responsible for enforcing it. Provides details on banking, insurance and securities market regulators in 137 countries, covering a total of 277 different agencies. For each jurisdiction the relevant regulators are identified, with full contact details plus information on internal organisation, and so on. For major markets there is also a detailed description of how the regulatory system works.

1.10.31 Periodicals

The compliance digest: quarterly journal of the Compliance Register. Milton Keynes: Compliance Register. £100 per year. Published by 'the international organisation for compliance professionals', with fairly substantial articles on aspects of financial services regulation aimed at the compliance officer. There's an emphasis on the United Kingdom but significant international content.

European financial services law. London: Kluwer Law International. £208 per year. Substantial articles of a fairly technical nature, e.g. 'An outsider's view of the Dutch penalisation of insider trading', 'The euro: redenomination and renominalisation of debt and share capital'. 10 issues a year.

Financial regulatory briefing: the monthly digest of official pronouncements. London: Financial Regulatory Briefing. £115 per year. Consists of sections on individual UK organisations in the financial services area, reproducing or digesting press releases and other official material. There's a related web site (section 1.10.75).

Financial stability review. London: Bank of England. Longish technical articles on aspects of financial stability. Focuses on the United Kingdom but with some international content. Two issues a year.

Journal of financial regulation and compliance: an international journal. London: Henry Stewart. £225 per year. Substantial articles from all corners of the globe, by both academics and practitioners and sometimes ranging beyond the areas of regulation and compliance to broader issues in financial services. Quarterly.

1.10.72 CD-ROMs

Financial regulations service. London: Butterworths.
Contains the rules of UK and US regulators plus commentary, covering financial markets, banking, retail financial services and takeovers and mergers. Also includes the text of *Butterworths company law handbook* and *Butterworths financial services law handbook*. Published in modules so you can choose the sections you require. System requirements: PC, Windows. Can be updated weekly or monthly.

Financial services compliance data. Bracknell, Berkshire: Technical Indexes. £695 per module per year (discounts for multiple modules).
Contains the text of legislation, rules and other documents on the regulation of investment business in the United Kingdom. Also includes the City takeover code, Bank of England regulations and money laundering regulations. System requirements: PC, DOS. In modules, updated monthly.

1.10.75 Web sites

The compliance exchange: the UK compliance officers' audit centre. Halsey, J. E. [UK]: J. E. Halsey. http://ds.dial.pipex.com/jhalsey. Free.
One-man site aimed at compliance officers and other professionals engaged in investment management or involved in the regulation of investment business. A selective, classified directory of related web sites. International in scope, with links to investment regulators by country.

The Compliance Register: the international organisation for compliance professionals and senior managers in the financial services industry. Milton Keynes: Compliance Register. http://www.compliance-register.com. Free (some sections members and subscribers only).
Corporate site including a quarterly online journal *The compliance digest* dedicated to financial regulation and related subjects internationally, though with a UK bias. In PDF format; later issues available to members and subscribers only.

Financial regulatory briefing. London: Financial Regulatory Briefing. http://www.frb.co.uk. Free.
Carries the same 'digest of official pronouncements' as the printed journal *Financial regulatory briefing* (see section 1.10.31), but accessible via a search engine. Plus links to the web sites of organisations involved in financial regulation.

Financial Services Authority. [London]: Financial Services Authority. http://www.fsa.gov.uk. Free.
Official site from the main UK regulator includes consumer information (e.g. a series of 'Investor alerts' on pensions misselling and other topics) and regulatory information (detailed descriptions of banking supervision, the regulation of investment business etc.). There's also online access

to the Central Register – a database of firms currently or formerly authorised to carry on investment business in the United Kingdom. Registration is required to access this facility; it's free for limited private searches but otherwise charged.

1.43 Intermediaries

To the economist a financial services intermediary is a bank, insurance company or other provider of financial services, but to the rest of the world the term refers to someone who intermediates between such providers – or financial markets – and the consumer. This section is concerned with the second definition. The Financial Services Act 1986 introduced the principle of polarisation with regard to investment intermediaries – either you sell one firm's products or you sell them all – and led to the development of two kinds of financial adviser: the independent financial adviser (IFA) and the tied agent or company representative.

Note that works for rather than about financial advisers will be found in section 1.00 and not here – unless they deal not only with financial services as such but also provide advice on how to manage your business, how to sell and so on.

1.43.03 Textbooks

Introduction to financial services: the giving of financial advice. Lake, Ted. London: Old Bailey Press, 1998. xiv, 126 p. (Law in practice series) £6.95.
Provides 'help and guidance on when and how to offer financial advice to members of the public'. Aimed at those starting a career in financial services or thinking of doing so.

1.43.21 Directories

The most comprehensive, official listing of UK financial advisers is the Central Register maintained by the Financial Services Authority. You can access this from the FSA web site (section 1.10.75).

The Matrix directory of independent financial advisers. London: Matrix-Data.
Alphabetical directory of around 11,500 firms of UK independent financial advisers, with indexes arranged by region. Gives contact details, memberships, senior personnel, areas of activity and other information. Over 2,000 pages per issue. Annual.

1.43.75 Web sites

Independent financial adviser promotion web site. [UK]: [IFA Promotion]. http://www.ifap.org.uk. Free.
Outlines the advantages of using an independent financial adviser and provides an online form you can use to request details of three IFAs in your area by email. The address http://www.unbiased.co.uk seems to lead to the same site by a different front door.

1.53 Information technology

Financial services have always been in the vanguard of the technological revolution and this is a rapidly changing area, which no textbook can satisfactorily pin down. Hence the importance of periodicals.

1.53.12 Market research

A number of significant reports on this area have been published recently by the **CSC Financial Services Group**, including *Virtual finance: a survivor's guide*.

1.53.31 Periodicals

Financial systems. London: Mitre House. £52 per year.
Magazine containing short articles on IT in financial services and on more wide-ranging IT issues. Quarterly, with some issues combined with other Mitre House titles. The subscription also includes issues of the slimmer but otherwise similar *Financial systems outlook*.

FT virtual finance report. London: FT Finance. £595 per year.
Newsletter covering the exploitation of the Internet by financial institutions, international but with a particular focus on the UK. Comprises news and fairly substantial articles 10 issues a year.

IT professional in finance. London: Pressfactory. £597 per year.
Newsletter covering IT developments in the global financial services sector. Market and product news, reviews of recent research and other developments. Weekly.

1.56 Marketing

These sources tend to deal with marketing from the point of view of the product provider rather than the adviser. A particular concern is the development of direct marketing methods employing mail, press, television, the Internet and other interactive media to reach out to the consumer rather than relying on an independent adviser. But 'direct marketing' can also refer to the use of a direct sales force.

1.56.03 Textbooks

Financial services marketing. Harrison, Tina. Harlow, England: Pearson Education, 2000. xix, 332 p. £24.99.
An introduction to the subject, structured around the basic principles of marketing. Includes a chapter on corporate financial services.

1.56.12 Market research

For distribution statistics per channel you might check *Financial adviser*, which has published useful figures in the past analysing the use of direct sales forces and other channels in individual companies.

1.56.31 Periodicals

Financial marketing: strategic marketing across financial services. London: Incisive Research. £465 per year.
UK-oriented newsletter on all aspects of marketing over all sectors. Includes some short articles. 10 issues a year.

Financial services distribution. Dublin: Lafferty. £460 per year.
Formerly *Distribution management briefing*, this newsletter offers global news on innovations in delivery and channel management strategies together with analysis and commentary. Includes country reports and and case studies. Monthly, with access to an online version included in the price.

Journal of financial services marketing. London: Henry Stewart. £155 per year.
Journal containing substantial articles, mostly from UK academics but not overly academic. Quarterly.

New media financial marketing: interactive marketing across financial services. London: Incisive Research. £249 per year.
Newsletter first published in October 2000. Carries news and features on electronic commerce in financial services and other interactive forms of marketing. With regular online financial services user statistics provided by Nielson/NetRatings.

Retail finance direct. London: Evandale. £575 per year.
Newsletter focusing on the direct marketing of retail financial services in the UK, including e-commerce. Mostly news. 24 issues a year.

1.56.75 Web sites

E-commerce@lafferty.com. Dublin: Lafferty. £1,250 per year.
Covering the delivery of financial services via e-commerce, this Lafferty newsletter is appropriately only available online. Updated daily, it com-

bines news stories from around the world with regular ratings of key web sites, together with research, in-depth analysis and comment.

Chapter 2

Banks and building societies

The subject of banks and building societies covers a vast terrain. Banking is not a well-defined, homogenous subject area and there are inherent difficulties in defining and separating the functions and activities of the myriad forms of banking operations. For example, the term 'retail banking' can be applied to both personal customers as well as business clients while the term 'commercial banking' can be used to describe the day to day money transmission functions such as cheque clearing through to the specialised corporate banking and clearing operations covering treasury functions and foreign exchange. Since the 'Big Bang' of 1986 it is increasingly difficult to view the various activities of the financial institutions as having discrete roles.

To a certain extent the term 'retail banking' has been replaced by 'retail financial services' and there is a growing emphasis on the products, distribution channels, customers and marketing rather than the type of institution or sector to which it belongs. Marketing and cross-selling of a broad range of financial products are now extremely important functions carried out by all players.

The published material therefore tends to be more general in scope than in the past. One indication of this was that there was once a substantial body of literature on building societies; now, since the deregulation of the industry and the diminishing size of the movement, building societies have small sections in general books or the focus of the material is the product, service or operations, rather than the type of service provider.

There was once a clear division between different types of financial institution (banks, building societies and insurance institutions) and a consequent demarcation between the products and services they offered. Building societies, for example, dominated the mortgage market until the demise of the Building Societies Association cartel in 1983 and until this time the interest rates for both mortgages and savings were fixed. In the early 1980s, banks began to enter the mortgage market (as a result of the abolition of exchange controls) and were able to offer high interest personal savings accounts (a market previously dominated by the building societies). In return, in the late 1980s, building societies were able to offer retail banking facilities. The 1986 Act also provided them with the opportunity to convert to banks, losing their mutual status.

The vast literature on banking overlaps considerably with general economics material and there is a considerable amount of academic literature. As well as market and company research, there are review and policy papers from the banks and building societies themselves, the central banks, international financial institutions, trade bodies and universities.

Subjects can range from the recovery of 'Nazi gold', funding of third world development to product information aimed at consumers (such as the latest interest rates on savings accounts). There has been increasing globalisation of the banking sector, evident from the growing number of banking web sites providing links across the world and the fact that the United Kingdom plays host to a large number of other banking institutions such as American and Japanese investment banks.

The purpose of this chapter is to provide an overview of the range and type of information available, rather than a comprehensive listing of all the sources. Many banking texts are expensive and it is not unusual to find useful text books costing in excess of £80. The resources listed in this chapter have been selected to reflect the broad spectrum of prices.

In addition to commercial sources some of the most important providers of information on the banking and building society sector are the trade and professional bodies: the **Chartered Institute of Bankers** (CIB), the **British Bankers' Association** (BBA), the **Association for Payment Clearing Systems** (APACS), the **Building Societies Association** (BSA) and the **Council of Mortgage Lenders** (CML). The CIB is a professional body whose members are individuals, not companies. Through its subsidiary, the **Institute of Financial Services**, it administers the professional qualifications for practitioners in the industry and publishes a substantial amount of study material.

The BBA is a trade body, representing banks (as corporate members) active in the United Kingdom, with over 300 member banks from more than 60 countries. APACS is the umbrella body for the UK payments industry. It manages the UK payments system and provides a forum to discuss non-competitive aspects of money transmission systems. The BSA is the trade body representing building societies in the United Kingdom while the CML represents the banks, building societies and other residential mortgage lenders, accounting for 98 per cent of the UK's residential mortgage market. The CML is the central provider of economic, statistical, legal, research and other information and analysis on the mortgage market.

2.00 General sources

2.00.01 Consumer guides

Personal finance on the Internet: a practical guide to savings, banking, investment, loans, insurance, pensions and tax. James, Graham. Plymouth: Internet Handbooks, 1999. 208 p. £16.99.
A comprehensive consumer guide to using the Internet for personal financial services: both to find information and to transact business and manage your money online. Packed with screen shots, web site evaluation (pros and cons of using a site) and search tips.

2.00.02 Career guides

Information on careers in banking is provided by the **Chartered Institute of Bankers** on its web site (see section 2.00.75). There are links to job-hunting sites, consultants and trainers in banking and finance, careers advice and details of CIB courses and professional development.

The **Banks and Building Societies National Training Organisation** publishes a small list of titles on professional development such as *Management skills*, *Competing through skills* and *Competency frameworks*.

Banking and the City. Holmes, Karen. London: Industrial Society, 1999. 80 p. £9.99.
Part of the *Insider career guide* series, the book is divided into three sections covering: the job, the person and 'getting in, getting on, getting out'.

Careers in banking and finance. Longson, Sally. 5th ed. London: Kogan Page, 1999. 131 p. £8.99.
Useful introduction to careers in all sectors of the financial services industry, with case studies, tips, useful addresses and guidance on skills, qualifications and types of jobs.

Getting into banking and finance: how to launch a rewarding career. Collins, Simon. Oxford: How to Books, 1998. 117 p. £7.99.
For first-time job-seekers and those already in work, but looking to switch to a career in banking and finance. A down-to-earth look at the opportunities available with advice on applications, qualifications and interview techniques.

2.00.03 Textbooks

The business of banking: an introduction to the modern financial services industry. Pond, Keith and Lipscombe, Geoff. Canterbury: Chartered Institute of Bankers, 1999. 268 p. £11.95.
A good starting point to the changing financial services environment, examining the impact of downsizing, technology and regulation.

The future of European banking. Danthine, Jean-Pierre, et al. London: Centre for Economic Policy Research, 1999. 118 p. £25.
An examination of the policy implications of the competitive environment in which European banks are operating (mergers, acquisitions and consolidation).

Introduction to the financial services environment. Brighouse, David. Canterbury: Chartered Institute of Bankers, 1999. 188 p. £20.
Outlines the environment in which financial services institutions operate. The text is divided into four sections: the macro-economic environment, regulation and legislation, an overview of the financial institution and personal financial services.

Modern banking in theory and practice. Heffernan, Shelagh. Chichester: John Wiley, 1996. 455 p. £19.99.
Good coverage of general banking matters such as competitive and strategic issues, regulation, the modern banking firm, international banking, banking structures around the world, management of risks and determinants of banking failure.

The monetary and financial system. Goacher, David. 4th ed. Canterbury: Chartered Institute of Bankers, 1999. £30.
In-depth treatment of the different financial markets and products and an analysis of the UK money and capital markets.

The recent evolution of financial systems. Revell, Jack, ed. London: Macmillan Press, 1997. 283 p. £57.50.
A series of papers from a meeting of the European Association of University Teachers in Banking and Finance. Academic coverage of pan-European banking activities.

The UK financial system: theory and practice. Buckle, Mike and Thompson, John. 3rd ed. Manchester: Manchester University Press, 1998. 411 p. £16.99.
Aimed at undergraduate students this text provides a clear explanation of financial theories and concepts and a comprehensive account of the workings of the financial system in the United Kingdom.

2.00.09 Official reports

Banking in Europe: data 1994–1997. Eurostat. Luxembourg: Office for Official Publications of the European Communities, 1999. 142 p.
Reviews the banking situation in Europe, with comparison to Japan. A thematic analysis of pan-European trends.

Competition in UK banking: report to the Chancellor of the Exchequer. Cruickshank, Don. Banking Review Team. London: Stationery Office, 2000. 344 p. £49.50.

The Review is an independent investigation of banking services in the United Kingdom, set up by the government in November 1998. It looked at the level of innovation, competition, and efficiency in the industry and how well it serves the needs of business, other consumers and, ultimately, the UK economy. It covers the markets for personal and business banking and the credit and debit card markets. The report sets out recommendations for a new pro competitive public policy framework and makes overarching recommendations on institutional structures and incentives. Analyses and recommends changes to the UK payments systems. Examines the UK retail markets for personal and retail customers. Considers the supply of equity to SMEs and the provision of basic banking services. The report is also available in PDF via the Stationery Office web site (http://www.the-stationery-office.co.uk/banking/index.htm).

2.00.12 Market research

Datamonitor is a major publisher of market research reports in financial services generally and also covers more specific banking and building society areas. In conjunction with **Reuters** it has published many titles under the Reuters Business Insight imprint. One example is *The future of UK banking to 2005*. This briefing report covers international comparisons, EMU and retail banking, new distribution methods, the future of the building society, the future of the finance house, new competitors, new retail banking products, retail banking in a UK recession. Another title in this series is *The future of European retail banking*. Other Datamonitor titles are: *UK retail banks and building societies* (£990) and *Student banking in the UK* (£495).

Market Assessment International and its subsidiary, **Key Note**, and **FT Finance** also produce a number of general banking market research reports. **Lafferty Publications** has a substantial list of titles such as its 'bank strategy' reports, which include: *Creating a winning Internet bank, Private banking and wealth management,* and *Mobile financial service*. Prices range from about £700 to £1,200.

The **Centre for the Study of Financial Innovation** (CSFI) produce a variety of reports on the banking sector. A series of reports published annually (except in 1999) entitled *Banking banana skins* attempts to 'spot the dangers lying in bankers' paths'. The format varies slightly each year but essentially the report is based on opinions from a broad range of senior management in the banking sector and is a source of good qualitative data. At the time of writing the 2000 report was in press and priced at £25. Another CSFI title is *Emerald City bank: banking in 2010* (1998, £25). This is based on responses from senior people in a range of different banking areas, both in the United Kingdom and abroad, on the future of banking. Topics discussed include: whether there is a need for traditional banking services and who will supply them, distribution, the role of the regulatory regime in helping or hindering financial services, and the likelihood of major discontinuity in the financial services between the present and 2010.

The **Chartered Institute of Bankers**, in conjunction with Andersen Consulting and Siebel, has produced a small list of market research reports, such as *Customer relationship management* (£200), *The network bank* (£125) and *Banking strategies beyond 2000* (£195).

The banking year ahead 1999/2000: a survey sponsored by the BBA and the Financial Times. London: BBA, 1999. 128 p. £180.
Data from a questionnaire survey of 500 institutions to discover issues of importance, threats and winners and losers in the industry. Thorough analysis of the main issues affecting banking in this period, based on opinions from key players.

UK banks: u-shaped, v-shaped or pear shaped? Samuels, Simon, Lord, Nick and Young, Stuart. London: Salomon Smith Barney, 1999. 116 p.
Analysis of the UK bank sector with forecasts for the future. Includes commentary on the main players in the market.

2.00.16 Company research

Annual reports are an important source of information. These can be found on many of the banks and building society's own web sites. In addition, a number of sites provide access to banks' and building societies' annual reports. CAROL (*Company annual reports on-line*) (http://www.carol.co.uk/) has a list of retail and merchant banks, although this is not a comprehensive list. The fee-based commercial online databases are often the most effective way of gathering company data.

2.00.21 Directories

The bankers' almanac. 155th ed. (Jan 2000). East Grinstead: Reed Business Information, 1999. 6 vols £475.
A core reference work for the sector. A directory of some 4,400 major international banks and their 238,000 branches worldwide. Also includes some 22,000 other authorised banks.

The CIB directory of corporate banking in the UK. Doggett, P. 1997 ed. Canterbury: CIB, 1997. 535 p. £140.
As well as providing a list of the number and nationality of banks active in the corporate market, this offers an analysis of the type of bank serving specific geographical areas of operation, preferred industry sectors and specialist industry expertise, target corporate sizes, products, services and skills offered, mission statements or banks' philosophy and number of employees.

Directory of consumer information and enquiry services in personal finance. London: Financial Services Authority, 1999. 128 p. Free.
Brings together in one source all the details and contact points for consumer bodies, trade bodies, regulators, charities and other voluntary organisations that provide advice and information to consumers in dealing with their personal finance. Also available on its web site (http://www.fsa.gov.uk).

2.00.24 Dictionaries

Dictionary of banking. Klein, Gerald. 2nd ed. London: Pitman Publishing, 1995. 348 p. £22.89.
Fairly detailed definitions but in a handy paperback size.

Dictionary of banking and finance. 2nd ed. London: Peter Collins Publishing, 1999. 344 p. £9.95.
9,000 terms in use in British, American and international banking and finance markets. Provides examples of the terms in context and includes quotes from newspapers and magazines. Supplements cover money, currencies, international banks and stock exchanges.

Dictionary of banking terms. Fitch, Thomas, P. 3rd ed. Hauppauge (New York): Baron's Educational Series Inc, 1997. 527 p.
Includes more than 3,000 key terms related to banking, electronic commerce, finance, money management, and legal regulations. United States focused but provides in-depth definitions – some entries are particularly lengthy.

Dictionary of banking terms and finance terms. Clark, John O. E. Canterbury: Chartered Institute of Bankers, 1999. 352 p. £15.
Over 4,500 definitions of retail and wholesale banking products and concepts. The explanations are brief but concise and United Kingdom-focused (although they include many new terms now established as part of the UK's banking and finance lexicon which originated in the United States).

Directory of financial sites on the Internet. London: Pitman, 1997. 242 p. £170.89.
A hybrid print and CD-ROM directory listing and reviewing over 1,000 web sites of banking and investment, including the relevant regulatory and governmental bodies. It includes all sites for UK-based financial institutions as well as the European, Asia/Pacific and North American institutions, although of course this is now getting a bit dated.

2.00.26 Bibliographies

Bibliography of banking histories. Vol I, Domestic banks. Wellings, Fred and Gibb, Alastair. Fife: The Authors, 1995. 167 p.

2.00.31 Periodicals

Applied financial economics. London: Routledge. £395 per year.
Peer-reviewed journal providing 'high quality research papers in empirical financial economics, with a particular emphasis on econometric studies of financial markets, asset pricing, and the interaction between financial and non-financial aspects of economic behaviour'. Six issues a year.

The banker. London: Financial Times Business. £189 per year.
A core title for the sector. Regular sections covering investment banking; banking services; retail banking and banking technology. Also packed with UK and international banking news and opinion pieces. Monthly.

CIB news. Canterbury: Chartered Institute of Bankers. Free to members, £50 per year to non-members.
Newsletter primarily for members of the Chartered Institute of Bankers, with CIB news and course information plus industry news and articles. Monthly.

Derivatives use, trading & regulation. London: Henry Stewart. £245 per year.
The official journal of the Futures and Options Association containing refereed articles and case studies covering options, futures, swaps and derivatives. Also features some book reviews. Four issues a year.

Economic trends. London: Stationery Office. £23.50.
Regular articles on general economic issues, so useful for background information. Contains statistics of interest to banking sector, for example selected financial statistics, sterling exchange rates, consumer credit and other personal sector borrowing, analysis of bank lending to UK residents. Monthly.

European banker. Dublin: Lafferty. £699.
Newsletter issued 12 times a year. News and market intelligence on national and cross-border developments in European banking, insurance and finance. Analysis of the performance of Europe's leading banks, looks at government intervention in the industry, changes in the regulation and structure of the banking system in the different countries of Europe, and the impact of EU directives on the industry.

Financial world. Canterbury: Chartered Institute of Bankers. Non-member subscription £75 per year.
Glossy monthly magazine aimed at banking and financial services professionals. Includes features, news, regular columns and special reports.

Journal of banking and finance. Amsterdam: Elsevier. 120.71 euro per year.
Provides an outlet for the flow of scholarly research concerning the finan-

cial institutions and the money and capital markets within which they function. The emphasis is primarily on applied and policy-oriented research. Monthly

2.00.36 Newspapers

The economist. London: Economist Newspaper Ltd. £86 per year.
Although this covers general current affairs and business news, it is included here for its substantial regular finance and economics section with news and articles on the banking sector. Weekly. Web version available (http://www.economist.com)

2.00.75 Web sites

There is an increasing number of web sites providing information on banking and finance. Most of the major search engines, directories and portals have a banking or personal finance sections. There are some specific banking portals also appearing, such as the Inmaze Bank Portal (http://www.bank-portal.com/), which is currently fairly limited in scope but does have a number of useful links.

The bankers' almanac. http://www.bankersalmanac.com.
This site has a comprehensive list of links to the world's banks in addition to a range of other information such as a ranking of the top 50 banks in the world, a list of international organisations, and the 'Information Bank', which includes links to the Web.

British Bankers' Association. London: British Bankers' Association. http://www.bba.org.uk. Free.
The site is divided into three sections, aimed at consumers, businesses, media and research. The site is good for news, press releases and coverage of forthcoming Parliamentary debates. It has a full list of BBA publications and at the time of writing a statistical section was about to be launched. There are no links to other banking sites, however.

The Chartered Institute of Bankers. Canterbury: Chartered Institute of Bankers. http://www.cib.org.uk. Free.
This is an extremely useful web resource. Its supersite (http://www.cib.org.uk/supersite/index.htm) provides links to resources on accountancy, banking, careers, jobs, training and self-development, central banking, city institutions, country information, electronic commerce, the euro, the future, history, the Internet, law, management and marketing, markets, mortgages and investment, research, technology in finance.

The European Union Banking and Finance News Network. London: LS Technologies. http://www.eubfn.com. Free.
A general banking news web site provided by L. S. Technologies in conjunction with the Chartered Institute of Bankers and the Institute of

Financial Services. Banking and financial services news items together with hundreds of articles, classified by subject, with an emphasis on banking IT issues. Also includes briefs on governments, institutions and country profiles.

Money extra. London: Insurance Trading Exchange Ltd. http://www.moneyextra.com. Free.
Umbrella personal finance site for consumers covering all areas of savings and investments as well as mortgages, loans, credit cards, online banking, tax, insurance etc. Includes calculator tools and product comparison tables.

Moneynet. Bromley: Moneynet. http://www.moneynet.co.uk. Free.
Interactive search facilities for comparison of financial products from over 100 lenders and savings and investment information from over 110 providers. Fast search response times and clear explanation of likely costs for each mortgage product.

2.00.78 Online services

Full pricing details should be obtained directly from the online providers listed here.

Bureau van Dijk. http://www.bvdsuite.com.
Among other databases, Bureau van Dijk provides BankScope (information on 11,100 banks worldwide with detailed reports, ratings, ownership and news with financial analysis functions); Scanned reports worldwide (5,000 scanned images of annual reports with interim and year-end accounts and full-text sections), and Capital intelligence for Gulf/Mediterranean, Asia/Pacific, Central/Eastern Europe, South Africa (bank analysis and bank rating reports).

Investext. [US]: Thomson Financial Securities Data. http://www.investext.com.
Research Bank Web has analyst reports, company reports, market research reports. Includes reports from investment banks and trade associations.

2.02 General sources (international)

The majority of banking texts published outside the United Kingdom are from the United States. The American Bankers Association is a major publisher and its web site is a good starting point for US focused material (see section 2.02.75).

2.02.03 Textbooks

Advances in international banking and finance. Vol 3. Khoury, Sarkis Joseph, ed. Greenwich (Connecticut): JAI Press, 1998. 1,173 p. £50.50.

A very scholarly approach for an academic (rather than practitioner) based audience.

EU and US banking in the 1990s. Lewis, Alfred and Pescetto, Gioia. London: Academic Press, 1996. 213 p. £45.
Useful comparison between US and EU banking systems at a period of considerable change. Analysis of the changing environment since 1980. Developments in banking regulation, marketing strategies and industry structure are related to growing globalisation of the banking sector. An examination of the effects of deregulation and integration on competition in addition to the future prospects for EU and US banking. Aimed at policy makers, practitioners and academics.

Global banking. Smith, Roy C and Walker, Ingo. Oxford: Oxford University Press, 1996. £19.95.
A comprehensive overview of the international banking and securities business with a focus on 'the determinants of competitive performance in the international financial service industry'.

Global banking. Oppenheim, Peter K. Washington DC: American Bankers Association, 1996. 338 p.
Intended primarily for a US audience but has a global focus. Study guide format with definitions of highlighted terms and explanations of concepts of international banking practice. Coverage includes money transfers, principles of foreign exchange, foreign exchange markets, principles of international credit, funding global finance, government agencies, country risk assessment and global financial risk assessment.

Global capital markets and banking. Walter, Ingo and Smith, Roy C. Maidenhead: McGraw Hill, 1999. 666 p. (The INSEAD global management series) £28.99.
This text is aimed at 'senior undergraduates'. Looks at the changing nature of global banking and capital markets and the array of new financial instruments. Includes a wide range of case studies.

Proceedings of the International Conference on Risk Management and Regulation in Banking (1997). New York: Kluwer Academic, 1999.

Papers from an international conference held in May 1997 on risk management and regulation in banking by 'top scholars, policymakers, and high-ranking banking officials from around the world'.

Universal banking: international comparisons and theoretical perspectives. Canals, Jordi. Oxford: Oxford University Press, 1997. 382 p. £18.99.
Covers the globalisation process of the capital markets. Considers the role of universal banks and financial markets in the context of deregulation and disintermediation and the role they play in modern financial markets.

2.02.09 Official reports

There are several international banking and economic organisations publishing material on the banking sector and its importance to monetary systems. The **Bank for International Settlements** (BIS) for example, is an international organisation fostering the co-operation of central banks and international financial institutions. It acts as a forum in hosting meetings of central bankers and in providing facilities for various committees, promoting international financial stability. It is also a centre for monetary and economic research and as such generates a substantial amount of literature

As well reporting the Bank's activities, the BIS annual report presents a global overview of the financial and economic situation, commonly listed under headings such as: developments in the advanced industrial countries, monetary policy in the advanced countries, developments in foreign exchange markets and international financial markets.

In addition to its annual report the BIS provides a number of regular publications, available in PDF format directly from its web site (http://www.bis.org/). These include: *Quarterly review: international banking and financial market developments, BIS consolidated international banking statistics*, the *Joint BIS–IMF–OECD–World Bank statistics on external debt* (formerly *Statistics on external indebtedness*), *Regular OTC derivatives market statistics* and *Central Bank survey of foreign exchange and derivatives market activity*. The various ad hoc and standing committees are responsible for generating a wealth of material. The web site lists the publications of these committees (for example the Basel Committee on Banking Supervision and the Committee on the Global Financial System). An annual conference of economists and representatives from central banks also generates regular papers, for example the March 1999 paper (no. 7) *The monetary and regulatory implications of changes in the banking industry* and the March 2000 meeting (no. 8) *International financial markets and the implications for monetary and financial stability*. There is also a substantial list of economic, policy and working papers, various historical data and methodology (for collection of statistics) and miscellaneous publications on various aspects of monetary policy and financial stability. The BIS generates a good deal of material on payment systems, primarily as a result of the work carried out by the Committee on Payment and Settlement Systems.

The **International Monetary Fund** (http://www.imf.int/) is an international organisation of 182 member countries, established to promote international monetary co-operation, exchange stability, and orderly exchange arrangements; to foster economic growth and high levels of employment; and to provide temporary financial assistance to countries under adequate safeguards to help ease balance of payments adjustment.

The IMF publishes material on bank soundness or crises, banking systems, and bank restructuring. Country specific reports are also produced, particularly from developing countries. Some examples of typical reports are listed in the section below.

The **European Central Bank** (http://www.ecb.int) has several publications of relevance to the banking sector (as well as to monetary systems), which are generally available in PDF format from the web site. The ECB Working Paper Series for example includes *A cross country comparison of market structures in European banking* by O. de Bandt and E. P. Davis, 1999 (ECB working paper no. 7). Other ECB publications are: *Asset prices and banking stability*, 2000; *EU banks' income structure*, 2000; *The effects of technology on the EU banking systems*, 1999, and *Possible effects of EMU on the EU banking systems in the medium to long term*, 1999.

The **World Bank** provides a research function on a range of development issues including international economics (capital flows, financial crises, monetary and fiscal policy) and as such publishes some material of relevance. One example is *Analyzing banking risk* (see entry below).

The **OECD** publishes *Financial market trends* (three times a year), which gives an up-to-date analysis of developments and trends in international and national capital markets. Each issue includes coverage of recent developments in financial markets, regulatory developments, economic and policy issues, new statistical information from OECD governments in areas such as international direct investment, overall bank profitability, institutional investment and privatisation. The OECD has also published *Bank profitability* (see entry below).

Analyzing banking risk: a framework for assessing corporate governance and financial risk management. Greuning, Hennie van and Bratanovic, Sonja Brajovic. Washington DC: World Bank, 2000. 305 p. $100.
A combined book and CD-ROM (with spreadsheet and analysis tools). Provides a comprehensive overview of topics dealing with the assessment, analysis, and management of financial risks in banking. The report emphasises risk management principles and stresses that key players in the corporate governance process are accountable for managing the different dimensions of financial risk.

Bank profitability: financial statements of banks 1999. Paris: Organisation for Economic Co-operation and Development, 1999. 352 p. £44.
Trends in bank profitability and factors affecting it are major indicators of changes in the state of health of national banking systems. These statistics, based on financial statements of banks, provide a tool for analysing developments in bank profitability.

Bank soundness and macroeconomic policy. Lindgren, Carl-Johan, Garcia, Gillian and Saal, Matthew I. Washington DC: International Monetary Fund, 1996. 215 p. $23.50.

In two parts. Part I covers why banking is such an important activity in most economies and how bank soundness may be defined, measured and predicted. Part II covers the macroeconomic causes and consequences of unsound banking systems. It provides a global view of the causes and consequences of banking sector problems pointing to ways in which banking systems can be strengthened nationally and internationally.

Banking soundness and monetary policy: issues and experiences in the global economy. Enoch, Charles and Green, John H., eds. Washington DC: International Monetary Fund, 1997. 542 p. $29.50.

Systemic bank restructuring and macroeconomic policy: papers presented at the seventh Seminar on Central Banking, Washington DC, January 27–31 1997. Alexander, William E., et al. Washington: International Monetary Fund, 1997. 181 p.

The follow-up to *Bank soundness and macroeconomic policy*, *Systemic bank restructuring* comprises a comprehensive programme to rehabilitate a significant part of a banking system so as to provide vital banking services in an efficient and sustainable way. The book builds on 'cross-country restructuring experiences'.

2.02.12 Market research

Market Assessment Publications produces some international studies, such as its *Strategic market intelligence for the professional: banking* (1998), which covers banking in France, Germany, the United Kingdom and the United States. Sections for each country typically include an executive summary and corporate overview, and cover market size, market sectors, share of market, distribution, market forecasts and sector forecasts.

In 1996 **FT Financial Publishing** and **Datamonitor** produced the *FT Guide to global central banks*, which includes central bank profiles from around the world, co-operation between banks, future trends and issues, regulatory roles, control of the markets and control of the domestic economy.

Lafferty Publications produces a number of regional reports. Recent titles include: *Retail financial services in Japan: critical review of an opening market* (£899), *Financial Europe '99: a brainscan of the financial services industry at the dawn of the millennium* (£1,299), *Masters of financial services: American benchmarks for the new millennium* (£1,599), *India – a land of a billion opportunities: personal financial services in the world's largest democracy* (£599), *Banking in Latin America* (£699), *Banking in Asia* (£699) and *Private banking for the Japanese* (£899).

Bankers almanac world ranking 2000. East Grinstead: Reed Information Services, 1999. 420 p.
Annual survey of the financial performance of more than 3,000 international banks in more than 200 countries, ranked by total assets in US$.

Flemings who's who in central banking 1999. Hennessy, Elizabeth, ed. London: Central Banking Publications, 1999. 198 p. £100.
Biographical guide to the world's leading central bankers with entries for 280 central bankers from 125 countries. Each entry includes job titles, age, education and full career history.

Morgan Stanley Dean Witter central bank directory 2000. Pringle, Robert. London: Central Banking Publications, 2000. 230 p. £135.
Information on each of the 173 banks listed includes a recent history and, where available, a description of the current legislative arrangements governing the central bank; also outlines the type of exchange rate system, and the monetary and supervision policy arrangements. Includes contact information on governors and key executives and full details of the banks' web sites and email addresses.

Tenth annual global banking conference: conference themes, presentation summaries. Leonard, John D and Sigee, Jeremy. London: Salomon Smith Barney, 1999. 100 p.
European banks were the focus of the conference and the themes were managing alternative delivery channels, delivering the promise of consolidation and instilling profit motivation in the organisation.

2.02.24 Dictionaries

See the *International dictionary of banking and finance*, section 1.02.24

2.02.26 Bibliographies

Internet sources for bankers: a selective guide to web sites. 2nd ed. Washington: American Bankers Association, 1999. $69 (ABA members), $110 (non-members).
Annotated list of banking information web sites. Comprehensive coverage of the United States but also an international focus. Includes disk of 'bookmarks'.

World banking abstracts. Oxford: Blackwell. £660 per year.
Short abstracts from articles published internationally in over 400 banking and finance publications, classified by subject and fully indexed. Key topics covered are: financial institutions; insurance and pensions; financial instruments and markets; financial operations and services; management; accounting and technology; policy, law and regulation; international and national economies, principles and methods. Also available online. Bimonthly.

2.02.31 Periodicals

ABA banking journal. Washington: American Bankers Association. $50 per year (outside US).
The official journal of the American Bankers Association and so content has a US bias but gives comprehensive coverage of the full range of banking activities. Monthly.

Central banking. London: Central Banking Publications. £245 per year.
Packed with numerous but fairly short articles, many written by key players from central banks around the world on various policy, markets and supervisory matters. Includes editorial, news in brief and focus on 'newsmakers'. Quarterly.

Euromoney. London: Euromoney International Investor. £205 per year.
Listed as the 'journal of the world's capital and money markets'. Wide-ranging and international focus on the financial sector. Useful for country or sector-specific material. Some news items but the real value is the breadth and range of the feature articles. Monthly.

Financial technology bulletin. London: Informa. £420 per year for 21 issues.
Billed as 'the international review of IT in the banking industry' this comes from the same stable as *Banking technology* (2.50.31). Has a mix of international news, new product information, company case studies and market research studies. Provides a good blend of technology with business news, and contains a regular section on innovative Internet applications and online banking initiatives.

International financial statistics. Washington DC: International Monetary Fund. $246 per year.
A standard source of international statistics on all aspects of international and domestic finance. It reports, for most countries of the world, current data needed in the analysis of problems of international payments and of inflation and deflation, international liquidity, international banking, money and banking, interest rates, prices, production, international transactions, government accounts, and national accounts. Information is presented in country tables and in tables of area and world aggregates. Monthly.

2.02.72 CD-ROMs

Thomson global banking resource. Skokie (Illinois): Thomson Financial. Price information is at http://www.tfp.com/index.html.
Also available via the Internet (http://www.tfp.com/index.html) this is a global database of financial institutions, including contacts, correspondents, subsidiaries, affiliates, financial, and payment information. Offered in modular format, the core service provides institution name, address,

phone and fax number; general information about an institution (ownership, branches, subsidiaries, affiliates and all correspondents); general routing codes, SWIFT and BIC addresses, as well as five years of financial profile information and institution ratings and rankings. The other modules provide historical data on institutions, payments data (such as sort codes) and contact details for officers of an institution.

2.02.75 Web sites

AAAdir. http://www.aaadir.com. Free.
A directory of banks, credit unions and financial information on the Internet. Comprehensive link to the banks of the world, listed by geographic region and country. Wide range of links, grouped by subject (such as to books and publications, newsletters, financial news, data and statistics, economic analysts and forecasters, e-commerce, dictionaries, software and hardware).

American Bankers Association. Washington DC: American Bankers Association. http://www.aba.com. Free.
This is an excellent site containing news, a comprehensive online catalogue of ABA publications, a 'consumer connection' section with financial planning information and calculators, World Wide Web links, a schools and conferences section and a very useful 'Center for Banking Information', the ABA's Library catalogue.

Banking on the World Wide Web. Institut fur Betriebswirtschaftliche Geldwirtschaft. http://www.gwdg.de/~ifbg/ifbghome.html. Free.
Generally considered one of the best banking sites on the Web. Among other information it provides a 'Banks of the world' link, which lists over 95 per cent of all worldwide banking sites, classified by region and country. Also has an excellent 'Currency and currency exchange' section with numerous links.

Qualisteam. http://www.qualisteam.com. Free.
Paris-based site. Claims to have the 'world's largest online financial bookstore'. Comprehensive coverage of bank links around the world.

2.10 Law

This section provides sources of material covering the regulatory and legal framework for banks and building societies. The most important pieces of legislation specifically for building societies are the Building Societies Acts 1986 and 1997. The Bank of England Act 1998 transferred the responsibility for banking supervision to the Financial Services Authority. It also established the framework within which the Bank of England exercises operational control over monetary policy.

2.10.03 Textbooks

Banking and financial services regulation. Blair, William, et al. 2nd ed. London: Butterworths, 1998. 546 p. £150.
Examines the implications of the move towards integrating the regulation of the UK's banking and financial services sector. It provides an overview of the regulatory system, a practical account of new financial instruments and explores the likely impact on those working in compliance and banking law. Has chapters on specialist subjects, such as derivatives and global custody, and capital adequacy.

Banking law in Scotland. Crerar, Lorne D. London: Butterworths, 1995. 220p. £72.
A comprehensive treatment of banking law and practice. Traces the development of banking in Scotland from the foundation of the Bank of Scotland in 1695 to the establishment of the Banking Ombudsman Scheme in the 1980s, the promulgation of the Good Banking Code in the 1990s and modern methods of money transmission. Practical emphasis but with reference to both primary and secondary sources and 'in-depth consideration of the specialities of the Scottish banking system'.

Banks and remedies. Blair, William, ed. London: LLP Professional Publishing, 1999. 356 p. £110.
Explains the various opportunities available to reduce risk and organise and administer rescue packages for ailing institutions. This edition addresses the new civil procedures rules in England, arbitration in banking and finance, rescues, EC remedies and English law remedies.

Building Societies Act 1986: a BSA summary. London: Building Societies Association. 9 p. Free.
Booklet providing background information on, and summaring the provisions of, the Act as amended at January 1999. Also available on the web site (http://www.bsa.org.uk).

Butterworths banking law handbook. McBain, Graham, ed. 4th ed. London: Butterworths, 1998. 1,177 p. £78.50.
The fourth edition takes account of extensive changes in banking legislation as a result of the enactment of the Bank of England Act 1998. The 1998 Act is set out in full together with the secondary legislation. European Council Regulations on the provisions relating to the introduction of the euro are also included as well as FSA guidance. A fifth edition was announced at time of writing, and a Banking Law Guide, to accompany this, is due for publication in 2001.

Butterworths international guide to money laundering: law and practice. Parlour, Richard, ed. London: Butterworths, 1995.
Provides an insight into the background of money laundering operations

and an understanding of the anti-money laundering laws and regulations of the key global financial centres. Arranged by country.

Electronic banking and the law. Arora, Anu. 3rd ed. London: IBC Business Publishing, 1997. 153 p. £95.
Developments in electronic funds transfer, cheque truncation, real-time gross settlement, ATMs, consumer protection, international money transfers and electronic purse. Includes an evaluation of important legal cases.

How not to be a money launderer. Cotterill, Nigel Morris. Brentwood: Silkscreen Publications, 1996. 254 p.
Easy to read journalistic style covering: how criminal money is generated, how it is laundered, what the UK laws mean, how to comply with them and how to implement changes in the organisation.

Introduction to law in the financial services. Largan, Mark. Canterbury: CIB, 1999. 208 p. £20.
Provides a general introduction to the legal issues relating to banks, building societies and elements of the insurance and investment sectors.

Law relating to financial services. Roberts, Graham. 3rd ed. Canterbury: Chartered Institute of Bankers, 1998. 350 p. £35.
A good choice for one single, reasonably priced book on the law as it affects the financial services.

Money laundering: guidance notes for the financial sector. London: Joint Money Laundering Steering Group, 1998. 1 vol. (looseleaf).
The *Guidance notes* are published subject to regular review on the understanding that they need to reflect changing circumstances and experience in order to be effective. The *Guidance notes* have the support of financial sector regulators and are issued on behalf of 13 financial sector trade associations who participate in the Joint Money Laundering Steering Group. A *Briefing note* to accompany the *Guidance notes* has been prepared by the British Bankers' Association and is available on the BBA web site at http://www.bba.org.uk/businesses/. Revised and consolidated June 1997, updated August 1998.

Paget's law of banking. Hapgood, Mark. 11th ed. London: Butterworths, 1996. 709 p. £275.
First published in 1904 and now a well-established and authoritative text on banking law.

Practical banking and building society law. Arora, Anu. London: Blackstone Press, 1997. 429 p. £24.95.
A very detailed and thorough approach with background material on the building society sector.

2.10.05 Manuals

The Building Societies Act 1986: practice manual. London: Building Societies Association. 8 vols (looseleaf). £1,000 per year (updates at £500 per year).
The manual is aimed at building societies and their professional advisers and provides all the relevant documentation on the Building Societies Act 1986 (as amended), relevant statutory legislation, and Building Societies Commission and Registry of Friendly Societies' prudential and guidance notes and other documents. The manual provides definitive guidance on the 1986 and 1987 Acts and gives considerable added value in the form of BSA commentaries on the legislation. It is somewhat unwieldy to use, but indispensable.

2.10.21 Directories

Encyclopaedia of banking law. Cresswell, Sir Peter, et al, general editors. London: Butterworths, 1999. 5 vols (looseleaf).
A comprehensive treatment of the modern English law relating to domestic and international banking. It includes a detailed table of cases and statutes, tables of contents by subject division, a subject index and also contains a full range of non-statutory materials. Comprehensively revised and updated from the end of 1999 in a rolling programme, the work draws together material from a wide range of sources including company law, trusts and investor protection legislation. Includes a monthly bulletin service with updates on current developments.

2.10.31 Periodicals

Butterworths journal of international banking and financial law. London: Butterworths. £550.
Aimed at practitioners and provides a global view of the latest developments in banking and financial law. Contains a mix of articles, briefings and book reviews and includes a monthly update on electronic commerce. Also an online version. 11 times a year.

The journal of international banking law. London: Sweet and Maxwell. £420.
Peer-reviewed articles dealing with international banking law with an emphasis on comparisons with different jurisdictions. Aimed at both academics and practising lawyers. Also 'punchy, topical, opinionated pieces often expressing a fairly radical or controversial view'. Monthly.

2.10.75 Web sites

Butterworths banking law direct. London: Butterworths.
Online banking law service containing a range of established works and

in-house databases and materials. The service includes: *Encyclopaedia of banking law; Paget's Law of banking; Journal of international banking and financial law;* UK primary and secondary legislation (updated daily); cases (specialist case reports and relevant *All England reports*); domestic, European and international materials; Butterworths *Banking law handbook;* the banking and bills of exchange volumes of *The digest;* the banking volume of *Halsburys Laws of England;* monthly bulletins (commentary on the latest news, legislative developments and cases); and a daily news update service. Further information from the Butterworths Direct Sales Support Team (tel. 0845 608 1188).

2.15 Regulation

The most important development in recent years is the change in supervisory structure for the banks from the Bank of England to the Financial Services Authority (under the Bank of England Act 1998).

The **Financial Services Authority** (FSA) previously known as the Securities and Investments Board, is an independent non-governmental body, which exercises statutory powers under the Financial Services Act 1986 and the Banking Act 1987 (and certain other legislation). The aims of the FSA are to maintain confidence in the UK financial system, to promote public understanding of the financial system, to secure an appropriate degree of protection for consumers, and to contribute to reducing financial crime. The web site is an important source of information (see section 1.10.75).

The **Building Societies Commission** is the regulatory body for building societies (this task was undertaken by the Registry of Friendly Societies until 1986). On a European level there is also, for example, the **Basle Committee on Banking Supervision**, which although it has no legal force represents broad supervisory standards, practices and guidelines.

The **British Bankers' Association** is an important source of information on retail banking compliance matters. A copy of *The banking code 1998* is available from the BBA web site (see section 2.00.75). This is a voluntary code of practice drawn up by the by the BBA, the **Building Societies Association** (BSA) and the **Association for Payment Clearing Services** (APACS), which sets minimum standards of service that personal customers can expect from all banks and building societies that subscribe to the Code. The BBA also publishes the full text of the *Code of Conduct for the Advertising of Interest Bearing Accounts* on its web site. *The new Data Protection Act 2000: a practitioner's handbook* is listed on the BBA web site, but was not available at the time of writing. *Implementing Part III of the Disability Discrimination Act: BBA guidance on banks' responsibilities to their disabled customers from October 1999* provides guidance to banks while a consumer leaflet, *Disability legislation: you and your bank*, provides guidance to consumers.

A lengthy list of titles providing guidelines or agreements for treasury functions and the wholesale money markets is available from the BBA. These are: *The International Currency Options Market – ICOM terms; International Exchange & Options Master Agreement – IFEMA terms; 1997 Foreign Exchange & Options Master Agreement (FEOMA); International Foreign Exchange Master Agreement; International Currency Options Master Agreement; Foreign Exchange & Options Master Agreement; Legal opinions; London market guidelines for certificates of deposit; International Deposit Netting Agreement – IDNA terms; International Deposit Netting Agreement – legal opinions; Forward Rate Agreements – FRABBA terms; Interest rate swaps – BBAIRS terms; BBA treasury terminology; The BBA credit derivatives report 1998; Credit derivatives report 1999/2000; London market guidelines: commercial paper; Internal modelling and CAD II: Qualifying and quantifying risk within a financial institution*.

2.15.03 Textbooks

Consumer protection in financial services. Cartwright, Peter. London: Kluwer, 1999. 292 p. £75.
Considers the role of the EU and UK ombudsmen schemes operating in the United Kingdom in improving consumer protection and examines the legal mechanisms protecting consumers in the banking, financial services, investments and insurance industries.

The emerging framework of financial regulation. Goodhart, C. A. E., ed. London: Central Banking Publications, 1998. 606 p. £95.
A collection of academic papers compiled by the Financial Markets Group of the London School of Economics.

Handbook of banking regulation and supervision in the United Kingdom. Hall, Maximilian J. B. 3rd ed. Cheltenham: Edward Elgar Publishing, 1999. 422 p. £95.
Very detailed coverage of banking regulation and supervision. Includes chapters on the Barings Bank collapse and the BCCI affair. Now in its third edition, this is a standard text on the subject.

The regulation of banking in Europe. Briscoe, Andrew, ed. London: Carlton Laws, 1999. 183 p. £45.
Written by an international team of lawyers, the book provides reports on the banking regulations of 21 countries in western and central Europe. Each report provides a brief and concise overview of the regulatory framework for banking.

2.15.05 Manuals

Banking supervisory policy. London: Financial Services Authority. 2 vols (looseleaf).
Also available from the FSA's web site, see section 1.10.75. Gives details of the FSA's prudential policy for its supervision of institutions authenticated under the Banking Act 1987. This is being superseded by the *FSA handbook of rules and guidance* made up of consultation papers and policy reports containing all the FSA's rules and guidance made under the new legislation (when the Financial Services and Markets Bill is enacted). The *Handbook* is published on the FSA web site.

2.15.12 Market research

Global financial regulation: myth or reality? McDowell, Robert. London: Reuters Business Insight, 1999. 108 p. £495.
An investigation into the regulation of global financial markets. Gives background material on the markets (their rationale, evolution, participants and financial instruments, and their impact on global and national economies) and has chapters on the scope of current regulatory supervision, impediments and consequences, the areas and substance of change, existing or new structures and organisations and the limitations of global financial regulation.

2.15.21 Directories

Who's who in financial regulation. Hennessy, Elizabeth, ed. London: Central Banking Publications, 1998. 120 p. £90.
Contains detailed bibliographies of 200 of the world's senior supervisors from central banks and regulatory agencies.

2.15.31 Periodicals

See also section 1.10.31 for similar journals with a broader focus.

Financial regulation report. London: Informa. £545.
Digest of worldwide regulatory developments and their implications for the financial services industry. 11 issues a year.

The financial regulator. London: Central Banking Publications. £240.
Global focus of developments in regulatory structures including interviews with key individuals and briefings from international forums. Quarterly.

2.33 Retail banks

In the UK the retail banks are often taken to mean the 'big four' clearing banks but because of the blurring of divisions between types of institution, it is becoming more common to talk of retail financial services, rather than retail banks. The entry of other players in to the personal financial services market such as retailers and travel companies has resulted in a growing information base for financial consumers, much of it Web-based. The more general sources will be found in chapter 1.

There are some books on individual banks, such as *Falling eagle: the decline of Barclays Bank* by Martin Vander Weyer (Weidenfeld & Nicolson, 2000, £16).

2.33.01 Consumer guides

The **British Bankers' Association** produces a number of FAQs on its web site (see section 2.00.75). These include a range of subjects grouped under 'BankFacts' (e.g. opening a bank account, running a bank account, banking abroad). There are also FAQs on dormant accounts, home banking and Internet shopping. The BBA's annual report concentrates on the past year's work of the Association rather than providing more general material on the banking sector. However, the Association produces a monthly eight-page newsletter with a useful round-up of news and developments.

Issues of relevance to banking and consumers (though not specifically directed at consumers) are also dealt with by the **National Consumer Council**, for example, one ad hoc report is: *In the bank's bad books: how the banking code of practice works for customers in hardship* (1997).

The annual report from the **Banking Ombudsman Scheme** (shortly to be subsumed under one central scheme, the Financial Services Ombudsman Scheme) provides some useful data on consumer complaints dealt with by the scheme such as detailed statistics and summaries of sample cases. The Scheme's web site is at http://www.obo.org.uk.

Dealing with your bank: how to assert yourself as a paying customer. Cain, Brian. Oxford: How to Books, 1997. 142 p.

A practical approach covering both personal and business banking, including case studies. Covers topics such as opening an account, borrowing money, managing money and banking online.

2.33.03 Textbooks

The big four British banks. Rogers, David. Basingstoke: Macmillan Press, 1999. 240 p. £25.
Aims to arrive at a picture of the banking sector by examining the strategies, cultures and organisational forms of Britain's big four banks.

The Internet and financial services: a CSFI report. London: Centre for the Study of Financial Innovation, 1997. 214 p.
Coverage includes retail banking, personal finance, payment and settle-

ment systems, regulatory matters as they affect the Internet in the United Kingdom, trends, future developments and implications of Internet banking. Takes both a UK and US focus.

The virtual banking revolution: the customer, the bank and the future. Essinger, James. London: International Thomson Business Press, 1999. 290 p. £60.
Emphasis on the strategic issues of using the new virtual delivery channels for banks and other financial services providers such as supermarkets. Includes case studies. International examples but the main focus is the UK sector.

2.33.12 Market research

Lafferty Publications produces regular market reports on retail banking, mainly with an emphasis on new delivery channels. Examples are: *E finance – Europe: new entrants in Internet financial services* (£1,999), *New entrants in financial services* (£1,199), *Retailers in financial services* (£799), *Delivery channel strategies* (£799) and *Bank branching 2010* (£699).

Datamonitor has produced regular reports on the UK retail banks, typically covering the structure of UK retail banks (branch numbers, ATMs, key ratios etc.), a market overview and competitive analysis of the main areas of activity (such as money transmission services, deposits and investments, loans and mortgages), together with key issues and forecasts and performance data for individual banks. A recent report is *UK retail banks and building societies 1999*, which is a very comprehensive market study of all aspects of the sector including market forecasts and statistical data. *IT in European retail banking distribution channels 1998* and *The Future of E-banking in Europe* (1999), both by Datamonitor, reflect the growing importance of new distribution channels in retail banking. Datamonitor also produces reports as part of the invaluable Reuters Business Insight Series, such as *The outlook for European retail banking 1999–2005: an industry at the cross-roads* (1998).

Key Note publishes a regular research report on retail banking, now in its 10th edition. *Personal banking 1999* (£279) provides a comprehensive analysis of the changing retail banking sector as new players enter the market. The report provides coverage of the industry background, market size, trends and forecasts, buying behaviour, current issues and company profiles. A 1997 Key Note report, *Retail branch banking* is useful for background material (analysis of market sector, trends and forecasts up to 2001). **Mintel** also covers retail banking and has produced a 1999 report, *Current accounts*.

Informa Publishing has a growing list of market research reports, as part of its Strategic Focus Reports Series, each priced at £695. Examples are

Ecommerce in retail banking, *Retail outlet banking* and *Retail banking and the Euro: what now?*

The **British Bankers' Association** produces an annual statistical digest, *Banking business: annual abstract of banking statistics*, providing the most comprehensive source on banking statistics (£49 non-members).

Bank sorting code numbers 1999. Reed Information, 1999. £3.50.

Creating tomorrow's leading retail bank. New York: Economist Intelligence Unit, 1999. 88 p.
Based on interviews with 51 senior bank executives from North America, the United Kingdom, continental Europe and the Asia/Pacific region. This research report explores the ways banks are trying to identify, attract, satisfy and retain a profitable customer base. It covers database marketing techniques, delivery channels, information management technology and Internet banking, and provides valuable qualitative data. Written in co-operation with PricewaterhouseCoopers.

Europe's new banks: the 'non-bank' phenomenon. Lascelles, David. London: Centre for the Study of Financial Innovation, 1999. 42 p. £25.
Examines the challenge of new banks and non-banks to the traditional European retail bank and the implications for employment in the financial sector. Includes European country profiles.

Online banking: effective strategies for success. Norfolk, D. London: Financial Times, 1999. 103 p. £495.
Provides the business case for online or e-banking, using various case studies and examining the infrastructure underpinnng the banks' relationship with their customers.

Online retail financial services. Wall, Matthew. London: FT Finance, 1997. 90 p.
Focuses primarily on financial services available to people via their personal computers. The online market is dominated by the United States so a study of US developments is useful in order to guess what is likely to happen elsewhere. Contains a large section on the United States, one on the United Kingdom and a chapter on continental Europe. Coverage includes technological developments, security and regulation.

Tearing down the walls: changing bank distribution. Lord, Nick, Samuels, Simon and Young, Stuart. London: Salomon Smith Barney, 1999. 60 p.
Examination of changes in distribution channels and the entry of new players into the market. Brief analysis of the main players regarding branch networks, telephone and PC banking.

2.33.16 Company research

The market research companies produce occasional company profiles as part of their market research data and occasionally publish more substantial company reports, for example, **Market Assessment Publications** produced *UK retail banks company profiles* (1997). Online sources are the most efficient way of gathering up-to-date company information (see section 2.00.78) and stockbrokers reports are also a valuable source of company data as are the annual reports and accounts of the banks themselves.

2.33.21 Directories

UK clearings directory: a directory of offices of banks and other financial institutions participating in the payment clearings operations under the auspices of APACS. East Grinstead: Reed Business Information, 2000. 418 p. £13.95.
Includes a list of sort codes.

2.33.31 Periodicals

Retail banker international. Dublin: Lafferty Publications. £799.
Newsletter issued every two weeks in both online and printed version. Covers news and analysis of developments in the global retail banking and consumer financial services industry. Critical management issues in financial services distribution, bank re-engineering, expansion and globalisation, mergers, acquisitions and alliances, competition, benchmarking and regulation. Includes interviews, country surveys, ranking tables, case studies and examination of quarterly and year-end results. A compilation of material from the newsletter is published annually as the *Retail banker international yearbook*: the 2000 edition is priced at £549 (250 p.).

2.33.75 Web sites

The Chartered Institute of Bankers web site (see section 2.00.75) provides links to the sites of UK banks. Typical content of the banks' web sites will be press releases, products and services for consumers, small business and corporate customers and online banking.

Financial Times. London: Financial Times. http://www.financialtimes.com.
Contains a section called 'FT your money' with consumer advice and information on the full range of retail financial services, with articles, FAQs, product comparison searches and links to providers.

2.35 Building societies

As a result of mergers and the conversion of many societies to plc status (following the 1986 Building Societies Act) the building society movement is diminishing. As of June 2000 there were only 68 societies. Building societies' ability to convert to company status has sparked considerable debate about the viability of mutuality, and this is reflected in much of the literature. There is a considerable difference between societies in terms of services and product range as well as in organisational structure, management and marketing strategies. Many societies, for example, retain a strong regional focus, concentrating their lending operations locally. Many of the texts on building societies were published before the more recent legislation (in the late 1980s) and are therefore considerably out of date (and therefore not listed here). The **Building Societies Association** is the major publisher of building society material although with the establishment of the **Council of Mortgage Lenders** in 1989 much of the regular material previously published by the BSA is now under the CML imprint.

2.35.01 Consumer guides

The **Building Societies Association** provide a range of fact sheets, FAQs and leaflets on its web site. These include: *Assets of authorised building societies, The Building Societies Act 1986: a BSA summary, History of the building society industry, Individual savings accounts and building societies, Protection of investors, Taxation of building society interest 1999/2000, Transfer of engagements, What EMU means for you, Why we need building societies.*

Taxation of building society interest. London: Building Societies Association. 18 p. Single copies free.
Leaflet explaining the tax treatment of the interest that building societies pay to investors. Also available on the Web (http://www.bsa.org.uk).

2.35.02 Career guides

A chapter on careers in building societies is included in the book *Careers in banking and finance* (see section 2.00.02).

Going for it. London: Building Societies Association.
Aimed at school leavers, features the jobs and career opportunities available in building societies. Only available on the BSA web site (http://www.bsa.org.uk).

2.35.03 Textbooks

Building society operations: the uniqueness of mutual societies and their role in the modern financial services industry. Souster, Bob. Canterbury: CIB Publishing, 1999. 182 p. £19.95.
A comprehensive account of the building society movement.

Introduction to building society operations. Souster, Bob. Canterbury: CIB, 2000. 156 p. £20.
A summary of the many changes that have occurred throughout the building society movement, from de-mutualisation, increased competition, new legislation, new technology and the diversification of the product base.

Mutuality for the twenty-first century. Gilmore, Rosalind. London: Centre for the Study of Financial Innovation. 28 p. £25.
An examination of the future of mutuals, which argues that they do have a future but need a modern legal structure to take advantage of the opportunities offered. The author proposes specific new legislation to allow mutuals to flourish.

To our mutual advantage. Leadbetter, Charles and Christie, Ian. London: Demos, 1999. 112 p. £9.95.
Covers building societies and other mutual institutions (friendly societies, mutual insurers etc.). A useful report that provides a comprehensive survey of the state of health of mutual organisations in Britain and a prognosis for the future. Includes case studies.

2.35.05 Manuals

See also the Building Societies Association's *The Building Societies Act 1986: practice manual* (2.10.05).

Building society annual accounts manual. London: Building Societies Association. 1 vol. (looseleaf). £115 per year, plus updates at £100 per year.

Investment manual. London: Building Societies Association. 2 vols (looseleaf). £180 per year, plus updates at £100 per year.
Provides guidance in relation to law and practice across a wide range of topics concerning investment and savings in building societies, primarily prepared for the BSA's members. Topics covered include: opening and running accounts for different types of investor, confidentiality and data protection, codes of practice, services to customers, events affecting account holders, cheques and money transmission, premises, the Ombudsman, and European aspects.

2.35.12 Market research

The market research companies do produce ad hoc reports on the sector but many include building societies in their more general market reviews.
Market Assessment International published a report in 1997 that provided a strategic overview, analysis of lending activities, historical background, and a SWOT analysis.

The future of the building society movement: a vibrant sector or a spent force? Imeson, Michael, Gould, Dan. London: FT Finance, 1999. 121 p. £450.
An assessment of the building society sector at a crucial time in the movement's history.

2.35.16 Company research

All societies are required to produce annual reports to the **Building Societies Commission** and these provide a good starting point for research. Abridged annual accounts data listed by society is also published in the *Building Societies yearbook* (section 2.35.21). Many societies have published their own histories and many produce regular newspapers, newsletters and journals. Press releases are also a good source of a society's operations, and can usually be accessed from the society's web site. The **Building Societies Association** publishes the annual *Building society annual accounts data* based on data drawn from the societies' annual reports and accounts.

Thedata provides a wealth of individual institutional data on building societies in a series of reviews covering various aspects of their financial and operational performance over a rolling five-year period and providing a page or two of data for each society. These are: *1994–1998 building society five year funding report* (November 1999); *1994–1998 building society five year profit report* (December 1999); *1994–1998 building society five year operational report* (December 1999); *1994–1998 building society five year credit report* (November 1999); *1994–1998 building society five year arrears and losses report* (December 1999).

BSA monthly statistics digest. London: Building Societies Association. £54 per year.
Figures on building society mortgage lending and savings, with a commentary. Monthly. Also available on the web site (http://bsa.org.uk).

Economics of mutuality and the future of building societies: [series of research papers]. Llewellyn, David. London: Building Societies Association, 1997.
A research exercise commissioned by the Building Societies Association in 1996 to provide an independent economic analysis and appraisal of some of the key issues in the debate about mutuality versus conversion to bank status. The study comprises seven papers, which can be purchased individually or as a complete set (£20 for the seven papers, £5 for individual reports, £3 per report if two or more are purchased together). The papers are: *The mutuality v conversion debate* (nos 1 and 2); *The economics of mutuality* (No. 3); *Corporate governance and the market for corporate control* (No. 4); *Trends in the British financial system: the context for building societies*

(No. 5); *The economics of diversification* (no. 6); *Contract banking and its potential for building societies* (no. 7).

2.35.21 Directories

Building societies yearbook. London: Professional & Business Information Publishing. £50.
Published annually in August. Provides data on each building society such as head office and branch addresses, a list of senior executives, staff numbers and branches, summary balance sheet, income and expenditure account and financial ratios. Plus review articles and statistical tables, a list of building society mergers and changes of name. The 1999/2000 issue contains 427 pages.

2.35.26 Bibliographies

Building society news. London: Building Societies Association. Free. Newsletter of the Building Societies Association covering developments in building societies and the financial services sector as a whole. Monthly.

Library bulletin. London: Building Societies Association. £150 per year. This monthly bibliography includes books and journal articles on building societies, the savings market, the mortgage and housing finance markets. Arranged by subject and including, for journal articles, a brief abstract.

2.35.31 Periodicals

Building societies are mainly covered in the general financial services and banking periodicals, listed in other sections. The *Mortgage finance gazette* (see section 2.78.31), previously the *Building societies gazette*, is still considered the main trade journal for the industry.

2.37 Investment banks

This section deals with both merchant and investment banks, as the two terms are often considered synonymous. The term 'investment banking' is generally defined as the advice given by banks on the raising of funds, mergers and acquisitions and a variety of other issues. As investment banks frequently form a subsidiary of a retail bank, the normal sources of information also apply.

2.37.02 Career guides

A chapter on careers in investment banks is included in *Careers in banking and finance* (2.00.02). The London Investment Banking Association has some careers information on its web site (http://www.liba.org.uk/).

2.37.03 Textbooks

All that glitters: the fall of Barings. Gapper, John and Denton, Nicholas. London: Penguin, 1997. 400 p. £9.99.
Typical of a handful of titles covering the Nick Leeson–Barings affair.

The business of investment banking. Liaw, Thomas. 2nd ed. Chichester: Wiley, 1999. 348 p. £44.50.
Designed to be a professional reference and graduate text covering a broad scope of banking activities. It is divided into four parts: basic banking, global perspectives, trading and risk management, and special topics.

Investment banking: theory and practice. Gardner, Edward and Molyneux, Philip, eds. 2nd ed. London: Euromoney Books, 1996. 377 p. £110.
22 chapters by academics and practitioners on how to succeed in investment banking. Coverage includes: gaining a competitive advantage; the supervision of investment banking; the international money markets; global forex markets and hedging exchange rate risks; Eurobond primary and secondary markets; derivative instruments and risk management; financial engineering using OTC products; mergers and acquisitions, corporate restructuring; syndicated lending and the syndicated loan markets.

The rise and fall of the merchant bank: the evolution of the global investment bank. Banks, Erik. Kogan Page, 1999. 300 p. £50.
Covers the development of merchant banking over two centuries up to 2000 and considers the future beyond that time. The text considers the environment and evolution of the merchant banks, the pace of innovation and the impact of globalisation on the historical banking institutions. Provides a very thorough and substantial treatment of the subject and includes an excellent bibliography.

The world's banker: the history of the house of Rothschild. Ferguson, Niall. London: Weidenfeld & Nicolson, 1998. 1,309 p. £24.

2.37.12 Market research

Datamonitor produced a two-volume report in 1995, *Merchant banks*, which covered competitive analysis (of the top merchant banks in their core areas of business), forecasts and issues, and company profiles.

Global investment banking strategy: insights from industry leaders. New York: Economist Intelligence Unit, 1998. 111 p.
Analysis of the forces affecting change by outlining the strategic decisions regarding customer and product focus. Written in co-operation with A. T. Kearney, Inc.

2.37.26 Bibliographies

Bibliography of banking histories. Vol II, Savings, merchant and overseas banks. Wellings, Fred and Gibb, Alastair. Fife: The Authors, 1997. 95p.
Lists the histories of the merchant banks and includes a very brief review of this literature.

2.37.36 Newspapers

Financial news. London: London Financial News Publishing Ltd. £199 per year.
Financial newspaper providing a source of information about Europe's investment banking, fund management and securities industries. News and regular features on: mergers and acquisitions; derivatives; private equity; fund management; equity capital markets; debt and credit markets; equity research; sales and trading; IT and e-commerce; global portfolio trading; custody and settlement. There is also an accompanying web version at http://www.efinancialnews.com. In addition to the core news provision the web version is developing a series of information tools and services such as search engines for archive or Web searching; a jobs database and career management facilities; and personalised news, which can be routed through an email address, hand-held computer or WAP mobile phone. Weekly.

2.37.75 Web sites

The London Investment Banking Association. London: London Investment Banking Association. http://www.liba.org.uk.
Has a list of its members on its web site, with some links through to the web sites of individual banks. The LIBA site also lists press releases and annual reports for the last two years.

2.39 Bank of England

The Bank of England Act 1998 ensured that the Bank's monetary policy was made legally independent of the government. It also transferred banking supervision to the Financial Services Authority. The **Bank of England** is a major publisher of banking material and its web site (http://www.bankofengland.co.uk) provides full coverage of its titles (and many documents are available to download in PDF format). This section provides a selective list of the main Bank of England material. The Bank's site allows searching for publications either by format (regular or ad hoc publications, Centre for Central Banking Studies training handbooks, Monetary Policy Committee minutes, consultative papers, fact sheets, speeches, press releases, statistics and working papers) or by subject (eligible securities, European matters, financial stability, London Approach, markets, monetary analysis and policy, small business and supervision).

There are fact sheets on the Bank and its role, banknotes, foreign exchange markets and monetary policy in the United Kingdom.

The Bank of England's Centre for Central Banking Studies delivers training courses, seminars, workshops and technical assistance for central banks and central bankers worldwide. A series of publications under the title *Handbooks in Central banking* has been published as a result of this training programme. The handbooks are aimed at staff taking on new responsibilities within a central bank.

2.39.03 Textbooks

Blackstone's guide to the Bank of England Act 1998. Blair, Michael, et al. London: Blackstone Press, 1998. 252 p. £24.95.
An in-depth commentary on the Act, which includes a background on monetary policy, the policy background of central bank independence and an overview of the Bank's constitutional history.

2.39.08 Technical reports

Practical issues arising from the euro. London: Bank of England.
Practical issues arising from the euro is a series of booklets providing a London perspective on the development of euro-denominated financial markets, financial services and the supporting financial infrastructure. The planning and preparation for possible future UK entry are also covered. This semi-annual publication follows on from its predecessor – *Practical issues arising from the introduction of the euro* (known as 'PIQ', which was published every quarter) – where the main focus was to assist the UK wholesale financial sector prepare for the euro.

2.39.12 Market research

Inflation report. London: Bank of England. As a single purchase (without the *Quarterly bulletin*) £12 per year.
Detailed economic analysis and inflation projections on which the Bank's Monetary Policy Committee bases its interest rate decisions, and presents an assessment of the prospects for UK inflation over the following two years. Published in February, May, August and November and is available on its own or as a combined package with the Bank's *Quarterly bulletin* (see below).

2.39.31 Periodicals

Bank of England quarterly bulletin. London: Bank of England. Priced as a combined package with the *Inflation report*, £40.

Structured in three main sections under recent economic and financial developments (markets and operations, the international environment); research and analysis; and speeches (of Bank of England officers). Articles are preceded with substantial summaries and are well illustrated with statistical data in graphs and tables.

2.39.75 Web sites

Bank of England. London: Bank of England. http://www.bankofengland.co.uk. Free.
An extremely comprehensive and well-designed site with substantial background information on the history, structure and role of the Bank. The publications section is particularly useful, with full details of items, including summaries. There is also a good deal of full-text information available (in PDF). The 'Links' section provides a list of the sites of central banks and other monetary authorities in the European Union and G10 countries as well as Internet addresses for information on the euro. The site also includes *The City handbook* (see section 1.00.75).

2.50 Management and operations

The changes in structure, operations and regulation in banking over the last decade have resulted in the emergence of new management imperatives. The management of IT features prominently in books and periodicals. As banking is essentially about risk, texts on risk management proliferate. Risk management has been included in this section because it is a fundamental aspect of the banking operation. It is a complex subject with a number of different facets (such as solvency risk, liquidity risk, credit risk, interest rate risk, price risk and operating risk). The **British Bankers' Association** has published its *Operational risk management survey 1999* (acknowledging that operational risk management as a new discipline has its own management structure, tools and processes). The survey is based on the current and emerging practices of 55 global financial institutions. Other titles under the BBA risk management heading are: *Credit derivatives: key issues, The environment – the challenge for business and banking, Banks' attitudes to local authorities: a business survey, Banks and businesses: working together – a statement of principles*.

2.50.03 Textbooks

The **Chartered Institute of Bankers** has produced an entire series of texts on risk management. Each text is between 150 and 180 pages, is priced at £30 and the series is subdivided into six different sections: cashflow management (*Cashflow forecasting and liquidity, Cashflow control, Cash collection and transmission*); credit risk management (*Framework for credit risk man-*

agement, Measuring credit risk, Corporate credit analysis); corporate finance (*Capital structuring, Mergers & acquisitions, Venture capital and buyouts, Leasing*); currency risk management (*Introduction to currency risk, Foreign exchange markets, Currency options, Currency futures, Currency swaps, Hedging currency exposures*); interest risk management (*Introduction to interest risk, Money markets, Interest rate options, Interest rate swaps, FRAs and interest rate futures, Hedging interest rate exposures*); and debt and equity markets (*Overview of the markets, Equity finance, Government bonds, Corporate bonds and commercial paper, Hybrid financial instruments, Bank finance*).

At the more expensive (and highly theoretical) range of the market, **Risk Books** publishes a number of titles, such as *Modelling and hedging equity derivatives* (£145), *Operational risk and financial institutions* (£179) and *Volatility: new estimation techniques for pricing derivatives* (£109).

A major series of text books has also been published by the **Chartered Institute of Bankers** to accompany its Diploma in Financial Services Management. The titles include: *Managing information, Managing people in organisations, The structure of accounts* and *Asset based working capital finance*.

Achieving transformation and renewal in financial services. Talwar, Rohit, ed. Cambridge: Woodhead Publishing, 1999. 221 p. £35.

Back office and beyond: a guide to procedures, settlements and risk in financial markets. King, Mervyn. Cambridge: GDP, 1999. 193 p. £40.

Bank management. Koch, Timothy W. and MacDonald, S. Scott. Fort Worth (USA): Dryden Press, 1999. 1,024 p. £28.95.
Although this is an American publication, and has a strong bias towards the US banking system, it has been included here because of its comprehensive treatment of the full range of banking management issues in a changing business environment. Aimed at students, it provides a thorough examination of financial concepts as they apply to the broad spectrum of credit, investment and funding decisions. Includes a valuable discussion of investment tools and strategies employed by banks, including financial futures, options on futures, interest rate swaps, and hedging.

Banking and finance on the Internet. Cronin, Mary J., ed. New York: Van Nostrand Reinhold, 1997. 352 p. £32.50.
An American perspective of the role of the Internet in banking and financial services (of value as the United States has been in the forefront of advances in this area). Shows how business models and customer relationships are changing.

Banking operations: regulation, practice and treasury management. Largan, Mark and Colley, Alan. Canterbury: Chartered Institute of Bankers, 1997. £30.

An emphasis on the operational side of the treasury function covering treasury management of financial services institutions, banking and investment supervision and regulation, market practice and procedures.

The banking revolution: salvation or slaughter?: how technology is creating winners and losers. Carrington, Mark St J., Languth, Philip W and Steiner, Thomas D. London: Pitman, 1997. 278 p.

Focuses on IT in banks and aims to provide insight into what technology is doing to the sector and to offer some guidelines on the management of technology in banks. Some of the issues covered include payment systems, credit cards, diversification of bank services, home banking and branch-less banking.

Banking: an industry accounting and auditing guide. Hitchens, John, Hogg, Mitchell and Mallett, David. 3rd ed. Milton Keynes: Accountancy Books, 1996. 731 p. £80.

Substantial and comprehensive treatment of the regulations and accounting developments and background to the main banking functions and risks involved. Aimed at banking professionals.

The commercial banking handbook: strategic planning for growth in the new decade. Chorafas, Dimitris N. Basingstoke: Macmillan Business, 1999. 463 p. £62.50.

Extremely comprehensive 'road map' of all the strategic planning issues aimed at banking professionals. Covers the role of marketing, relationship banking, pricing of products and services, the branch office network, private and direct banking, credit and risk. Includes case studies.

Fundamentals of financial institutions management. Cornett, Marcia Milton and Saunders, Anthony. London: McGraw-Hill, 1999. 762 p. £25.99.

Information technology and financial services: the new partnership. Gandy, Anthony and Chapman, Chris. Chicago: Glenlake, 1997. 224 p. £35.

An examination of the benefits that can be developed between banking and information technology. Explanation of technological processes, terms and key concepts and an analysis of the way technology can alter the dynamics of financial services. Covers retail, wholesale banking and investment banking. Global approach, packed with case studies from around the world.

Internal controls in banking. Kinsella, Ray, ed. Dublin: Oak Tree Press, 1995. 140 p. £35.

Eight papers, which bring together the perspectives of the banks, the supervisory authorities and the accountant or auditor and that examine how the nature of internal controls in banking has 'been changed and refined and how this has impacted on organisational and management structures'. The main focus is on the UK banking system.

Leadership in financial services: lessons for the future. Davis, Stevan. Basingstoke: Macmillan Business, 1997. 198 p. £52.50.
Profiles of 26 leaders of financial service institutions and their insights and experiences in addressing the challenge of change.

Management in the financial services industry: thriving on organisational change. Croft, Liz, Norton, Ann and Whyte, Jan. Canterbury: Chartered Institute of Bankers, 1999. 428 p. £25.

Managing banking risks. Cade, Eddie. Cambridge: Gresham Books, 1997. 256 p. £85.
A wide-ranging primer for generalist reading giving 'a practising banker's overview of the full spectrum of risks that a modern bank needs to manage'.

Managing information: understanding the impact of IT on the financial services. Fawcett, Phillip. Canterbury: Chartered Institute of Bankers, 1999. 252 p. £19.95.

Managing the new bank technology: an executive blueprint for the future. Seymann, Marilyn R., ed. Chicago: Glenlake, 1998. 293 p. £45.
American focus but covers a wide range of banking technology management issues of interest to bank executives in the United Kingdom. Topics covered include: understanding bank technology, bank technology strategies, the role of the Internet, fraud and security, outsourcing, managing the bank's networks, technology's impact on the mortgage industry and technology's role in mergers and acquisitions.

Risk management in banking. Bessis, Joel. Chichester: John Wiley, 1997. 448 p. £24.95.
Value for money coverage of all aspects of financial risk management in banking.

Treasury management. Hudson, Alan, with Largan, Mark and Colley, Allan. 3rd ed. Canterbury: Chartered Institute of Bankers, 1998. 460 p. £45.
Cited by CIB in its 'classic' reference list, this text covers treasury operations, supervision and control, financial instruments and financial, derivative and capital markets.

Understanding volatility and liquidity in the financial markets: building a comprehensive system of risk management. Chorafas, Dimitris N. London: Euromoney Books, 1998. 219 p. £125.
Practical examples to explain the impact of volatility and liquidity on the financial markets.

2.50.12 Market research

Informa Publishing has produced a number of reports in its *Strategic focus reports* series, including *Modelling and managing bank credit risk* (£695); this gives an 'overview of recent developments in the rapidly evolving fields of risk management and measurement, with an emphasis on commercial lending'.

2.50.31 Periodicals

Banking technology. London: IBC Business Publishing. £190 per year. Well-established journal covering a very broad range of banking technology issues, with a heavy emphasis on news and latest developments as well as surveys and numerous feature articles. Examples of subjects covered are: Internet and digital banking, mobile banking, smart cards, IT architectures, financial data distribution, data warehousing, electronic payments, neural networks, exchange trading systems, dealing room technology, artificial intelligence. 10 issues a year.

Financial IT. London: Incisive Research. £465 per year.
Newsletter with global IT news in the financial sector. One or two very short articles, mainly a round-up of the systems being used by financial organisations, targeted at 'IT decision-makers' in the banking, finance and building society sector. 20 issues a year. Alternate issues are entitled *FT IT monthly update*.

Financial sector technology. London: Perspective Publishing. £89 per year. Aimed at senior IT managers it reports on IT developments within the perspective of business trends. In addition to news and features each issue of the magazine contains an in-depth supplement on subjects such as IT security, networking, cabling, telecomms, business continuity. Bimonthly.

Virtual finance international. London: Evandale. £575 per year.
Newsletter concentrating on the growing trend for financial services providers to 'virtualise' their operations. Short news items, global coverage. 24 issues a year.

2.50.75 Web sites

The Chartered Institute of Bankers' supersite (2.00.75) has links to resources on management and marketing.

Reuters. London: Reuters. http://www.reuters.com. Free.
The web site provides a 'Reuters risk management' section, which includes articles and an archive of risk news for the previous year.

2.56 Marketing

2.56.03 Textbooks

The art of marketing mortgages. Knight, Stephen. London: Collins & Brown, 1997. 320 p. £75.
Written by the founder and chairman of Private Label Mortgage Services Ltd, the United Kingdom's first specialist mortgage design and distribution company, this book charts that company's marketing strategies in a competitive environment. Includes the views on the mortgage market by 14 major industry figures.

Customer services: marketing and the competitive environment. Jones, Steve and Palmer, Sally. Canterbury: Chartered Institute of Bankers, 1996. 330 p. £30.
Explanation of how general marketing theory can be applied to head office and branch functions. Published to accompany CIB's Professional Investment Certificate.

Financial services marketing: a reader. Meiden, Arthur, Lewis, Barbara and Moutinho, Luiz, eds. London: Dryden Press, 1997. 375 p. £18.95.
Collection of 24 academic essays, which is designed to meet the needs of undergraduate and masters level students, as well as researchers. Aims to serve as an overview of the critical aspects of marketing of financial services as well as an analysis and discussion of new concepts and trends.

Introduction to marketing, customer service and sales. Watkins, Charley. Canterbury: CIB, 1999. 166 p. £20.
This text provides an introduction to the basic principles, terminology and concepts of marketing with 'a focus on service to personal customers through retail networks, direct selling and other direct marketing techniques'.

Marketing financial services. Meiden, Arthur. Basingstoke: Macmillan Press, 1996. 324 p. £15.99.
A basic text aimed at students and practitioners. It covers all areas of financial services offered by banks and building societies as well as insurance and other finance companies and credit card issuers. Also includes many exhibits, descriptions of situations, examples or the results of research and studies in the United Kingdom and overseas.

Marketing financial services. Ennew, C., Watkins, T and Wright, N. 2nd ed. Butterworth Heinemann, 1995. £21.99.

2.56.12 Market research

Lafferty Publications produces a varied range of market studies under the general heading of bank marketing. These are typically priced from around £599 to £1,199 and titles include *Customer relationship management on the web* (£1,199), *Database marketing for retail banks and financial services companies* (£999), *Targeting customers for profit* (£699), *Distribution and marketing strategies in action* (£599), *Growing brand loyalty* (£699) and *Internet financial services* (£699). Two of **Mintel**'s financial services report deals with marketing: *Banks and building societies: fight for distribution* (1997) and *Branding in financial services* (1999). **Informa Publishing** has published *Brand strategy in retail financial services single, multiple and online* (£695) as one of its Strategic Focus reports.

Branding in retail financial services: capitalising on untapped value. Kaiser Associates. London: FT Finance, 1998. 125 p. £450.
Discusses how brand management must be adapted for the particular characteristics of the retail financial services sector in the United Kingdom, in Europe and the United States – an explanation of how to go about building, maintaining, extending, globalising and measuring strong retail financial services brands, before finally considering the likely prospects for brand management in the sector.

The future of marketing retail financial services. Field, Christopher. London: FT Financial, 1997. 196 p. £450.
Covers the competitive, consumer and technology dynamics that are impacting on the consumer financial services sector, looks at the new channels of distribution, the marketing strategies, country reports (with case studies), and future prospects.

Marketing strategies in retail banks: current trends and future prospects. Watkins, Trevor. London: FT Finance, 1999. 104 p. £495.

2.56.31 Periodicals

Bank marketing international. Dublin: Lafferty. £599.
Newsletter issued 10 times a year both in print and online versions. A global perspective on bank marketing with an emphasis on best practice bank marketing. Coverage includes product development, branding, service quality, segmentation, pricing, competition, direct marketing, customer retention, advertising, relationship-based marketing, branch design and sales force management.

2.72 Payment systems

This section deals with payment systems in the broad sense of the term, falling into two general areas: the bank clearing systems and money transmission services (such as the use of electronic payments and plastic card services). A primary source of data on UK payments is provided by APACS (the **Association for Payment Clearing Services**). One of APACS' principal tasks is to manage the major UK payment clearing systems and to maintain its operational efficiency and financial integrity (carried out by three operational clearing companies: Cheque and Credit Clearing Company, CHAPS, and BACS, which operates the bulk electronic clearing).

APACS forecasts payment trends, conducts market research and maintains a large body of statistics. The most recent payment clearing statistics are published on its web site (http://www.apacs.org.uk/). The *Yearbook of payment statistics* (£100) provides an overall view of the UK payments market giving clearing and payment statistics (plastic card holding and usage, including fraud losses, statistics of branch networks of financial institutions). The Association's annual report (*APACS annual review*) provides an overview of the clearing companies and payments sector including market data and statistics (such as plastic card fraud). APACS also publishes an annual *Plastic card review* (£50), which analyses plastic payment card trends in the United Kingdom for the previous seven years (primarily statistical data). The APACS payments market briefing is an annual briefing sheet giving forecasts and trends for volumes to 2008, and a yearly booklet *The UK payments industry: key facts and figures*. There are several publications concerning plastic card fraud. *Fraud in focus* is an annual publication aimed at 'opinion formers in the banking and retail industries, government, police and media, as well as the public and students'. There is a series of best practice guidelines on the use of cheques and credit and a list of standards and security guidelines (such as for processing debit and credit vouchers).

The **Bank for International Settlements** publishes a considerable volume of material under the auspices of its Committee on Payment and Settlement Systems. For example: *Survey of electronic money developments* (2000) and *Statistics on payment systems in the group of ten countries: figures for 1998*. This is an annual publication that provides data on payments and payment systems in the G-10 countries and is an update to the data contained in *Payment systems in the group of ten countries* (last published in 1998). *Managing change in payment systems* (1998) publishes presentations from a global conference on managing change in payments systems.

Other policy and research material on payment systems is generated by the International Monetary Fund. For example, *Payment systems, monetary policy and the role of the central bank* (1998, $25).

2.72.03 Textbooks

Digital cash: commerce on the net. Wayner, Peter. 2nd ed. London: Academic Press, 1997. 359 p. $39.50.
Published in the United States, but it includes examples from British sys-

tems and a UK version is available. A fairly general guide to exchanging money over the Net.

Introduction to money transmission. Hillier, David. Canterbury: Chartered Institute of Bankers, 1999. 190p. £20.
A good basic introduction to money transmission services.

The payment system in the European Union: law and practice. Malaguti, Maria Chiara. London: Sweet & Maxwell, 1997. 388 p. £96.
Primarily a legal study of the European payments system, which takes account of the two major innovations in recent years: the technology has enabled payment systems to be radically altered and new financial services have been established. Very thorough treatment of the basic legal concepts of payment systems in the European Union, with substantial reference to case law, national and international legislation. Contains comparative material on the domestic systems of the United Kingdom, France, Germany, Italy and the United States.

Virtual money: understanding the power and risks of money's high-speed journey into electronic space. Solomon, Elinor Harris. New York; Oxford: Oxford University Press, 1997. 286 p. $27.50.
Examines how financial markets are being 'tailored to the new reality of cyberspace'.

2.72.12 Market research

As part of its *Strategic focus reports* series, **Informa Publishing** has produced *International payment systems 2000* (£799).

2.72.31 Periodicals

Card world independent. Corby: C&M Publications. £435 per year.
An international journal for the plastic card, financial and retail services industries. Monthly newsletter format, which contains mainly short news items and industry developments, calendar of events and one or two lengthier articles.

Cards international. Dublin: Lafferty. £799.
Newsletter issued every two weeks and price includes both printed and online versions. News, analysis, profiles and case studies covering all aspects of the card market.

Electronic payments international. Dublin: Lafferty. £799.
Newsletter issued 10 times a year. Global news coverage and analysis on ATMs and EFTPOS, payments processing, clearing and settlement, outsourcing, new players in the payments world, mergers and acquisitions, Internet payments, new forms of electronic money, cross-border payments, EDI, debit cards, electronic purses and smart cards.

2.72.75 Web sites

Money and payment systems. Institut fur Betriebswirtschaftliche Geldwirtschaft. http://www.wiso.gwdg.de/ifbg/geld.html.
A collection of links on various aspects of money, both paper and coins and electronic money, with an emphasis on digital cash and Internet electronic payment systems.

2.75 Investment

This section primarily deals with retail investment products such as bank and building society savings accounts, that is those products not considered as 'investment business' as defined by the Financial Services Act 1986. For publications dealing with the full range of investment and savings products see chapter 1.

2.75.12 Market research

Mintel has produced a regular and varied range of reports on the savings market. A 1999 report *Deposits* has been followed with *Deposits and savings* (2000). *Empty nesters: savings and investments* (1997) looked at the savings market for mature investors. For a perspective on the role, strategies and future of European savings banks **Lafferty** has published *European savings banks – coming of age?* (£699). **Datamonitor** is probably the most prolific market research company to study the savings market. It has researched the European savings market with its *European savings and investment 2000* report and the UK market in *UK savings and investments 1999, Consumer trends in UK savings and investments 1998* and *UK savings and investments distribution 1999*.

Savings and investments for low-income consumers. National Consumer Council. London: National Consumer Council, 1997. 68 p.
An investigation into how the financial services sector provides for the needs of customers who have only small amounts of money to save.

2.78 Lending

The majority of sources in this section deal with lending in the broad sense of the term, with a focus on mortgage lending and general credit issues. The mortgage market is often referred to under the broader subject of 'housing finance', which can cover fairly broad ground spanning general housing market issues and even construction. House price information for example is available from a number of different sources, such as the **Halifax** bank, the **Nationwide Building Society** and the **Northern Rock Building Society**. A broad range of housing market data is published by the **Council of Mortgage Lenders** (CML), which includes regional mix-adjusted house prices. The most recent housing market data is on the CML's web site (http://www.cml.org.uk) and includes a list of the largest mortgage lenders, statistics on mortgage arrears and possessions, and monthly mortgage lending data.

2.78.01 Consumer guides

The **Office of Fair Trading** (OFT) has leaflets on consumer credit and these can be downloaded from its web site (http://www.oft.gov.uk). For example, the leaflet *Credit charges and APR* gives details on how to calculate the total charge for credit and the annual percentage rate. This booklet has been updated and expanded to take account of new regulations that came into force on 14 April 2000. The regulations governing credit advertising is explained in the OFT leaflet *Credit advertising*. Other advice and information for consumers can also be found on the OFT web site.

The **Financial Services Authority** provides various consumer fact sheets, available free of charge from its web site. For example, *FSA guide to repaying your mortgage* (November 1999), *Is an endowment mortgage right for you?*, *Your endowment mortgage – what you need to know (for people who already have an endowment)*.

The **Council of Mortgage Lenders** publishes a range of consumer booklets and information sheets and FAQs on home buying, mortgages and other related topics. These are available free to individual members of the public, but a charge is made for bulk ordering. They are also available free via its web site (http://www.cml.org.uk). Examples are: *How to buy a home, How to buy a home in Scotland, The Mortgage Code, You & your mortgage, Mortgage complaints, Mortgage indemnity: a borrowers guide, Assistance with mortgage repayments, The Possessions Register, Handling of arrears and possessions, Debt following mortgage possession, Mortgage product information sources, Take cover for a rainy day, Thinking of buying a residential property to let?: a check-list for investing landlords, Stamp duty and residential property: key facts* and *Mortgage interest tax relief-key facts*.

Money-saving mortgages: how to take years off a mortgage and save thousands of pounds. Cornell, Tony. 2nd ed. Oxford: How to Books, 1999. 136 p. £9.99.
Advice on reducing the time it takes to pay off a mortgage and reducing mortgage payments. An examination of various mortgage reduction techniques, how to choose a lender and select a mortgage.

Slash your mortgage. Banks, Robin. Kogan Page, 1999. 173 p. £7.99.
Pitched as an 'exposé of the lender's secrets, showing how homeowners can save money. It challenges conventional wisdom and presents a new mortgage model, mapping out how savings can be made in both the short and long term.'

2.78.03 Textbooks

The **Chartered Institute of Bankers** produces a series of three books on credit risk management as part of its Risk Management Series and has published the following text books to accompany its Diploma in Financial Services Management: *Lending & securities* and *Principles and practice of consumer credit risk,* both priced at £19.95.

Banking operations: UK lending and international business. Jones, Steve. Bankers Books, 1996.
Designed to instil among bankers a more detailed knowledge of how banks operate in international and lending fields.

Credit management handbook. Edwards, Burt, ed. 4th ed. Aldershot: Gower, 1997. 486 p. £65.
A standard text on credit management, which provides comprehensive coverage of the subject including the history and future of credit, key credit control issues and practical guidance on the Consumer Credit Act.

Credit risk: models and management. Shimko, David, ed. London: Risk Books, 1999. 330p. £145.
An edited collection of papers aimed at the practitioner covering 'risky bonds, valuation of risky debt, credit ratings, migration alternatives and management of credit risk'.

EMU and the UK housing and mortgage markets. Maclennan, Duncan and Stephens, Mark. London: Council of Mortgage Lenders, 1997. 54 p. £20.
A study of the role that housing and the mortgage markets play in the macro-economy and how they will be affected by EMU.

Internal credit risk models: capital allocation and performance measurement. Ong, Michael. London: Risk Books, 1999. 372 p. £80.
Pitched as a 'practical, accessible step-by-step analysis of the theory and practicalities of credit risk measurement and management'. Topics covered include: default probabilities, expected and unexpected losses, time effects, default correlations, and loss distributions.

A regional analysis of mortgage possessions: causes, trends and future prospects. Muelbauer, John and Cameron, Gavin. London: CML, 1997. £15.

Residential lending and property law. Souster, Robert and Wibberley, Philip. 4th ed. Canterbury: Chartered Institute of Bankers, 1998. 310 p. £30.

Retail credit and banking fraud: fraud risk exposure in the retail credit industry. Quadrant Risk Management Ltd. London: FT Finance, 1997. 141 p. £430.

Attempts to highlight the development of fraud within the retail credit industry.

2.78.05 Manuals

Mortgage law and practice manual. London: Council of Mortgage Lenders. 2 vols (looseleaf). £150 per year.
Brings together relevant aspects of consumer credit legislation, common law and practice and other legislation, aimed at lenders. Topics covered include insurance of mortgaged properties, new house schemes, valuations, consumer credit, mortgage advertising, mortgage forms and procedures, data protection, conveyancing and the Insolvency Act 1986.

2.78.09 Official reports

A cost-benefit analysis of statutory regulation of mortgage advice. London: Financial Services Authority, 1999. 46 p.
An objective assessment of the impacts of regulating mortgage business under the legislation that will result from the Financial Services and Markets Bill. Includes a brief overview of the size and scope of the mortgage market, number of intermediaries, variety of products and recent market developments.

Mortgage arrears and possessions: perspectives from borrowers, lenders and the court. Ford, Janet, et al. Department of the Environment. London: HMSO, 1995. 124 p. £25.
Reports research into establishing the characteristics and reasons for mortgage arrears and investigates the different policies and practices of lenders in making loans, recovering arrears and dealing with possession and voluntary surrenders.

Mortgage repayment methods: a report by the Office of Fair Trading. London: Office of Fair Trading, 1995. 49 p.

2.78.12 Market research

The market research companies such as **Datamonitor**, **Key Note** and **Mintel** publish reports on this sector, for example Mintel's *Personal loans* (1999) and *Mortgages* (1999).

Brokers' reports are a source of ad hoc market research, such as an edition of Merrill Lynch's *UK bank sector bulletin, trends in the UK mortgage market* (April 1999). The **Council of Mortgage Lenders** (CML) is a primary publisher of mortgage and related housing market research reports. These include: *Private sector housebuilding: structure and strategies into the 21st century; The rise and fall of residential transactions in England and Wales; Attitudes to moving and debt: household behaviour in the 1990s; Mortgage payment protection insurance take-up and retention: evidence from existing research;*

E-commerce and the Internet: the future for mortgage distribution?; The potential for mortgage securitisation in the UK and Europe; Why mortgage payment protection insurance? principles and evidence; Voting & the housing market: the impact of New Labour; Dynamics of owner-occupation; UK and the euro: housing and mortgage market perspectives; Trends, attitudes and issues in British housing; Housing subsidies and tax reliefs in Britain: trends and prospects and *Ageing, home-ownership and the mortgage market: an analysis of costs and subsidies.* These reports are all priced at £25.

The **European Mortgage Federation** (EMF) is a major source of information on housing finance. Its annual report (for 1998, published in 1999) is entitled *Mortgage credit in 1998* and covers recent developments in EU mortgage markets, including data on outstanding mortgage figures, mortgage interest rates, number of new mortgage loans, outstanding mortgage bonds etc. There is also a comprehensive update on all 1998 initiatives by European institutions affecting the activities of mortgage lenders.

Hypostat 1988–1998 provides comprehensive statistics on mortgage credit and property markets dating back to 1988 from the 15 EU member states as well as Norway. In addition to the numerous statistical tables, a commentary compares the European mortgage credit and property markets and examines recent trends including mortgage interest rates, gross and net mortgage lending, outstanding mortgage loans, market shares by type of lender, mortgage bonds, levels of owner-occupation, building permits issued, housing starts and completions, housing transactions, dwelling and construction price indices. The full list of EMF publications with their prices is given on its web site at http://www.hypo.org.

Compendium of housing finance statistics 1997. London: CML, 1997. £75.
Annual publication featuring a wide range of statistics relating to housing finance. Contains historical data on topics such as housing tenure, house prices, property transactions, mortgage lending activity, funding, regional comparisons, building society performance and rates of interest.

2.78.16 Company research

Thedata produces a range of titles from its Mortgage Sector Information Service. For example *Top 20 mortgage lenders* provides market share and league tables based on the published reports and accounts of institutions. As the banking institutions report on their mortgage business in different ways, a degree of estimation and interpretation has been used.

2.78.21 Directories

CML directory of members. London: CML. Free.
Updated fairly frequently. This lists all members of the Council of Mortgage Lenders, giving their head office address and telephone numbers.

The official CML yearbook 99. London: Charterhouse Communications, 1999.
The official yearbook for the Council of Mortgage Lenders, but ceased publishing after the 1999 edition. Includes in-depth coverage of industry and product development, market forecasts and statistics. Also provides details of relevant regulation and codes of practice, reviews technological developments and profiles individual members of the CML.

2.78.26 Bibliographies

See the Building Societies Association's *Library bulletin* (2.35.26).

2.78.31 Periodicals

Some of the more general titles listed in section 1.00.31 contain detailed information on mortgage and other lending products.

CML market briefing. London: CML. £170 per year.
A monthly commentary on developments in the housing and mortgage market, including essential statistics.

CML news & views. London: CML. £40 per year.
Newsletter providing a digest of information, opinions and perspectives on current issues in the mortgage and housing markets in the UK. Excellent as a single source of developments in the sector. Fortnightly.

Credit. London: Risk Publications. £695 per year.
News and features covering the swaps market, credit research, corporate finance, bond covenants and credit risk. Monthly.

Credit today. London: Blue Moon Publishing. £59 per year.
The magazine for the commercial and consumer credit industry. News, analysis and features in addition to an advice section providing information, comment and guidance in key aspects of credit law and procedures. Monthly.

European mortgage review. London: CML. £120 per year.
A bimonthly review providing up-to-date information on mortgage developments at the EU level and in national markets relevant to mortgage lenders in the United Kingdom and the rest of Europe.

Housing finance. London: CML. £95 per year.
A core source of information covering in-depth articles on a wide range of mortgage and housing market issues. Contains a statistical section fea-

turing 33 tables of up-to-date information on housing tenure, house building, property transactions, house prices, mortgage lending and the personal sector. Quarterly.

Journal of credit management. Oakham (Leicestershire): Institute of Credit Management. £55 per year.
A monthly journal aimed primarily at members of the ICM but has a broader appeal with feature articles on a broad range of credit management issues. News, book reviews and news from the ICM.

Mortgage finance gazette. London: Charterhouse Communications. £54 per year.
The main trade journal for the mortgage finance sector (previously entitled *Building societies gazette*). Offering a comprehensive coverage of all aspects of the mortgage market the magazine features news, diary items and shortish articles written both in-house and by key individuals in the market. Monthly.

Mortgage info. Brussels: European Mortgage Federation. 95 euro per year.
A subscription-based information service designed for those who monitor developments at European level. Subscribers receive regular up-to-date information on recent EU initiatives affecting the business of mortgage lenders. The subscription covers around 20 communications a year.

Mortgage introducer. London: PBI Newmedia. £2.50 per issue.
The magazine for mortgage advisers. Includes a 'Market monitor' for mortgage product data. News, features. Monthly.

Mortgage solutions. London: City Financial Communications. £75 per year.
Aimed at professionals in the mortgage market. A blend of news, features and product data. Monthly.

Quarterly figures 2000. Brussels: European Mortgage Federation. 160 euro per year.
A six-page newsletter covering tables, charts and comments on mortgage interest rates, net and gross lending, housing construction activity, housing transactions and dwelling price indices.

What mortgage. London: Charterhouse Communications Group. £23.50.
Contains a wealth of consumer data on mortgages such as comparison tables and a directory of lending criteria; features on various aspects of selecting a mortgage and home buying such as re-mortgaging, guides to different types of mortgages, home insurance and other related products. Monthly.

2.78.36 Newspapers

The newspapers listed in section 1.00.36 generally include mortgage and other lending products in their coverage. In particular, *Financial adviser* (q.v.) includes a regular supplement *FA mortgage extra*.

2.78.75 Web sites

The general financial services sites described in section 1.00.75 will also contain substantial information on mortgages and other lending products. For example, *Interactive investor international* has a 'mortgage centre' providing consumers with the information they will need in the run-up to buying a home. The *Find* web directory has a 'mortgage and loans centre' providing links to mortgage lenders and brokers, providers of personal loans, sources of commercial and corporate finance, credit card companies, rate and product comparisons and sites providing mortgage and loan calculators.

Business credit news UK. Southampton: Business Credit Management UK. http://www.creditman.co.uk/news. Free.
Email newsletter for 'credit managers/credit controllers, credit management consultants and trainers, accountants, solicitors, credit information companies, debt collection companies, factoring companies, credit insurance companies and brokers, insolvency and bankruptcy professionals, software companies, export/import companies, businesses generally and the public'. Useful round-up of latest business credit news. The web site also has links to banks, information on conferences and bibliographical links (books, journals and newsletters).

E-loan. http://www.e-loan.com/uk. Free.
An independent site, which enables customers to choose the mortgage that is right for their individual needs and to process the transaction online (giving updated information about the progress of a mortgage application). It lists products from over 50 lenders.

Your mortgage. http://www.yourmortgage.co.uk.
Useful mortgage finding and house buying web site with calculators (including a house price calculator), checklists, news and articles.

Chapter 3

Insurance

Compared with some financial services insurance is a well-defined subject area. This is partly because of the way insurance is regulated. In the United Kingdom firms must be specifically authorised to transact insurance business so there is little scope for a blurring of boundaries. However, there are *some* fuzzy edges and they are becoming fuzzier.

Firstly, it is normal to exclude national insurance. With the creation of the welfare state immediately after the war insurance grew to encompass the new area of national insurance and this was reflected in the introduction by the Chartered Insurance Institute of separate examinations for civil servants working in this field. But these examinations were eventually dropped and national insurance in the United Kingdom has now become a form of social security with little evidence of a true insurance mechanism at work. It would be unusual today for a general work on insurance to include this area, although such a work might mention the new opportunities expected to open up for the private insurance industry as the responsibility of the state for social welfare is redefined.

Secondly, it is common to include 'risk'. Insurance is essentially about risk and, to an insurer, risk (or *a* risk) can mean the thing that is being insured as well as the chances of a loss. Thus to the marine insurer shipping is part of marine insurance; to the liability insurer the law of tort is a part of liability insurance – particularly so, as it is normal practice for liability insurers to take responsibility for the defence of cases brought against their policyholders. This general pattern is reflected in the literature of insurance and it is not unusual for a book ostensibly on, for instance, 'directors' and officers' liability insurance' to contain six chapters on the law relating to the liability of directors and officers and one chapter on insurance policy conditions. Such works are included here but works solely on risk are not.

Thirdly, the boundaries between insurance and other financial services are becoming blurred. Banks are moving into insurance either by selling policies over the counter or by buying or setting up their own insurance companies. This phenomenon is known as 'bancassurance' and this term is sometimes used to include the reverse procedure – insurance companies moving into investment, developing hybrid products like unit-linked life polices, and into banking (for instance Prudential or Standard Life).

At the same time the traditional life insurance salesman with his foot in the door has become a qualified financial adviser, offering advice on a whole range of investment products as well as traditional life assurance. But this convergence is taking place on another front altogether as capital market instruments such as derivatives and bonds are being used as an alternative way of financing risk (see section 3.64).

Within insurance there are some very disparate areas, to the extent that sometimes the same word means something different in each. Traditionally insurance has been divided into branches that reflect the way the business is organised and the cover afforded under particular kinds of policy. The original branches in the United Kingdom were marine, fire, life and accident, the latter including health, liability and aviation. Today the main branches can be divided into three groups, each very different from the other: marine, aviation and transport; property, pecuniary and liability; life and health. Note that motor insurance belongs to the second group and not to transport insurance, which is concerned with goods in transit. More broadly two divisions are recognised: life (including health) and general (the rest). There tends to be a sharp polarisation of interest within general insurance in the United Kingdom between highly pre-packaged domestic 'retail' business such as motor and household and the more global kind of business (marine, aviation and large commercial risks) transacted on the London market. And with the gradual integration of life assurance with other financial services a newer division has emerged: general insurance (insurance other than life and health) and 'financial services' (life and health plus anything else that life insurers choose to concern themselves with).

In addition to commercial sources the two most important providers of insurance information in the United Kingdom are the **Association of British Insurers** (ABI) and the **Chartered Insurance Institute** (CII). The ABI is a trade association of insurance companies. It performs a key role in the industry, but it doesn't represent Lloyd's, insurance intermediaries and certain other entities operating within the market. The other principal trade associations are the **British Insurance and Investment Brokers' Association**, the **Institute of Insurance Brokers** and the **Association of Insurance and Risk Managers**. The CII is a professional body whose members are individuals, not companies. Its members come from all areas of the industry but there are also two more specialist professional bodies: the **Chartered Institute of Loss Adjusters** and the **Institute of Risk Management**. The CII has around 80 local institutes of which the largest is the **Insurance Institute of London**.

3.00 General sources

3.00.01 Consumer guides

The **Association of British Insurers** produces a useful series of free information sheets for consumers. These are also available on the ABI web site (section 3.00.75).

Arranging insurance: how to manage policies and claims for everyday personal and business purposes. Hallett, Terry. Oxford: How To Books, 1997. 174 p. (Business Basics) £9.99.

Perfect insurance: all you need to get it right first time. Jennings, Marie. London: Arrow, 1997. v, 80 p. (The Perfect Series) £5.99.

The Sunday Times personal finance guide to the protection game: a straightforward guide to insurance. Pratt, Kevin. London: HarperCollins, 1996. 152 p. £6.99.

The Which? guide to insurance. Wallis, Virginia. 1ˢᵗ ed. London: Which? Books: distributed by the Penguin Group, 1998. 316 p. (Which? Consumer Guides) £10.99.
Subtitled on the cover 'how to get the best deal on insurance and make a successful claim', this book was commissioned and researched by the Consumers' Association.

3.00.02 Career guides

There are also substantial careers sections on the web sites of the **Association of British Insurers** and the **Chartered Insurance Institute**. See section 3.00.75. The CII also publishes careers literature and can offer careers advice.

The inside careers guide to insurance. London: Cambridge Market Intelligence. (Inside Careers) £15.
Includes a very short directory of 'key recruiters', a directory of 'associations, institutes and professional organisations' and articles on insurance education and training, the different kinds of jobs in insurance and other careers-related information. Published in association with the Chartered Insurance Institute, from whom a limited number of free copies may be available. Annual.

3.00.03 Textbooks

The biggest publisher of insurance textbooks in the United Kingdom is the **Chartered Insurance Institute**, with over 40 works covering three different sets of examinations – the introductory Insurance Foundation Certificate, the intermediate Certificate of Insurance Practice and the professional Associateship – in addition to a range of financial planning titles. Although designed as student coursebooks for specific examination subjects these works are of use to a wider audience and some are virtually the only substantial publications on their subjects. The insurance titles are as follows: *Insurance practice* (P01), *Long-term insurance practice* (P02), *Legal aspects of insurance* (P03), *An introduction to commercial general insurances* (P10), *An introduction to personal general insurances* (P11), *An introduction to long-term business* (P12), *An introduction to marine and aviation insurance* (P13), *An introduction to private medical insurance* (P15), *Transacting private medical insurance business* (P75), *Risk and insurance* (510), *Risk and insurance with special reference to Lloyd's* (511), *Company and contract law and their application to insurance* (520), *Life and disability underwriting* (555), *Financial aspects of long-term business* (570), *Risk management* (655), *Life assurance* (735), *Principles of property and pecuniary insurances (incorporating construction and engineering insurance)* (745), *Commercial property and pecuniary insurances: assessment and underwriting (incorporating construction and engineering insurance)* (750), *Liability insurance* (755), *Personal insurances* (760), *Motor insurance* (765), *Principles of marine insurance* (770), *Marine insurance underwriting and claims* (775), *Aviation insurance* (780), *Reinsurance* (785), *Underwriting management* (815), *Claims management* (820), *Lloyd's regulatory requirements* (920), *Insurance and the single European market* (925), *Insurance broking* (930), *Principles and practice of management in insurance* (935), *Accounting and finance for managers in insurance* (940), *Accounting and finance for managers in insurance with special reference to Lloyd's* (941), *Marketing* (945), *North American general insurance practice (with special reference to the US market)* (950). All the coursebooks are in looseleaf format, between 250 and 750 pages long and updated once or twice a year as necessary. Wordings and other source material are included where appropriate. £60 each, £50 to members.

For new recruits and those requiring the briefest of introductions to insurance subjects the CII publishes a series of training guides in pamphlet form. Individual guides cover insurance in general, business interruption insurance, commercial fire insurance, engineering insurance, household insurance, liability insurance, life assurance, motor insurance and reinsurance.

Insurance non-marine: an introduction. Davis, Margaret, Hood, John and Stein, Bill. 1st ed. London: Witherby, 1997. ix, 774 p. £40.
Includes 500 pages of appendices giving sample policy wordings. Published for the Institute of Risk Management, aimed at students.

Introduction to insurance. Hansell, D. S. 2nd ed. London: LLP, 1999. xxii, 389 p. (Practical insurance guides) £30.
Includes progress tests at the end of each chapter, but the book is not just

for students. According to the blurb it is 'Designed for those working *within* the industry'.

3.00.05 Manuals

Handbook of insurance. Kingston upon Thames, Surrey: Kluwer. 2 vols (looseleaf).
The most substantial general work on insurance published in the United Kingdom, comprising some 1,500 pages in all. Concentrates on a detailed treatment of different kinds of cover and will be the best source of all for some of the less well documented areas, e.g. contingency insurances. Biased towards non-life, with just one chapter on 'Life, pensions, health and medical insurance' – albeit a chapter of some 100 pages. Updated by quarterly looseleaf amendments, with a newsletter *Kluwer insurance briefing* forming an additional component of the update package. This newsletter is actually more than it sounds, each issue containing two or three full-length articles on recent developments.

The insurance manual. Susman, Brian, ed. Stourbridge, West Midlands: Insurance Publishing & Printing Co. 1 vol. (looseleaf).
Very much a work of reference, with numbered sections, tables and lots of bullet lists. Updated by looseleaf amendments twice a year. Around 500 pages.

3.00.07 Source materials

The primary sources in insurance are policy documents and policy wordings – or clauses, as they tend to be called in areas like marine insurance where the product is less prepackaged. A number of bodies are involved in the production of standard wordings, notably the **Association of British Insurers**, the **International Underwriting Association of London** (now responsible for the so-called 'institute' clauses in marine insurance as well as reinsurance wordings) and **Lloyd's Underwriters' Non-Marine Association**. See also the *Market wordings database*, section 3.00.72.

UK & overseas policy forms. [London]: Non-Marine Association, [1999]. 665 p. £250 plus VAT (free to NMA members).
Latest edition in a long succession of policy books from the Lloyd's Underwriters' Non-Marine Association. Contains standard non-marine policy forms, proposal forms and clauses used in the London insurance market for UK and overseas business. Also available as a CD-ROM. See also the US and Canada volume.

USA & Canada policy forms. [London]: Non-Marine Association, [1999]. 834 p. £250 plus VAT (free to NMA members).
Contains standard non-marine policy forms, proposal forms and clauses

used in the London insurance market for US and Canadian business. Also available on CD-ROM. See also the UK volume.

3.00.08 Technical reports

On grounds of longevity alone top of the league as a UK publisher of technical insurance reports must be the **Insurance Institute of London**, whose advanced study group scheme has led to the publication of nearly 100 reports since the first in 1949. Recent titles in print are *Liability insurance and accident compensation* (ASG 225), *Insurance against inherent defects in buildings* (ASG 230), *Directors and officers liability insurance* (ASG 234), *Estimated maximum loss assessments: London market practice* (ASG 236) and *Construction insurance* (ASG 208B).

The IIL is one of the 80 or so local institutes that form part of the national **Chartered Insurance Institute**. More recently the CII itself has become a publisher of research, particularly through its Society of Fellows, whose report *The impact of changing weather patterns on property insurance* has been especially well received. A number of research projects are currently in progress and several are expected to lead to published reports, including one on alternative risk transfer.

Internationally among the biggest publishers of this kind of material are large specialist reinsurance companies. Reinsurers of all sizes have a direct financial interest in the competence of the insurance companies they service and for public relations reasons wish to sustain an image of professionalism and technical mastery. Accordingly this material is usually free or reasonably priced although some firms may limit circulation. The most important reinsurers in this respect are **Swiss Re** and **Munich Re** and the annual catalogues published by these firms are well worth obtaining. Recent titles include *Product recall and product tampering insurance: the escalation in product liability and its insurance* from Swiss Re and *The international situation of disability insurance* from Munich Re. Reports are often published in several languages.

Some large firms of accountants and consultants are also significant publishers of technical insurance material. Among the more broad-based firms **PricewaterhouseCoopers, Ernst & Young** and **KPMG** are notable in this respect. There are also two firms of consultants specialising in risk and insurance, **Jim Bannister Developments** and the **Risk and Insurance Research Group**, which publish occasional reports.

Etudes et dossiers. [Geneva]: Association Internationale pour l'Etude de l'Economie de l'Assurance. SwFr40 per issue.
Series of reports from the 'International Association for the Study of Insurance Economics', also known as the Geneva Association. Over 200 titles have been published in this series since its inception in the 1970s.

Reports are often drawn from conferences, workshops, and so on, and recent items include papers from the sixth Strategic Issues in Insurance conference (no. 218) and from the 25th Seminar of the European Group of Risk and Insurance Economists (nos 220 and 221).

General insurance research report. London: Association of British Insurers.

A series of research reports commissioned by the ABI with a view to advancing the insurance industry's knowledge and handling of a wide range of risk-related factors. The first seven titles, published in 1999 and 2000, are *Subsidence: a global perspective*, *Criminal decision-making*, *Effectiveness of CCTV*, *Land use planning and insurance risks*, *Crime statistics underwriting*, *Appraisal of the performance and cost effectiveness of using factory produced metal faced sandwich panels in building applications* and *Future crime trends in the United Kingdom*. Priced at £10 or £15 each.

Occasional paper. London: Association of British Insurers. Free.

Series of pamphlets first published in 1998 and now comprising more than 10 titles. Wide-ranging in subject matter, including *Financing pensions: funding versus PAYG* (no. 3), *UK insurance companies' overseas business* (no. 4), *A compendium of arson in the UK* (no. 8) and *Alternative performance measures of life insurance firms for management control and performance management* (no. 10).

SCOR tech. Paris: SCOR.

Occasional series of reports from the French reinsurer, all or most available in English. Recent titles include *Compensation for bodily injury by annuity settlements in Europe* and *Millennium claims symposium*.

3.00.12 Market research

There are three primary sources for aggregate, market-wide statistical and descriptive data on the insurance industry in the United Kingdom.

The first source is the annual returns submitted by insurers. These are described in section 3.00.16, but the returns are also a potential source for *market* data, such as total premium income for motor insurance – provided the category of business you are interested in corresponds either to a statutory accounting class or to a risk group used by most companies transacting that type of business, and provided you can identify all the companies involved and obtain annual returns for them all. This is clearly impractical. However, some of the electronic sources described in section 3.00.72 allow you to create your own aggregates, and some of the printed sources described in section 3.00.16 attempt to give totals per class – although it is important to question whether this is a total of all companies transacting this class or just a total of selected firms, that is those listed in that source. Note, however, that although there are over 800 companies authorised to transact insurance business in the United Kingdom many of these do not submit annual returns to the FSA so no total will be 100 per cent. This is generally for one of two reasons. An increasing number of firms operating in the United Kingdom and domiciled in other parts of the European Economic Area are now authorised only in their home state, and some firms while retaining their authorisation may have ceased underwriting new business.

The second primary source of market research is the statistical work of the principal trade association of insurance companies, the **Association of British Insurers**. The ABI regularly collects statistical data from its members, covering premium income, claims experience and so on, and publishes aggregated figures in a range of formats (nothing is published for individual firms). In general these aren't true totals as they do not include the small number of non-ABI members (although some attempt is made to estimate the missing figures from these) and with one or two exceptions they do not include the Lloyd's insurance market. Some of the more sensitive data is only available to members. The main printed titles are listed below, but some information appears first or only in press releases and the ABI's journal *Insurance trends* has a useful statistical section at the back. The association has also co-operated with Lloyd's and other market bodies in commissioning a study *The London insurance market* from Robert L. Carter and Peter Falush. Some statistical information is available on the ABI web site (section 3.00.75).

The third source of market research is a small number of commercial publishers. These firms draw heavily on the sources mentioned above but for consumer data in particular will often commission or undertake their own sample surveys. The most important firms are described below.

FT Finance has been producing management reports on insurance for several years. Recent examples include *UK health and welfare insurance* (£595) and *EMU & the insurance industry* (£795). Increasingly these reports are focused at a pan-European or global level: see section 3.02.12. The more highly priced *FT market trends* series also includes some insurance titles, e.g. *Insurance online*. With effect from 2000 these reports are published by **Informa**, who also produce a *Strategic focus* series including some insurance titles.

Datamonitor has a long pedigree in this area and is perhaps the most prolific UK publisher of market research in insurance. Many of its titles tend to be published annually in new editions while others are ad hoc. Recent examples of UK research reports cover distribution, health insurance, motor insurance, household insurance, commercial general insurance, individual long-term insurance, personal general insurance, extended warranty insurance, liability insurance, loan-related insurance, 'tele-insurance', 'personal niche insurance', consumer trends. Prices range from £795 to £1,995. There are many other titles that are international (see section 3.02.12) or company-by-company studies (3.02.16).

Recently Datamonitor has joined forces with **Reuters** to publish a series of management reports at a lower price range under the Reuters Business Insight imprint. Examples include *The future of UK insurance to 2005* (£495) and *Trends in global commercial insurance: the impact of ART* (£495).

Mintel also publishes market research on insurance, available in print or (by subscription) on the Mintel web site. Recent titles include *Motor insurance*, *Travel insurance* and *Pet insurance*. More occasional contributors are **Market Assessment International** and its subsidiary **Key Note**. The former has recently published *Personal lines insurance 2000* in its *Strategic market report* series; the latter publishes the overlapping reports on insurance companies and the UK insurance market, both reissued from time to time in new editions.

Finally, a new firm **Insurance Research & Publishing** has recently been set up by a small group of insurance journalists and writers. Its first title is *Effects of insurers' mergers and acquisitions on market share throughout the world* by Sue Copeman.

Insurers sometimes commission their own private research and a **General Insurance Market Research Association** has been set up by a number of firms partly to co-ordinate this effort. It doesn't publish research itself.

British insurance premium index. [Basingstoke, Hants]: AA Insurance Services.
Little more than a leaflet but potentially very useful. Shows average premiums for household and motor insurance for a range of sample locations and insureds. Also gives inflation indexes. Quarterly.

Insurance companies', pension funds' and trusts' investments. London: Office for National Statistics. (Business monitor; MQ5) £70 per year. Broader than the title suggests, including general figures for insurance company income, expenditure, assets and liabilities as well as detailed investment statistics. The publishers state that 'the estimates are derived from statistical enquiries to these financial institutions'. Quarterly.

Insurance pocket book. Henley-on-Thames: NTC. £35.
Very useful reference guide to the UK insurance industry, primarily a compilation of statistics from a range of other sources. Includes market statistics, figures from annual returns for the largest companies, rankings and ratios. Also short sections on other major markets. Published in association with Tillinghast-Towers Perrin. Literally pocket-sized but with a lot of information packed into around 300 pages. Annual.

The insurance report. [London]: Swiss Re.
A review of the UK personal lines insurance market, focusing on consumers and distribution channels and incorporating original consumer research. Includes detailed statistics. In two volumes, life and non-life. Annual.

Insurance statistics yearbook. London: Association of British Insurers. £50.
Based on data collected from ABI member companies and other co-operating UK insurance companies. The publishers estimate that the figures cover almost 100 per cent of the long-term insurance company market and over 90 per cent of the general insurance company market, with respect to business written worldwide by insurance companies authorised in the United Kingdom. The major exception is Lloyd's, but two or three key tables are expanded with Lloyd's figures. Statistics given include premium income, claims paid, benefits paid and revenue accounts (all analysed by class of business), plus investment figures, distribution figures and so on. Many tables cover 11 years. There's also a listing of major events over the past year.

Insurance: facts, figures and trends. London: Association of British Insurers.
A useful descriptive account of the UK market with many statistics. Annual.

Statistical bulletin. London: Association of British Insurers.
A series of statistical publications on different topics, each title generally appearing annually or quarterly. The main general insurance titles are *General insurance statistics: sources of premium income* (distribution channels), *Indices of prices affecting motor insurance, Occupational disease enquiry, General insurance: motor claims results, Analysis of ... UK liability market* and *Analysis of UK motor market*. On the long-term side there's a single title, *New long term insurance results,* which analyses premium income and number of contracts by both class of business and distribution channel. The titles *Insurance overseas earnings* and *Family expenditure survey* cover all branches. The latter presents insurance expenditure statistics taken from the government survey, including some data not published in the official report of the same title. Much if not all of the figures in these bulletins will subsequently appear in the ABI's *Insurance statistics yearbook* (q.v.), but the bulletins will often be more up to date.

3.00.16 Company research

The primary source of company information is the companies themselves – or rather, the documents they are required by statute to produce. Like all companies UK insurers are bound by the companies acts to submit an annual report and accounts to shareholders. Unlike other companies they are also required – under insurance companies legislation – to submit a much more detailed annual return to the Financial Services Authority. These annual returns, which are commonly referred to as 'DTI returns' after the name of the body to whom they were submitted until recently, contain a wealth of detail on insurance transactions. Information given includes number of policies, premium income and number and cost of claims, all broken down into statutory classes of business. These categories are important because they represent the normal limits in terms of specificity to published financial data both on individual companies and (aggregated) for the whole insurance market, although the ABI's membership surveys (see section 3.00.12) may pinpoint certain other areas.

The accounting classes for general (non-life) business are less detailed than the authorisation classes, that is the categories in terms of which insurers are authorised to transact business. The accounting classes are accident and health; motor; aviation; marine; transport; property; third party liability; miscellaneous and pecuniary loss; non-proportional treaty reinsurance; proportional treaty reinsurance; and marine, aviation and transport treaty reinsurance. These accounting classes are further divided into 'risk groups'. These are not prescribed but there is sufficient uniformity of practice from company to company to allow some comparison at this level.

The division of long-term business is more complex, but the main categories are life assurance and general annuity business; pensions business; permanent health insurance; and 'other' (mainly capital redemption business).

The annual returns can often be obtained by writing to the company secretary of the insurer concerned. The only public collection is maintained on microfiche at **Companies House** in Cardiff. Copies can be obtained on fiche or online as image files.

A small number of firms produce commercial research on UK insurers. Some statistical studies derive their data from the annual reports and accounts only and this is often the case where the publishers produce similar research across a wide range of industries. But the more in-depth studies are based on the annual returns. Such works frequently include ratios and other analysis applied to the raw data and a few venture to add their own ratings or assessment of financial strength. There are over 800 companies authorised to transact insurance business in the United Kingdom and inevitably the most comprehensive of such works are only available in electronic format. For these see section 3.00.72.

In addition to the works listed below recent insurance company research from **Datamonitor** includes *General insurance company profiles 1999, Life* *office company profiles 1999, Market leaders in UK life assurance 1999* and *Market leaders in UK general insurance 1999*.

A range of company surveys is self-published by **Ian Youngman**. Recent titles include *A market guide to health cash insurance* and *A market guide to retailers and insurance*. Some reports are annual, including *UK direct writers*. The reports concentrate on services, strategy, etc., rather than financial data.

In a league of its own is a small group of investment banks producing in-depth research on the UK insurance industry aimed at investors. This material focuses on the limited number of insurers and intermediaries with a public listing, but there is also valuable background research on the broader market environment within which these companies operate. Firms significant in this respect include **BZW Research, Charterhouse Securities, Credit Suisse First Boston, Merrill Lynch** and **Warburg Dillon Read** (whose *Insurance monthly* has been published continually since 1983). But as firms merge and remerge names change weekly. If you are a client of one of these companies you will be able to get their valuable research free and this may also include useful material on the Web. If you are not a client you may have to look elsewhere.

Best's UK insurance security analysis service: ISAS. London: A. M. Best International. £545 per year.
In two very large looseleaf volumes, life and non-life. Each volume covers over 100 UK insurers, with financial statistics (from the annual returns), graphs, ratios, comparative data, ratings and commentary. Each company report comprises four pages and is replaced annually.

Britain's largest insurers. Norkett, Paul. 3rd ed. Walton-on-the-Naze, Essex: Tekron, 2001. 347 p. £200. Detailed reports on the largest insurance groups (life and non-life), chiefly derived from annual returns, plus comparative tables. About 20 pages per group, including some descriptive as well as statistical data, e.g. on directors (with pictures too). Lavish production quality – unusual for a work of this type. There's also a quarterly newsletter, *Insurance news review*.

Insurance. Middlesbrough: Plimsoll.
Consists of two issues per year, each issue comprising a main report plus supplement, obtainable separately. Both the main report and the supplement are in two volumes and consist of one-page analyses of insurance companies, underwriting agencies and some intermediaries. There are around 1,000 firms in the main report and another 1,000 smaller firms in the supplement. The data is based on annual reports: statistics plus Plimsoll ratios, contact information, names of directors etc. There are also comparative tables ranking firms by sales, assets, and so on, although the disparate nature of the firms included (with no distinction made between

insurers and intermediaries) makes these less useful than they might be. A separate series of reports covers insurance intermediaries only (see *Insurance brokers etc.*, section 3.43.16) and it is unclear why some are included here.

Insurance company performance: a statistical summary of the top 200 UK insurers. [Nottingham]: University of Nottingham Centre for Risk and Insurance Studies. £225.
In two volumes. The first consists of worldwide results based on data from annual reports and accounts; the second contains more detailed information on UK business only, taken from annual returns. Annual.

The insurance competitor intelligence service. London: Datamonitor. £495 per report.
Series of 16 reports on major UK insurance companies. Each covers strategy, structure, performance, advertising and overseas operations and includes statistics from annual returns. A bespoke service is also available: reports can be commissioned on any UK insurer.

The insurance industry. Hampton: Schober Direct Marketing. (Financial Survey) £220.95.
In two volumes, around 1,700 pages and 6,000 entries in all. Covers insurers, intermediaries, underwriting agencies, and so on, in one alphabetical sequence. Data is from annual reports and accounts: contact details, directors, summary financial statistics etc. Annual.

Market analysis of insurance companies: UK property/casualty & UK reinsurers. London: Fitch IBCA.
Surveys over 100 companies (two pages per company), with statistics from annual returns, including analysis by class of business. Also has comparative tables by class.

Post index: UK general insurance market analysis: insurers, brokers, loss adjusters. London: Timothy Benn. £275.
New reference source from the publishers of *Post magazine* and the *Insurance directory*. The first, 2000, issue offers in 367 pages a market survey, comparative tables, rankings and detailed profiles on 106 insurers plus the top brokers and loss adjusters. The insurance company profiles each consist of a page or two incorporating data from the annual returns together with an additional two-page narrative supplied by the company itself, for those who chose to avail themselves of this opportunity. Compiled by Peter Falush and Neil Withington. Annual. Excerpts are available free of charge at http://www.postmag.co.uk.

Standard & Poor's UK insurer ratings service. London: Standard & Poor's Insurance Ratings.
Consists of separate reports for Lloyd's motor syndicates and around 100 UK non-life insurance companies. Each report is typically one page and

contains statistics (usually from annual shareholder reports) and commentary, with S&P solvency ratings. In a ring binder, each report replaced annually. There's also a supplement on floppy disk, *Classic*, which provides additional statistics.

UK insurance premiums. Nottingham: University of Nottingham Centre for Risk and Insurance Studies. £50.
Shows worldwide premium income of over 180 of the largest UK insurance groups. An excerpt appears on its web site (section 3.00.75). Annual.

UK non life insurance industry: results.... Jim Bannister Developments. London: Rhine Re. Free.
Summarises annual returns for around 100 UK non-life insurers, with two pages of figures per company. Annual.

3.00.18 Product research

See also the electronic product *Policygen*, section 3.00.72.

Financial Times world insurance policy guide. London: LLP Professional. £495 per year.
Under its revised format this service comprises a monthly newsletter *Policy news: world insurance product developments* plus the twice-yearly *Policy wordings summary: the comparative guide to selected insurance company contracts by class of business* and an accompanying CD-ROM. The *Policy wordings summary* surveys selected UK products in certain classes, comparing wordings for each class, analysed by section or aspect. The CD-ROM gives the text of the actual wordings, broken down under the same headings. The first issue under the new format covers computer insurance, contractors' combined policies, directors and officers, engineering, goods in transit and motor fleet. The summaries are typically two pages each; the corresponding PDF files on the CD-ROM range from 17 to 65 pages. These files are also available on diskette.

The insurance buyer's guide: a guide to schemes, packages and unusual risks. Kingston upon Thames, Surrey: Croner. £79.50.
Covers 'nearly 2,000 schemes', mostly from brokers or underwriting agencies. Arranged by subject, giving brief details of cover for each scheme, with contact details and a detailed subject index at the back. Annual; over 600 pages per issue. You also get a useful newsletter.

Special risks: the UK's comprehensive guide to specialist and bespoke policies. London: Timothy Benn. £75.
Arranged by subject, with detailed information on cover available for over 2,000 plans from more than 590 providers. Includes indexes by subject and firm. Unlike its close rival *The insurance buyer's guide* contact details are given in each product entry instead of just at the back. The first annual issue was published in 2000 with 241 large-format pages.

3.00.21 Directories

Evandale's London insurance market directory. London: Evandale. £155.
A directory of firms operating in or providing services to the London insurance market: insurance companies, brokers, Lloyd's syndicates, underwriting agents, lawyers, loss adjusters, consultants, contact offices, accountants etc. Also includes 'Where are they now' listings of defunct insurance companies, brokers and underwriting agents and sections on media contacts and web sites. For each firm gives contact details, senior personnel, brief financial data etc. In sections by kind of firm, with combined indexes at the back. Annual.

The insurance directory: the definitive guide to the insurance industry. London: Timothy Benn. £250.
Published annually since 1842 and still referred to in many insurance offices by its earlier name the *Post magazine almanack* or by its earlier appearance *The green book*. Has traditionally rested on the substantial laurels of its long pedigree and extensive content with few concessions made to user-friendliness, but in recent years this has begun to change. Comprises a large number of different sections with a new master index at the back. The first section lists around 1,500 UK insurance companies, underwriting agencies, syndicates, and so on, followed by a short listing of Irish companies, a useful index by class of business and a guide to historical company changes. Information given includes contact details, senior personnel and brief financial data. A separate section on brokers and intermediaries lists over 2,000 UK firms, arranged geographically, and a similar section covers loss adjusters and assessors. Other sections include legal and specialist services, institutions and associated bodies, European government departments and associations and universities offering insurance and related studies. Annual. Also available on CD-ROM as *ID.se@rch gold*: see section 3.00.72

The insurance register. Kingston upon Thames, Surrey: Croner. £126.95.
Lists UK insurers, brokers, underwriting agencies etc. in one alphabetical sequence. Around 1,500 entries, including some 300 insurers. Gives contact details, senior personnel, brief financial information, class of business and main distribution channel. There are classified indexes at the back and a short section on specialist services. Annual.

3.00.24 Dictionaries

For those looking for a straightforward and fairly comprehensive (British) English insurance dictionary there is a straight choice between Bennett's *Dictionary of insurance* and *Witherby's dictionary of insurance*. The former scores higher on both breadth (number of entries) and depth (length of entries) and it's one penny cheaper. But an examination of the two reveals a surprisingly low overlap, with many terms appearing in only one. So buy both.

Be warned that US insurance terminology differs in many respects from British and this difference will be reflected in other English-speaking insurance markets where practice follows the US rather than the British model. There are many American insurance dictionaries available, including the extensive *Dictionary of insurance* by Lewis E. Davids.

For an insurance dictionary on CD-ROM only see *Onscreen insurance terms*, section 3.00.72.

Dictionary of insurance. Bennett, C. London: Pitman, 1992. 385 p. £19.99.
Over 3,500 terms explained in detail. Includes abbreviations, useful addresses and some specimen policies.

Dictionary of insurance and finance terms. Clark, John O. E. Canterbury: Chartered Institute of Bankers, 1999. 342 p. £15.
Covers all classes of insurance, commercial and personal. Includes agencies and associations. Shares many entries with the companion volume, *International dictionary of banking and finance* (section 1.02.24).

Glossary of insurance terms. Sevenoaks: Insurance Industry Training Council, 1997. 75 p. £10.
Short explanatory paragraphs on around 100 terms. Now published by the Chartered Insurance Institute.

Witherby's dictionary of insurance. Cockerell, Hugh. 3rd ed. London: Witherby, 1997. vi, 377 p. £20.
Brief definitions of over 2,000 terms. Includes separate sections on abbreviations and 'institutions of insurance'. Also available on CD-ROM.

3.00.26 Bibliographies

Libraries are inevitably the best source for comprehensive bibliographies, but now that most library catalogues are automated the elaborate printed catalogue is becoming an anachronism and even the printed subject bibliography is being dispensed with in favour of ad hoc catalogue printouts, which are more up to date and can be tailored for a particular enquirer, or better still by direct, online access. This is the approach adopted by the library of the **Chartered Insurance Institute** (see chapter 7), whose extensive insurance database combines the functions of a catalogue of holdings with the detailed indexing of journal articles. Tailored printouts can be provided on request and access to the Web, supported by a range of document delivery options, is available from *CII Library online* (see section 3.00.75).

For listings of recent publications there is still a case to be made for the published bibliography and some examples are listed below. In addition to these there are listings published as features within particular periodicals, in particular the CII Library's 'In print' listing in *The Journal* (see section 3.00.31), 'Worldwide insurance abstracts' in the *Global insurance bulletin* (section 3.02.31) and 'Media fortnight' in the *Jim Bannister report* (section 3.00.31).

Daily press summary. London: Association of British Insurers. Consists of short abstracts of press items on insurance. Two or three leaves a day; arranged by subject headings.

Media contact directory. London: Association of British Insurers. £60. A directory of insurance and other financial journals and journalists, with a section on insurance industry press contacts. Annual.

3.00.31 Periodicals

There aren't many competing titles here; most of these items occupy separate niches of their own. The clear market-wide leader as a trade magazine is *Post magazine* and this title has seen off several rivals over its century and a half of existence. However, if you are an intermediary you will find the broking titles listed in section 3.43.31 rivals for your attention; there is very little to distinguish them from some of the items in this section, save for a slightly more focused targeting. Similarly if you are a reinsurer you will find competition in the reinsurance titles listed in section 3.69.31. Aside from commercially published titles, a range of specialist newsletters is produced by the Association of British Insurers. These include *Benchmarking newsletter, Electronic commerce newsletter, Parliamentary newsletter, Regulatory newsletter* and *Research newsletter*. Non-members can get them by subscription.

General insurance. London: Mitre House. £48 for two years.
Magazine aimed at the domestic retail market. Product and other news plus short articles, typically by practitioners and on particular kinds of product. The subscription includes two other titles: *Commercial insurance* and *Computing for insurance*. Ostensibly six issues a year but it's difficult to pin down as it merges and demerges all the time with the two other titles and others in the Mitre House range.

The Geneva papers on risk and insurance, issues and practice. Oxford: Blackwell. £99 per year.
Published for the Association Internationale pour l'Etude de l'Economie de l'Assurance, also known as the Geneva Association. One of two successor journals to the original *Geneva papers on risk and insurance*, which was first published in 1976, the other being *The Geneva papers on risk and insurance theory* (section 1.07.31), which took the mathematics with it. This non-mathematical companion contains substantial articles (a typical issue runs to over 100 pages) of an academic nature from a wide

geographical range of contributors. Though academic in orientation the articles are not usually overly theoretical and can provide useful descriptive information on overseas markets, especially European. Quarterly.

Insurance age: first choice of the insurance professional. London: Informa. £58 per year.
Tabloid-size magazine on general insurance only – both the domestic and the London market, but especially the former. Includes news, very short articles, some special features under the 'Insight' banner (e.g. on technology, commercial lines), 'Product link' (a product directory) and 'Policy portfolio' (classified advertising for special schemes). Some special supplements, and there's also a web site (section 3.00.75). Monthly.

The insurance insider: insight and intelligence on the London insurance market. London: Hastie. £350 per year.
Formerly *The London insurance insider* and before that *SoN*, the Society of Names newsletter, but now aimed at a wider audience – both Lloyd's members and other investors in the insurance industry. Contains news, articles and a regular central section 'Insider vital insurance statistics'. This combines company results with an intriguing survey on directors' own share dealings. See also the related web site, section 3.00.75. 10 issues a year.

Insurance research & practice. London: Chartered Insurance Institute. £25 per year (£10 to CII members, free to fellows).
The journal of the CII Society of Fellows, an organisation made up of members who have achieved the Institute's highest qualifications. The articles in its official organ are substantial and practical, usually by practitioners in the industry and often supported by statistics. Achievement of the fellowship is most commonly by dissertation and many of the articles in the journal are edited versions of these documents, offering an eclectic and geographically diverse range of subject matter while remaining firmly focused on insurance and related subjects. Two issues a year. Recent articles are available on *CII Library online* (section 3.00.75).

Insurance trends: quarterly statistics and research review. London: Association of British Insurers.
Substantial, authoritative articles from the ABI political and economic research staff and external contributors. Wide ranging, often supported by statistics. Plus regular statistical tables at the back, updating other ABI statistical publications with market aggregates (see section 3.00.12). Quarterly.

The Jim Bannister report: covers all that matters in insurance. London: Jim Bannister Developments. £295 per year.
Newsletter from an industry veteran, responsible for the development of a range of insurance and related newsletters subsequently acquired by

Lloyd's of London Press (LLP). Wide ranging in coverage: insurance and risk management internationally. News, some articles, comment, statistics. Regular features include a summary of company results and 'Media fortnight', useful reviews of recent reports and other publications. The subscription package includes occasional special reports, such as *Alternative risk financing* and *How brokers win*. Fortnightly.

The journal. Chartered Insurance Institute. London: Informa. £18 per year (free to CII members).
Distributed to around 70,000 CII members throughout the world, this must be one of the mostly widely circulated British insurance periodicals. Successor to the CII's annual bound journal, published since 1898 – but very different in content. This is a magazine containing short articles on insurance and related subjects (wide ranging, in keeping with CII membership) together with institute news. Includes two useful regular features: 'Legal', case summaries, and 'In print', a select list of new acquisitions from the CII Library. Six issues a year.

London market newsletter. London: LLP. £495 per year.
The longest established title in the LLP family of insurance newsletters, first published in 1982 by the now-defunct Risk Research Group. Focusing on the London insurance market, includes market news, market statistics, company news, company results and occasional short articles (often conference speeches). Two valuable annual statistical features are published, each spread over several issues: UK broker league tables and a summary of UK insurers' annual returns. Weekly.

Post magazine & insurance week. London: Timothy Benn. £118 per year.
With a weekly circulation of over 60,000 and published since 1840, this is commonly recognised as the principal trade magazine for the whole of the UK insurance market. Wide ranging in its interests, catering for the domestic non-life market, the global London market and the merging areas of life assurance and related investment business. A substantial news section includes 'Broker news', 'Claims news', 'Technology', 'Product news' and 'International'. Plus short articles, case summaries, some special features (e.g. 'Claims supplement') and over 20 pages of situations vacant. There's also a web site, section 3.00.75.

Weekly insurance news. Danbury, Essex: Lodge Information Services. Two pages of news summaries arranged by broad headings. Focuses on insurance in the United Kingdom, especially company news. Delivered weekly by fax.

3.00.36 Newspapers

Insurance day. Colchester: Informa. £325 per year.
Slim tabloid-size newspaper that started life in 1995 as a supplement to

the long-lived shipping and insurance broadsheet *Lloyd's list*. Has since become a separate publication, which means that today the older publication is best regarded as a shipping paper, the insurance content having been syphoned off into *Insurance day*. Note 'day' and not 'daily': issues appear on Tuesdays, Wednesdays and Thursdays, with an optional news sheet *Insurance day Friday* faxed or emailed to your office. Perspective is international and although one suspects a lingering attachment to the *Lloyd's list* focus on the interests of the global London market it is fairly wide ranging in its subject interests. Includes some short articles, daily insurance share prices, substantial situations vacant (Thursdays) and occasional magazine-style supplements. Also available by subscription on the LLP web site (section 3.00.75).

Insurance times: the general insurance industry's largest circulating weekly newspaper. London: MSM International. £115 per year. Glossy tabloid aimed at the domestic retail market. News and short articles on insurance and related subjects, an extensive directory of specialist insurers, situations vacant. Some special supplements, e.g. *Top 50 European general insurers*. See also the web site (section 3.00.75). Weekly.

3.00.72 CD-ROMs

Two printed insurance dictionaries are also available in electronic formats. See *Witherby's dictionary of insurance* (section 3.00.24) and the multilingual *Elsevier's dictionary of insurance and risk prevention* (section 3.02.24). The NMA policy books are also on CD-ROM: see section 3.00.07.

For computer-based training on insurance the primary source in the United Kingdom is the CII Training Technology range produced by the **Unicorn Training Partnership** in association with the **Chartered Insurance Institute**. These programs are designed to address particular examinations but are also appropriate for more general training needs. The range includes four CD-ROMs at the Associateship and Certificate of Insurance Practice level: *Basic principles & practice of insurance, Commercial & personal lines insurance, Advanced principles & practice of insurance* and *Technical insurance*. There's also a multimedia presentation *Risky business* providing a general introduction to insurance and linked to the syllabus of the Insurance Foundation Certificate. As a separate venture Unicorn also produce insurance-based strategic business models.

Best's Insight. London: A. M. Best International.
Comprises four separate products: *Insight life, Insight non-life, Insight brokers* and *Insight global*. The first two contain full statistical data from the annual returns of 339 UK non-life insurers from 1981 onwards, 270 UK life insurers from 1988 onwards and 35 friendly societies from 1996 onwards. The brokers service provides data from the annual reports and accounts of 184 Lloyd's brokers, 402 provincial brokers and 91 Lloyd's

holding companies. For *Best's insight global* see section 3.02.72. These services allow you to manipulate data to produce customised reports. System requirements: PC, Windows, Microsoft Excel. Prices for each service in four figures. Regularly updated.

Global finbase insurance. London: Datamonitor. £795 per country. A series of products covering over 40 individual insurance markets worldwide. Provide market and company data in Microsoft Excel format, allowing you to produce customised reports etc. System requirements: PC, Windows 95 or higher, Microsoft Excel. On diskettes or by email.

ID.se@rch gold: the insurance database on CD-ROM. London: Timothy Benn. £475 plus VAT per year.
Covers UK insurers, intermediaries, loss adjusters and associations – based on the same listings in the printed *Insurance directory* (section 3.00.21), but searchable by company name, class of business, location, key personnel, and so on. Printing and downloading beyond an initial allowance requires the purchase of additional 'units'. System requirements: PC, Windows 3.1 or higher. One replacement disk every six months.

Market wordings database. Chatham, Kent: MWD Administration, Technical Services, Lloyd's Policy Signing Office.
Library of over 8,000 of the most commonly used policy wordings, clauses, forms and schedules in the London insurance market. A joint market initiative to promote the speedier production of policies and cover notes, with access limited to organisations directly or indirectly involved in the insurance industry, either in the United Kingdom or overseas (a translation service is available). Updated monthly with a replacement disc. Also available online via the Lloyd's extranet (the Lloyd's Insurance Network) with fortnightly updates. Pricing depends on customer requirements.

Onscreen insurance terms. London: Cartermill, 1996. 1 disk (CD-ROM). Short definitions of 1,800 terms. You can search by entry word or for words occurring within definitions; cross-references are usefully hyperlinked. System requirements: PC, Windows 3.1 or higher. Also available on diskette.

Policygen. Haddenham [Buckinghamshire]: Research Department. £1,188 plus VAT per year.
Designed as a research tool for insurance intermediaries and financial advisers, providing detailed product information covering household, motor, package, commercial and general liability business. Information given includes general policy analysis, standard features, optional covers, added benefits, sums insured and limits of indemnity, exclusions and excesses. Based on a series of product tables supported by a benchmarking and ranking system and with further data in the form of

policy wordings and commentary from product providers. Updated by monthly CD-ROMs, with an option of more frequent updating online.

Synthesys. London: Standard & Poor's Thesys.
Full statistical data from the annual returns of 334 UK non-life insurers and 298 UK life insurers from 1985 onwards. Allows you to manipulate the data to produce customised reports. Also includes a preconfigured Excel worksheet containing summary data and a form-view facility that allows you to see data as submitted on the official forms. System requirements: PC, Windows, Microsoft Excel. Issued on multiple diskettes but a CD-ROM version is expected soon. Available as two separate products, life and non-life. Prices for each in four figures. Usually more than one issue per year.

3.00.75 Web sites

At first sight there seem to be a lot of web sites on insurance. But most of these are commercial sites from individual insurance companies and although these firms may try to lure browsers into their private webs by offering little nuggets of information for the most part they are negligible as sources of technical or market data on insurance. That accounts for perhaps 90 per cent of insurance sites. Most of those remaining are from the United States with purely domestic concerns – which leaves the handful listed below and in other sections of this chapter. These do not, however, include the enormous number of sites providing risk-related information that may be of use to insurers. Some of the web directories mentioned here provide a useful signpost to these, and to the other exclusions mentioned above.

Association of British Insurers. London: Association of British Insurers. http://www.abi.org.uk. Partly free.
In three sections: free, subscription-only and members-only. The free section includes press and media information (ABI news releases, briefing material, representations and position papers), consumer advice and information (including PDF versions of printed information sheets on different kinds of cover) and a section on insurance employment and vacancies containing 'useful information on the insurance industry, the jobs it offers and how you can join' (including employment statistics and links to specialist recruitment consultancies). The subscription-only section contains additional market statistics, daily press summaries, company circulars, newsletters and a web directory of related organisations. The members-only section provides further information of a more confidential nature.

Centre for Risk and Insurance Studies. [Nottingham]: [University of Nottingham]. http://www.nottingham.ac.uk/unbs/cris. Free.

Includes details of ongoing research projects in insurance at the University of Nottingham Centre for Risk and Insurance Studies and a useful extract from the centre's printed report *UK insurance premiums* (section 3.00.16) ranking UK insurance companies by premium income.

The Chartered Insurance Institute. London: Chartered Insurance Institute. http://www.cii.co.uk. Free with e-commerce services. In addition to general news and information about the CII there is extensive material on its research programme, online tuition support and digital versions of the Institute's range of insurance and financial planning textbooks (see sections 1.00.03 and 3.00.03). These can be purchased as individual PDFs and companies can also subscribe to the whole set as a single searchable database. See also *CII Library online*, below.

CII Library online. London: Chartered Insurance Institute. http://www.ciilo.org. Free with e-commerce services.
Designed as a single point of access to all published information on insurance, risk and related financial services, both online and offline. Incorporates within an integrated searchable interface a digital journal archive, a directory of web sites and other web-based documents, an online bookshop, a journal index (supported by an online photocopy ordering facility) and full access to the CII Library catalogue. The journal archive includes the full text of recent articles from *The journal, The journal of the Society of Fellows, Insurance research & practice* and *STI times*. See also the entry for the library, chapter 7.

Evandale insurance online. London: Evandale. http://www.evandale.co.uk. £3,995 per year for single users (free trial available).
News service with sections on insurance, reinsurance worldwide, e-commerce and direct selling in insurance and in financial services generally. Updated daily, with a searchable 10-year archive and an email alert facility. Also offers searchable and downloadable contact databases on non-life insurers worldwide and on the London insurance market.

The global risk management network. [London]: EMAP Business Communications. http://www.emap.com/grmn. Mostly free (registration required).
Covers both insurance and risk management. Includes a news database, recruitment advertising, a discussion forum, a series of Bermuda-oriented information papers, a searchable full-text archive of back issues of *The review* and *International risk management* magazines (sections 3.69.31 and 3.62.31), an annotated directory of professional bodies, links to other insurance, risk management and related web sites ('Winfolinks', also available in pamphlet format) and pay-to-view country reports from Axco. The latter are priced at £285 per report but this is much cheaper than the

printed format if you just want one report (see *Insurance market report*, section 3.02.12).

Insurance age electronic. [London]: [Informa]. http://www.insuranceage.com. Free (registration required).
Includes browsable but not searchable market and product news from issues of the printed magazine *Insurance age* (section 3.00.31), links to other sites and 'Product link', a subject directory of general insurance products also taken from the printed publication.

The insurance insider. [London]: London Insurance Insider Ltd. http://www.lii.co.uk. Free.
News and features from the printed magazine of the same title (see section 3.00.31), aimed primarily at Lloyd's members and other insurance investors. For the most recent issues excerpts only are available online, although all items are listed. Articles are in PDF format.

The Insurance Institute of London. London: Insurance Institute of London. http://www.iilondon.co.uk. Free.
Includes a 'lecture archive' containing the full text of recent lunchtime addresses organised by the institute, in PDF format. There are several of these lectures each year on a wide range of topics, delivered by practitioners from within and without the insurance industry. For example the archive contains three lectures for March 1999, on the marine market, government changes affecting the insurance industry and 'Lloyd's and the FSA'.

Insurance news net.co.uk: the online resource for the insurance industry. [UK?]: InsuranceNewsNet.com, Inc. http://www.insurancenewsnet.co.uk. Free.
UK version of a longer-established US insurance news site. Includes a range of news on the UK industry together with links to individual news items on other web sites, a few longer articles – mostly contributed by product suppliers – and a free email newsletter.

Insurance newslink. [UK]: Shillito Market Intelligence. http://www.insurancenewslink.com. £300 per year.
A database of market news comprising short abstracts from the national press, press releases and so on, especially strong on IT developments. You can use a simple search engine or browse news by category: 'Markets', 'Company news', 'Seminars & research', 'Information technology news' and 'Electronic trading'. Within each category you get a choice of further subdivisions, e.g. 'Results' or 'Mergers and takeovers', making this an effective tool for regular browsing of new items. The site includes links to other insurance-related sites. Free trial available.

Insurance times online. London: Newsquest Media Group. http://www.insurancetimes.co.uk. Free (registration required for daily news service).

In addition to current and archive material from the printed *Insurance times* (section 3.00.36), includes a daily news service and a regularly updated version of the printed *Insurance industry handbook*, a guide to specialist insurers and schemes. Chiefly general insurance, aimed especially at intermediaries.

Insurance-first.com: for news, views and information. [UK]: Insurance-First. http://www.insurance-first.com. Free.

UK-oriented insurance news site. You can search the news archive and also find brokers and lawyers by class of business.

LLP. [London]: LLP. http://www.llplimited.com. Partly free. Includes information about LLP publications and online versions of *Insurance day* (section 3.00.36) and the shipping paper *Lloyd's list*. News summaries from the latest issue of each can be browsed free of charge; you can browse the last week's issues for £275 a year (*Insurance day*) or £515 a year (*Lloyd's list*), or you can opt for fully searchable archives at £350 or £620 a year respectively.

Post magazine online: insurance information for insurance professionals. [London]: Timothy Benn. http://www.postmag.co.uk. Free (some sections subscribers only).

Includes a searchable database of jobs, which anyone can access, but some of the best parts of this site are available only to subscribers to the printed *Post magazine & insurance week* (see section 3.00.31) or related products. These sections include news and features from the current issue of the printed magazine, a searchable archive of back issues and a 'Marketpl@ce' facility. This allows you to search for UK insurers, special schemes, legal and other specialist services by class of business. Full contact details are provided.

3.00.78 Online services

Reuters insurance briefing. London: Reuters.

Brings together a number of specialist insurance sources, including the full text of several UK and US insurance newsletters and magazines (including *Asia insurance review, Business insurance, Insurance day* and *Post magazine*), daily insurance and risk news from Reuters, specialist insurance-related news wires like *BestWire* and *LLP casualty wire*, insurance market reports from Axco and credit ratings from Standard & Poor's and A. M. Best. In addition, users of RIB can access the full *Reuters business briefing* database, containing up to 10 years of news from Reuters and over 4,000 other publications from around the world. RIB is available as a searchable database or a customisable briefing service. The Search service can be accessed via the Reuters web site or via dial-up Windows or

Macintosh software. You can search free-text or use selection lists to combine companies, countries, topics, industries and sources. The minimum charge for the Search service is £500 plus VAT per month for up to 20 hours access.

3.02 General sources (international)

Although insurance practice can vary greatly from country to country there is a big international trade in insurance, with the United Kingdom one of the biggest players. Comparative data on the insurance market internationally is of interest to insurers and reinsurers looking to expand abroad or monitoring their risk exposure. The **Association of British Insurers** has an International Division of which a primary function is to monitor overseas markets. It publishes a useful *International newsletter*. The ABI also hosts the **British Insurers' European Committee**, which aims to represent all UK insurers – companies, Lloyd's, P&I clubs etc. – at a European level. It publishes its own *Bulletin* (see section 3.10.31), a particularly useful source for those wishing to monitor progress on EU directives affecting the industry.

This section covers works that are explicitly international, typically containing data on a range of different insurance markets or on a worldwide spread of companies.

3.02.12 Market research

FT Finance has been producing a steady stream of management reports on insurance internationally. Titles include *Distribution channels in European insurance: innovation and diversification* (£595), *European health and long term care insurance* (£450), *The European life insurance market* (£450), *Insurance in Asia* (£595), *Insurance in South Africa: ready to compete* (£595) and *Japanese insurance: the impact of deregulation* (£595).

Much of the insurance output from **Datamonitor** is pan-European or global. Recent European reports have covered life insurance and pensions, personal general insurance, commercial general insurance, distribution, 'tele-insurance', EMU, health insurance and captives. Other reports have dealt with the insurance market in Belgium, France, Germany, Italy, the Netherlands and Spain, life, pensions and health insurance in Central and Eastern Europe and global reinsurance. Several titles have been published on the US market. Prices range from £795 to £1,995.

Datamonitor has also published some pan-European titles with **Reuters** under the Reuters Business Insight imprint, and the Dublin-based **Lafferty** publishes some insurance titles, typically with a European or international focus, e.g. *Life insurance 2010* (£999).

At the European level the **Comité Européen des Assurances** (CEA) is an important publisher of insurance market research, collating a wide range of comparative data sourced from its member organisations – national trade associations like the Association of British Insurers. Its *Annual report* provides a useful survey of pan-European developments (legislative and market), with a more frequent briefing provided by the bimonthly *CEA info*. The *CEA eco* series consists of more detailed surveys on particular topics; recent titles include *The European motor insurance market in 1997* (no. 6), *The European life insurance market in 1997* (no. 7) and *European insurance employment in 1997* (no. 8). Other recent reports from the CEA include *Indirect taxation on insurance contracts in Europe* and *Taxation of life insurance in Europe*. Most CEA material is available in multiple editions for different languages. See also *European insurance in figures*, below.

European insurance in figures. Paris: Comité Européen des Assurances. £44.
Statistics from CEA member states, i.e. the European Union plus several other European markets. Includes premium income (analysed by class of business and also per inhabitant and in relation to GDP), investments, number of companies, largest companies, number of employees. Most tables consist of an analysis by state, with totals. Annual.

Global insurance directory. [New ed]. [London]: Royal & SunAlliance, [1998]. ca 350 p.
A lavishly produced country-by-country guide to the availability of different kinds of insurance and relevant legal requirements. An updated version is available on the Web: see section 3.02.75.

Insurance market report. London: Axco Insurance Information Services.
Series of reports on individual insurance markets. There are 125 reports on non-life markets and more than 76 on life markets. It is the publisher's intention to extend the life range to match the non-life and many new titles are being issued each year. Reports cover all continents and some surprisingly small or obscure countries. Each report covers the market in general, regulation, distribution etc., as well as individual branches of insurance and general country information. The life reports also cover pensions, employee benefits and social security. There are market statistics and figures for the larger insurers as well as a select directory of insurers. Each report comprises between 75 and 150 pages and is replaced every year or two (occasionally longer). The series is also available on two CD-ROMs (life and non-life) in PDF format. Reports can be purchased individually but the normal arrangement is by subscription, which can be for the whole range or by continent, life and/or non-life, print and/or CD-ROM. Under the subscription you get quarterly releases of replacement volumes and new (life) titles and/or replacement discs. Subscriptions will generally be in four figures.

Insurance statistics yearbook. Paris: Organisation for Economic Co-operation and Development. £49.

Contains both comparative tables and sections on individual countries. Statistics include premium income, investment and number of companies. All figures cover a range of several years. As a compilation from a large number of national sources the figures are surprisingly detailed and up to date: the 1990/1997 issue was published in summer 1999. Also available on CD-ROM. Annual.

Insuring foreign risks: a guide to regulations world-wide. Crockford, D. N., ed. Kingston upon Thames, Surrey: Croner. 1 vol. (looseleaf).

Arranged by country, each country section giving brief background information, details of insurance regulation, useful addresses, lists of relevant legislation etc. Updated quarterly by looseleaf amendments; about 750 pages.

Sigma. Zurich: Swiss Reinsurance Company. Free.

If this item were commercially published you would be paying several hundred pounds for it and not complaining. Issued since 1968 this is a series of individual reports on aspects of insurance and reinsurance from an international perspective, with the accent on statistical and economic analysis. The six or seven reports a year include three annual regulars: *World insurance in...*, which appears mid-year, analysing premium income by country, branch (life and non-life), percentage of GDP etc.; *Natural catastrophes and man-made disasters*, which appears earlier, with a tabulated review of losses plus commentary; and *Sigma-prospect*, a forecast for world non-life markets. One warning: if you rely too much on *Sigma* for individual market statistics you may sometimes be working a year behind: sources from individual countries are inevitably going to appear first, since Swiss Re uses these as raw material. That said, there are many commercial publications that use *Sigma* as their raw material. In the United Kingdom this series is available from Swiss Re (UK) and recent issues can also be downloaded from the Swiss Re web site (section 3.02.75). Available in English, French, German, Italian and Spanish.

Standard & Poor's Insurance Solvency International market profiles. European ed. London: Standard & Poor's Insurance Ratings. £245. Covers 15 European countries, providing for each a market survey plus rankings and statistics for the larger insurers. Annual.

3.02.16 Company research

See also the CD-ROMs in section 3.02.72 and Moody's web site, section 3.02.75. There are also certain investment banks and similar organisations producing insurance company research on an international scale. Of particular importance in this respect are **Moody's Investors Service** and **Fox-Pitt Kelton**. The latter is now a subsidiary of Swiss Re and especially valuable for European research.

Best's insurance reports. International ed. Oldwick, NJ: A. M. Best. $779. An international version of the well-known and much respected US insurer reports. Profiles around 1,200 insurers, arranged alphabetically by country. For each insurer gives summary financial information and commentary (including a potted history), but unlike the US editions most profiles do not include ratings. In two volumes, around 3,000 pages in all. Also available on CD-ROM. Annual.

Moody's credit opinions. Insurance: insurance holding companies, life & health insurers, property & casualty insurers.... New York; London: Moody's Investors Service.
International in scope though with a bias to the United States. Summary statistics, ratings and comment. One page per company; nearly 500 pages per issue. Two issues a year

3.02.21 Directories

Assecuranz-compass: the worldwide insurance directory. Brussels: Assecuranz Compass. £408.
Published since 1893 and now listing around 15,000 insurance companies. Arranged by country with a company index and a classified section giving brief entries under class of business. Gives contact details plus, for some companies only, senior personnel and year of establishment. Also on CD-ROM. Annual.

Evandale's directory of world underwriters. London: Evandale. £235. Arranged by country, with a company index. Lists around 9,000 non-life insurance companies, with contact details, senior personnel, brief financial data and other information. Annual.

Global insurance directory. London: Financial Times Business. (Financial Times Business Directories) £225.
Aims for depth rather than breadth, with around 500 company entries arranged by country (with a company index), three or four per page. Gives contact details, summary financial data, subsidiaries, ownership, classes written etc. There are also sections listing over 200 service companies (with subject index) and over 4,000 key personnel. Formerly *The Financial Times world insurance yearbook*. Also on CD-ROM (see section 3.02.75). Annual.

International insurance directory. London: LLP.
The main section of this directory lists ca 4,000 insurance and reinsurance companies, arranged by country. Gives contact details and brief financial information for each firm. Subsidiary sections cover P&I clubs, brokers

(by country) and Lloyd's; there's also a glossary and an alphabetical index. Annual.

3.02.24 Dictionaries

Elsevier's dictionary of insurance and risk prevention: in English, French, Spanish, German and Portuguese. De Lucca, J. L. Amsterdam; London: Elsevier, 1992. 429 p.
Gives equivalents for 3,962 terms. Arranged by the terms in English, with indexes for the other languages. A separate section covers abbreviations. Also on CD-ROM.

Insurance dictionary. Müller-Lütz, H. L., ed. Karlsruhe: Verlag Versicherungswirtschaft. £15 per volume.
A series of pocket-sized multilingual dictionaries. Each gives equivalents for around 1,300 terms in English, French, German and one other language: Arabic, Bulgarian, Chinese, Croatian, Danish, Dutch, Finnish, Greek, Hebrew, Hungarian, Indonesian, Italian, Japanese, Norwegian, Polish, Portuguese, Romanian, Russian, Slovene, Spanish, Swedish or Turkish. New editions occasionally produced.

Lexicon: risk, insurance, reinsurance: French–English/American, English/American–French: including abbreviations, initials and tables. Lesobre, Jacques, Sommer, Henri and Cave, Frances J. 3rd ed. Paris: SEP l'Assurance Française, [1993?]. 375 p.
Gives equivalents in French and English.

3.02.26 Bibliographies

Catalogo de obras de seguros y seguridad. 1992/1996 [ed]. Madrid: Fundaçion Mapfre Estudios, 1996. 408 p.
A detailed catalogue of the collection of the Centro de Documentación of the educational foundation run by the Spanish insurer Mapfre. Around 4,000 references in classified order with author and subject indexes. International; particularly strong on Spain and other European countries.

CEA doc. Paris: Comité Européen des Assurances.
Covers EU countries only. Short references to new publications, with subject headings in English and French. In two parts: *Book list*, published six times a year, and *Articles*, monthly. Each issue is a few pages. Also available on the CEA web site at http://www.cea.assur.org.

Insurance and employee benefits literature. [US]: Insurance and Employee Benefits Division, Special Libraries Association.
Annotated listings of new books and web sites, chiefly American but with some UK and other material. Six issues a year. The publishers are 'moving towards' email distribution only.

International Insurance Library, Louvain: catalogue. [5ᵗʰ ed]. [Louvain?]:
ABB, [1998]. 4 vols (2,127 p.).
Catalogue of a collection split between various sites of the University of
Louvain, the Belgian insurer ABB (now part of the KBC group) and other
locations. Detailed catalogue records arranged in classified order. For
searching leave it on the shelf and consult the web version, at http://
www.kbc.be.

3.02.31 Periodicals

European insurance market. London: LLP. £436 per year.
Newsletter containing market and company news, statistics and some
longer items, such as market surveys. Fortnightly.

Global insurance bulletin: incorporating Worldwide insurance abstracts.
London: Risk & Insurance Research Group. £315 per year.
An internationally oriented newsletter with market news, shortish arti-
cles and some country surveys. The regular feature 'Worldwide insurance
abstracts' provides fairly long summaries of selected articles from US and
UK insurance periodicals. Monthly.

Insurance international. London: Mitre House. £48 per year.
From the same stable as *General insurance* (section 3.00.31) and exhibits
the same eccentric publishing behaviour. The package includes issues of
Commercial risk and some issues are combined with other titles. Consists
of short articles on insurance aimed at an international audience, typically written by practitioners. Quarterly.

Insurance research letter. Lake Forest, Illinois: International Research
Services. $660 per year.
Very useful international newsletter published since the 1960s. Arranged
by continent and then by country; comprises short news items and longer
features with a high statistical content – often summaries of the annual
reports of insurance supervisory authorities (particularly helpful if the
original is not in English) – plus special reports (often second-hand, e.g.
from *Sigma*). Comes loose and hole-punched so you can arrange it by
continent in ring binders and an annual index provides convenient access. There's an optional *Flash report* service whereby you get important
items sooner, and an optional *US insurance news*. It's $1,000 a year to in-
clude both. Also available by subscription on the Web: see *Insurance services
network*, section 3.02.75. Monthly.

Journal of international insurance. The Hague: Kluwer Law International.
£94 per year.
Substantial new journal (launched in 1999) with contributions from academics and practitioners. Articles are typically between 10 and 20 pages
and cover a wide range of topics and geographic areas.

World insurance report. London: LLP Professional. £795 per year. International newsletter focusing on market news arranged by broad category rather than country: law and supervision, marine and aviation etc. Since its inception in 1975 two other FT newsletters have been absorbed and these live on as separate sections at the back: *World loss report* (tabulated data on large losses) and *World insurance corporate report* (company news). Following the purchase of this title from FT Finance in 2000 the LLP newsletter *Reinsurance market report* has also been absorbed. The initial result of this absorption seems to be a thicker issue and some more substantial features (as opposed to news). The subscription includes useful quarterly indexes; an annual index would be a good idea too. Fortnightly.

3.02.72 CD-ROMs

Four major international reference works are available in both printed and electronic formats. See the OECD *Insurance statistics yearbook* (section 3.02.12), the *Global insurance directory* (section 3.02.21), *Assecuranz-compass: the worldwide insurance directory* (section 3.02.21) and *Best's insurance reports* (international edition, section 3.02.16). The Axco *Insurance market report* series (section 3.02.12) is also available on CD-ROM.

Best's Insight global. London: A. M. Best International.
Contains information and ratings for over 4,900 insurers from more than 60 countries. Statistical data is taken from the companies' annual reports and extracts from the Best's rating reports are also included. You can make cross-border and comparative analyses, as well as evaluate individual companies in detail. Functionality includes ranking, graphing, peer group totals and averages, ratio building, market share and percentage change. You can subscribe to the standard version, covering over 1,300 insurers outside the United States, or can add an optional US database, covering over 3,600 US insurers. Updated monthly.

Best's key rating guide international. Oldwick, NJ: A. M. Best International. $225 per year.
Contains company profiles, contact information, balance sheet and operational data as well as ratings and profitability, leverage and liquidity tests for insurers and reinsurers worldwide. You can search for particular companies, create and sort lists based on selected criteria, export and import data. Annual, Windows-based CD-ROM.

Classic ratings database. London; New York: Standard & Poor's Insurance Ratings.
Financial statistics and ratings on over 4,000 insurers and reinsurers in 72 countries. Data can be manipulated to produce customised reports. Price in five figures.

EuroThesys life & non-life. London: Standard & Poor's Thesys. £1,495 per year (single user).
Detailed data from the reports and accounts of over 1,700 European life and non-life insurance companies, from 1994 (where available) to the latest published year. Supplied on CD-ROM in Microsoft Excel spreadsheet format. Includes profit and loss, balance sheet and ratio analysis; standardised to facilitate cross-company and cross-country comparisons. Updated monthly.

ISIS: insurance information and statistics. London: Thomson Financial.
Up to eight years of financial data on over 4,000 insurers in 71 countries. Formatted to allow analysis and manipulation. Also includes ratings, class of business, ownership and other descriptive data. Created by Bureau van Dijk from data provided by Thomson. Price in four figures.

Search2. [London]: Thomson Financial. £3,450 plus VAT per year. Financial statistics, ratios and ratings (from several agencies) on over 5,000 insurers and reinsurers worldwide. Covers non-life business only. System requirements: PC, Windows 3.1 or higher. You get a replacement disk every month.

3.02.75 Web sites

A. M. Best Company: the insurance information source. Oldwick, NJ: A. M. Best. http://www.ambest.com. Mostly free.
Extensive site including a searchable database of Best's insurance company ratings, the full text of recent special reports, news and features from the printed *Best's review*, a searchable news database and details of other A. M. Best products. Chiefly US-oriented but includes some international content, for instance large non-US firms are included in the ratings service.

Global insurance directory. [UK]: Royal & SunAlliance. http://www.royal-and-sunalliance.co.uk/gid. Free (registration required).
A country-by-country guide focusing on the availability of different kinds of cover and legal requirements. 'Provides a snap shot of the latest insurance and country related information for virtually every country in the world.' Also available – but not updated – as a printed volume (section 3.02.12).

Insurance services network. Lake Forest, Illinois: Insurance Services Network. http://www.isn-inc.com. Mostly free.
Offers information on the insurance market in over 50 countries (details of cover available, demographic and economic information plus links) together with news articles and online access to the international *Insurance research letter* (section 3.02.31). Free except for the latter, which is by

subscription. Also includes an online bookstore and insurance and related links.

International facts. New York: Insurance Information Institute. http://www.internationalinsurance.org. Free.
Collection of useful facts about insurance internationally, culled from various mostly published sources. Includes economic and premium data, number of companies, regulatory bodies and other information per country, regional data and worldwide rankings of different kinds of firm. There are also links to other sites.

Moody's Investors Service. Insurance. New York: Moody's Investors Service. http://www.moodys.com/insurance. Free.
Section of the Moody's site providing debt and financial strength ratings, summary statistics and comment on around 1,000 insurers, together with details of printed publications. Coverage international though strongest on the United States.

RSX: the world insurance portal. [Sussex]: WIRE. http://www.rsx.co.uk. Free.
International site with a UK slant. Consists of links to recent news stories on other sites, a detailed web directory and a company information feature called *RSX marketview*. This provides tabulated links to the sites of individual insurers and reinsurers, each analysed into 'News', 'Financials', 'Products', 'People' and 'Contacts' so that particular web pages can be accessed directly. Ratings from Standard & Poor's are also included.

Swiss Re. [Zurich]: Swiss Re. http://www.swissre.com. Free.
The standard features of a large corporate site are augmented by online versions of a wide range of recent Swiss Re publications in PDF format. These include issues of *Sigma* (section 3.02.12), which provides detailed economic and statistical analyses of the insurance industry internationally. An 'Insurance links library' is also being developed, listing companies and associations by country, and a new Swiss Re portal (registration required) provides news and other information within a personalisable framework.

3.07 Quantitative methods

From being insurance mathematicians actuaries have now extended their range of interests into investment and further afield. The actuarial literature has moved with them and will accordingly be found in section 1.07 and not here.

3.07.31 Periodicals

Insurance: mathematics & economics. Amsterdam; Oxford: Elsevier Science.
Fairly long, theoretical articles with lots of algebra. Since its inception the mathematics in the subtitle seems to have beaten the economics.

3.10 Law

Insurance law to those outside the industry means – not surprisingly – the law as it relates to insurance. This is chiefly a subdivision of contract law, comprising the law relating to the insurance policy, its construction and interpretation. But it also includes an element of agency law – the law relating to insurance intermediaries – and of company law – the regulation of insurance companies.

To those within the industry insurance law tends to mean any aspect of the law of interest to the insurer or insurance intermediary. This will include in particular the law of civil liability and most especially tort. Thus an insurance practitioner would expect a book on the law of employer's liability insurance to go into great detail on the Health and Safety at Work Act and the important case law defining an employer's liability to his or her employees.

The Marine Insurance Act 1906 enumerates painstakingly, clause by clause, how the marine insurance contract should be interpreted. This is, however, a special exception (although of some relevance to other branches of law) and by and large insurance contract law is case law. On the other hand the law of insurance companies – their authorisation and supervision – is predominantly statute law, enshrined in insurance companies acts and regulations. Works on insurance law tend to concentrate on insurance contract law. For items focusing on the authorisation and supervision of insurers see section 3.15.

A small group of legal firms are particularly active in this area and are a useful source of newsletters and papers (see section 3.10.31). These firms are strongly represented on the **British Insurance Law Association**, a broad-based organisation of individuals with an interest in this area and the UK member of the **Association Internationale de Droit des Assurances** (AIDA).

Both organisations produce important publications on insurance law (see below). In addition AIDA organises the World Congress of Insurance Law every four years, and the reports from these events form a substantial corpus of information particularly for those interested in comparative works on insurance law internationally.

3.10.03 Textbooks

Colinvaux's Law of insurance. Colinvaux, Raoul. 7th ed. London: Sweet & Maxwell, 1997. lxxx, 567 p. (Insurance practitioners library) £130.
Chiefly on contract law, with one chapter on the regulation of insurance companies and one on agents. Includes chapters on individual branches. Aimed at both practitioners and students.

EC insurance law. Merkin, Robert and Rodger, Angus. London: Longman, 1997. xxiv, 195 p. (European law series) £15.99.
Straightforward account of EU law as it affects insurance. Includes chapters on the single insurance market, insurance intermediaries and jurisdiction.

General principles of insurance law. Ivamy, E. R. Hardy. 6th ed. London: Butterworths, 1993. 1,211 p. £145.
Not quite as large a book as it seems at first sight, as it includes 500 pages of appendices – statutes, statutory instruments and EU directives. Covers all branches of insurance, with a chapter on the regulation of insurance companies and five chapters on agency.

Insurance law: doctrines and principles. Lowry, John and Rawlings, Philip. Oxford: Hart, 1999. lxii, 454 p. £20.
A general survey on insurance law, aimed particularly at undergraduates but suitable for a wider audience.

The law of insurance contracts. Clarke, Malcolm A. 3rd ed. London: LLP, 1997. cxxxiii, 909 p. (Insurance law library) £170.
Covers insurance contract and agency law; all branches. Also published as part of the *Electronic insurance law service* CD-ROM (see section 3.10.72).

MacGillivray on insurance law: relating to all risks other than marine. MacGillivray, E. J. 9th ed. London: Sweet and Maxwell, 1997. cli, 1,024 p. (Insurance practitioners library) £175.
Chiefly on insurance contract law, with chapters on the regulation of insurance companies, agency and Lloyd's. Includes chapters on each branch of insurance.

Modern insurance law. Birds, John. 4th ed. London: Sweet & Maxwell, 1997. lxi, 422 p. £25.

Aimed at both students and practitioners, 'an introduction to this complex area of law'. Chiefly on insurance contract law, with one chapter on intermediaries. Covers all branches.

Policies and perceptions of insurance: an introduction to insurance law. Clarke, Malcolm. Oxford: Clarendon, 1997. xxviii, 326 p. (Clarendon law series) £16.99.
An 'introduction to insurance contract law in the United Kingdom'.

Aimed at college students, with a somewhat different approach from most works on this subject.

The single market in insurance: breaking down the barriers. McGee, Andrew. Aldershot: Ashgate, 1998. vi, 151 p. (European business law library) £40.
'Explores the difficulties inherent in the concept of the single market in insurance, as well as the practical difficulties of implementation.' Aimed at lawyers and academics.

Tolley's Insurance handbook. Merkin, Robert M. 1st ed. Croydon: Tolley, 1994. xxxiii, 274 p. £39.95.
'A comprehensive first point of reference to the full range of insurance matters and insurance principles.' Divided into a lot of short chapters, arranged alphabetically – almost a short encyclopaedia of insurance law. Includes a chapter on the regulation of insurance companies.

3.10.05 Manuals

Insurance and EC law: commentary. Empel, Martijn van and Drabbe, Humbert, eds. The Hague; London: Kluwer Law International. 1 vol. (looseleaf). (Amsterdam financial series) £110.
Comprehensive description of EU law as it affects insurance, with contributions from several authors. Comprises around 750 pages in all, updated irregularly by looseleaf amendments.

Insurance contract law. Merkin, Robert M. Brentford: Kluwer. 2 vols (looseleaf).
A substantial work, particularly as it restricts itself to insurance contract law only, though covering all branches of insurance. Comprises around 1,500 pages, with quarterly looseleaf updates and the useful *Kluwer insurance & reinsurance law briefing*.

Insurance contract law. Fontaine, M., ed. Karlsruhe: Verlag Versicherungswirtschaft, 1992. 2 vols (320; 267 p.).
A country-by-country survey of insurance contract law. Of nearly 30 chapters on individual jurisdictions 14 are in English: those on Australia, Denmark, England, Finland, Greece, Hungary, Japan, the Netherlands, Poland, South Africa, South Korea, Sweden, the United States and Yugoslavia. Published in conjunction with the Association Internationale de Droit des Assurances.

International encyclopaedia of laws. [Insurance law]. Fredericq, Simon and Cousy, Herman. The Hague; London: Kluwer Law International. 3 vols (looseleaf). £236.
A series of monographs on individual countries covering both contract law and regulation, the former predominating. Currently comprises chapters on Australia, Canada, Chile, Denmark, Greece, the Netherlands,

Nigeria, Poland and the United Kingdom, with an appendix ('Codex') providing the text of the main EU directives on insurance. Each chapter comprises between 150 and 400 pages. Publication is in progress, with irregular updates (one in 1998, three in 1999) providing amendments and new chapters. Published in conjunction with the Association Internationale de Droit des Assurances.

International insurance law and regulation. Campbell, Dennis, ed. [New ed]. Dobbs Ferry, NY: Oceana. 2 vols (looseleaf).
Covers contract law and regulation in around 40 jurisdictions, with a chapter on the European Union and eight further chapters on 'Transnational aspects'. Around 1,500 pages, updated approximately twice a year with amendments and occasional new chapters.

Single licence vademecum for operators. Paris: Comité Européen des Assurances, 1997. 2 vols (412; 312 p.). £65 per volume.
Analyses relevant EU law affecting insurance then looks in detail at how this has actually been implemented in each member state. Comprises a life and a non-life volume, *The life single insurance market* and *The non-life single insurance market*, each subtitled *access and conditions of exercise under freedom of establishment or freedom of services on European markets*. Also published in French and German.

3.10.07 Source materials

Butterworths insurance law handbook. Wood, Jeremy, ed. 5th ed. London: Butterworths, 1998. xv, 1,936 p. £70.
Contains annotated statutes and statutory instruments, solicitors' professional indemnity rules, Motor Insurers' Bureau agreements, Association of British Insurers statements, codes and understandings, FSA Insurance Division guidance notes and European directives, decisions and regulations. Exemplifies the alternative approach to the updated looseleaf for this kind of material: a fat, cheapish paperback you can just throw away when it gets out of date. Apart from the wait for the next edition the main downside is the amazingly thin paper.

Compendium of insurance law. Merkin, Robert. London: LLP. 2 vols (looseleaf). £364.
Unlike the competitors from Sweet & Maxwell and Butterworths this compilation is arranged by subject, with an editorial introduction to each chapter followed by the relevant sources: annotated legislation (UK statutes and SIs), EU material (directives, some draft directives, decisions), ABI statements of practice etc. Approximately 1,500 pages, updated by looseleaf amendments twice a year, plus the same text on CD-ROM, replaced twice a year.

EC insurance directives. Maitland-Walker, Julian. London: LLP. 1 vol. (looseleaf). £195.

Arranged by subject with short introductions summarising directives followed by the full text. Includes a useful table showing how directives have been implemented in national law. Also some draft directives. Around 750 pages in all, updated two to three times a year by looseleaf amendments.

Encyclopedia of insurance law. O'Dowd, Anthony, ed. London: Sweet and Maxwell. 2 vols (looseleaf). £370.

An annotated collection of statutes, statutory instruments, EU directives, Insurance Division guidance notes, ABI statements of insurance practice and MIB agreements – together with a section on case law, providing short summaries arranged by subject area. Comprises around 1,500 pages, updated by looseleaf amendments twice a year.

Insurance law: text and materials. Hodgin, Ray. London: Cavendish, 1998. xxxix, 722 p. £24.95.

Aimed at students. Each chapter begins with an introduction to the topic, followed by case summaries, extracts from legislation, articles and other relevant documents. Covers all branches; chiefly contract law but with one chapter on intermediaries and another on the Insurance Ombudsman.

Legal decisions affecting insurance 1729–1991. Hodgin, Ray, ed. London: Butterworths, 1992. 4 vols + 1 index. £590.

A selection of ca 250 of the most important English insurance cases, arranged chronologically from 1729 to 1991. Full reports are given, with short editorial notes. The index volume includes listings by name and subject. Around 4,000 pages.

Lloyd's law reports. Insurance & reinsurance. London: LLP. £199 per year.

A merger of *Reinsurance law reports* and *Lloyd's reinsurance reports*, this now forms a section of the full *Lloyd's law reports* series, which covers a wider range of commercial cases. Each issue contains the full reports of selected English cases (typically six or seven). With a bound cumulation annually.

3.10.31 Periodicals

In addition to the commercially published journals listed below you could create a modest law library for nothing courtesy of several large firms of UK solicitors – who in their anxiety to impress the industry with their specialist experience and competence in insurance vie with each other in producing often quite substantial client newsletters focusing on insurance law and in particular recent cases. Top of the list must be **Barlow**

Lyde & Gilbert, whose *Insurance law quarterly* is also available on its web site, but other solicitors publishing serviceable insurance newsletters include Cameron Markby Hewitt, Clifford Chance, D. J. Freeman, Lawrence Graham, Reynolds Porter Chamberlain, Wansbroughs Willey Hargrave and Wilde Sapte.

Bulletin. British Insurers' European Committee. [London]: The Committee. This newsletter provides a useful update on the progress of directives and other EU developments affecting insurance, together with information on the other aspects of the committee's work.

Insurance law monthly. Sudbury, Suffolk: Monitor Press.
Newsletter containing shortish articles on aspects of insurance law, mostly summarising recent English cases on insurance. These are often unreported cases making this a valuable work of reference, particularly in view of the annual index. Monthly.

The international journal of insurance law. London: LLP. £125 per year (£195 with annual cumulation).
Published in association with the Association Internationale de Droit des Assurances. Substantial articles from an international range of contributors, plus an 'AIDA section' containing shorter contributions and news from the association and case comments, reports and notes. Each issue has a cumulative index to cases, legislation and subjects. Quarterly.

Journal. British Insurance Law Association. London: The Association. Free to members.
Substantial articles on insurance law and related subjects (i.e. insurance and law), often presentations made at meetings of the association. Not available to non-members but membership is inexpensive and fairly open. Three issues a year.

3.10.72 CD-ROMs

The electronic insurance law service. London: LLP. £495 (single user), £995 (2–10 users) per year.
Contains the text of several LLP printed publications (some of them looseleaf updated items): *The law of insurance contracts, Reinsurance practice and the law, Compendium of insurance law, Insurance disputes* and *Good faith and insurance contracts*. Also carries selected cases

Lloyd's law reports. System requirements: PC, Windows 95 or higher. Two disks a year.

Insurance company law handbook for Windows. London: 3d Consulting.
Contains the complete text of UK insurance legislation, EU directives and other official documents: prudential guidance notes, 'Dear director' letters, actuarial guidance, ABI guidance, consultative documents etc. System

requirements: PC, Windows 3.1 or higher. Regularly updated and consolidated. Price in four figures.

Insurance law service. London: Butterworths. £350 per year (single user). Collection of source material relating to insurance law. Comprises in the main statutes and statutory instruments (without annotations); the insurance volume (vol. 20) from the 5th edition of the *Encyclopaedia of forms and precedents* (but without some forms); law reports from the *All England law reports* as well as some unreported transcripts; directives and other EU materials; guidelines and codes (ABI, MIB, DTI etc.); FSA materials. Uses the 'Books on screen' interface. Updated quarterly.

3.15 Regulation

The agency now responsible for the regulation of insurers in the United Kingdom is the **Insurance and Friendly Societies Division of the Financial Services Authority**. This department has been tossed around a lot recently, having moved from the Department of Trade and Industry to the Treasury to the FSA in the course of two or three years. It produces a valuable stream of guidance in the form of 'Dear director' letters, 'Prudential guidance notes' and other documents. These are essential sources on the legislative requirements, for instance on the preparation of annual returns; an additional source is the largest firms of chartered accountants and management consultants, several of which publish useful materials on this subject. As an example the recently merged PricewaterhouseCoopers produces a short guide *The route to authorisation* as well as the more substantial *The insurance annual return: a guide through the maze*. Also recently merged, **Deloitte & Touche** produce a pamphlet, *Insurance in the UK: a guide to authorisation*.

3.15.05 Manuals

Regulation of insurance in the United Kingdom and Ireland. Ellis, Henry and Wiltshire, James A. London: Kluwer. 2 vols (looseleaf).
The only substantial work on this subject published in the United Kingdom, comprising some 1,500 pages with quarterly looseleaf updates and a useful newsletter *Kluwer insurance & reinsurance law briefing*. Contents: The idea of insurance regulation – Regulation of insurers in the United Kingdom [ca 500 p] – Regulation of insurers in Ireland – Regulation of insurers in EC member states [with separate chapters on France and Spain] – Supervision of insurance intermediaries [United Kingdom and Ireland] – Supervision of insurance contracts [United Kingdom and Ireland] – Representatives of government, insurers, intermediaries and consumers [a survey of individual bodies] – Legislative sources [listing only].

3.15.09 Official reports

Insurance: annual report. HM Treasury. London: Stationery Office. £17.95.
The official report from the Insurance Directorate of HM Treasury (now
relocated within the Financial Services Authority). Surveys legislative
and supervisory developments over the past year, with lists of authorised
insurance companies and statutory instruments in force. The company
listings are particularly useful but have unfortunately become rather complex with the introduction of the European single market. Companies
allowed to operate in the United Kingdom on the basis of home state
authorisation (i.e. in another country within the European Economic Area)
are listed in a separate section from UK-authorised companies. Information given is minimal – name, state of incorporation etc., authorisation
class – and the listing is already over six months out of date when it
appears, but this is still an invaluable source. There are also useful statistics derived from these listings giving number of authorised companies
by each class.

3.17 Taxation

The introduction of insurance premium tax in the United Kingdom has
added to the breadth and diversity of this subject. Other aspects include
the direct taxation of insurers, the taxation of insurance benefits and VAT
in relation to insurance claims. Works on insurance taxation will also be
found in material on regulation and accounting. Some works may also
deal with background subjects, for example general features of corporation tax. The large firms of accountants can be useful sources of
information.

3.17.03 Textbooks

Taxation of insurance business. MacLeod, James S and Levitt, Arthur. 4th
ed. London: Butterworths, 1999. xxxix, 3, 461 p. £150.

On the taxation of insurance companies (life and general) and policyholders (including income tax, capital gains tax, insurance premium tax,
VAT).

3.17.31 Periodicals

Insurance tax review. Croydon: Insurance Tax Review. £345 per year.
News and fairly substantial articles on tax aspects of insurance and back-
ground tax information, usually written by expert practitioners.
Production quality could be improved with a couple of staples. Monthly.

3.22 Takeovers and mergers

Mergers and acquisitions continue at a fast pace in the insurance industry, with specialist publishers reflecting this trend in their own corporate manoeuvrings.

3.22.31 Periodicals

Insurance M&A report. London: LLP. £195 per year.
Newsletter featuring regular surveys of mergers and acquisitions in the insurance industry worldwide. A useful source of data. 10 issues a year.

Insurance M&A weekly. London: Thomson Financial Insurance Solutions. £590 per year.
Newsletter covering insurance mergers and acquisitions internationally. Mostly short news items, arranged by area. A supplement, *M&A quarterly update*, includes tabulated summaries.

3.23 Troubled companies

Troubled companies are not necessarily insolvent and there are many firms in 'run off' – firms that have discontinued actively underwriting but which continue to pay claims, sometimes through a run off specialist or consultant. There are two kinds of published information in this area: legal data on litigation involving troubled companies, particularly concerning the payment of insurance or reinsurance claims when the insurer or reinsurer is insolvent or in run off, or both; and material recording the fast moving chain of events, usually by company. Some insurance directories now have sections on 'companies ceased underwriting'.

3.23.31 Periodicals

Insurance security watch. London: LLP. £195 per year.
International newsletter with news and regular surveys by country and company of liquidations and run offs, etc. Monthly.

3.25 Lloyd's

Lloyd's is an insurance exchange and not an insurance company and thus differs in many important respects from the rest of the UK insurance industry. As a subject Lloyd's used to be a subdivision of marine insurance but today well over 50 per cent of its business is non-marine. The **Society of Lloyd's** is the collective name for the underwriting members or 'names' and the underwriting firms that constitute the market. The **Corporation of Lloyd's** is the organisation that provides the extensive administrative machinery to support the society. Its responsibilities include the provision of information to those working at Lloyd's, including the maintenance and development of the Lloyd's intranet. In the last few years it has cut back its provision of information to the outside world, with the sale of its publishing subsidiary Lloyd's of London Press (now **LLP**) and reductions in other areas. But its public web site (see section 3.25.75 below) is an extensive resource.

There are a number of other organisations associated with Lloyd's, in particular **Lloyd's Underwriters Non-Marine Association**, a grouping of non-marine underwriters working in the market, which publishes policy wordings and other useful data, and the **Association of Lloyd's Members**, a grouping of the 'names'. Lloyd's Register has no connection with the insurance market.

3.25.03 Textbooks

An introduction to Lloyd's. Lloyd's Training Centre. 3rd ed. [London]: Lloyd's, 1998. ca 180 p. in various pagings.
Aimed at those studying for the Lloyd's Introductory Test, but of value to anyone wanting a basic introduction to how Lloyd's works.

3.25.07 Source materials

Lloyd's acts, byelaws and regulations. London: LLP Reference. 2 vols (looseleaf). £395 per year.
Annotated texts. Comprises some 750 pages, updated quarterly by looseleaf amendments with more frequent bulletins, which aim to provide subscribers with new items as soon as they are available (later consolidated into the main work). Includes the same text on CD-ROM.

3.25.12 Market research

Statistics relating to Lloyd's. London: Lloyd's Commercial Policy Unit. Includes Lloyd's global accounts and statistics on premium income, market share, market expenses, membership, capacity and security. Also data on the largest syndicates, brokers and underwriting agencies. Most figures are given for a wide range of years. Annual.

3.25.16 Company research

Best's guide to Lloyd's market results & prospects. London: A. M. Best International. £250.
Provides detailed statistical and other information on the Lloyd's market derived from syndicate reports and accounts, questionnaires, Companies House data (agents) and Lloyd's itself. In five sections: syndicates, managing agents, members' agents, MAPAs and quoted Lloyd's corporates.

An annual paperback of some several hundred pages produced in association with the Association of Lloyd's Members.

Moody's Lloyd's syndicate rating guide. [London?]: Moody's Investors Service. £500.
Statistics, graphs and commentary on individual syndicates, agencies and other Lloyd's entities, Originally published by Syndicate Underwriting Research, now taken over by Moody's. Annual. Also on CD-ROM.

Standard & Poor's Lloyd's syndicate performance measures. London: Standard & Poor's Insurance Ratings. £1,950.
Detailed financial information and performance measures on all syndicates trading at Lloyd's. Includes brief histories and other background material.

Syndicate profiles. London: SBW Insurance Research.
Detailed statistics and other data on all trading syndicates 'to which traditional names have access'. Usually two pages per syndicate, each issue around 300 pages. Annual.

3.25.21 Directories

Directory of Lloyd's & London insurance market. London: Chatset. £45.
Formerly the *Chatset/Ocarina directory of Lloyd's of London* and still primarily of use for its coverage of Lloyd's. In separate sections for insurance companies, Lloyd's brokers, underwriting agents and other entities, with full contact information plus some statistics. Also includes descriptive chapters on Lloyd's membership. Issued every two years.

3.25.31 Periodicals

See also the slightly broader *Insurance insider*, section 3.00.31.

Digest of Lloyd's news: the monthly review of news for members of Lloyd's and their advisers. London: Ocarina. £90 per year.
Small-format newsletter from a firm that has made a specialisation of publishing for the Lloyd's member / adviser. Contains Lloyd's market news and statistics. Monthly.

3.25.72 CD-ROMs

Lloyd's acts, byelaws and regulations (section 3.25.07) is also available on CD-ROM.

Best's Marksman 4: the Lloyd's market analysis system. London: A. M. Best International.
Contains data from annual and quarterly returns for all syndicates in addition to the syndicate portfolios of major corporate investors plus some commentary from A. M. Best. Allows you to manipulate data to produce

customised reports. System requirements: PC, Windows, Microsoft Excel. Regularly updated.

Lloyd's syndicate results: also known as Limelight. London: Thomson Financial Insurance Solutions.
Contains detailed statistics per syndicate as well as facsimiles of individual syndicate reports. In Adobe Acrobat format, reader supplied. System requirements: Windows 3.1 or later. Annual.

3.25.75 Web sites

Lloyd's. [London]: Lloyd's. http://www.lloyds.com. Free.
Extensive information on the Lloyd's market including a links directory of Lloyd's underwriters (*Lloyd's marketview*), data on the market's ratings, solvency and performance, listings of underwriters and brokers by name and risk type and a virtual reality model of the famous underwriting room.

3.36 Mutuals

Mutual insurers are insurers that are owned by their policyholders. They include friendly societies, a dwindling number of mutual life offices (sometimes mutual only in name, sometimes mutual but without the name), the shipowner mutuals known as protection and indemnity clubs, and a number of 'group captives' run on an industry-wide basis, for instance, to cover professional indemnity risks. Outside the United Kingdom mutuals are frequently found in agricultural insurance.

3.36.31 Periodicals

Mutuality. Paris: Association Internationale des Sociétés d'Assurance Mutuelle.

Contains articles in four languages – English, French, German and Spanish – and thus not as big as it at first looks. There are perhaps 40 pages per language per issue. Notwithstanding, articles are fairly substantial, often supported by statistics. Authors tend to be practitioners and the articles are practical. Focuses on all kinds of mutual insurance, particularly in mainland Europe. Annual.

3.37 Captive insurers

Captive insurers are one of the earlier forms of alternative risk transfer. In essence a captive insurance company is a subsidiary set up for the express purpose of insuring the parent company. Material on captives will often be found in works on both risk management and alternative risk transfer.

3.37.03 Textbooks

Captive insurance companies: establishment, operation and management. Bawcutt, Paul. 4th ed. London: Witherby, 1997. xvi, 495 p. £75. By the head of the Risk and Insurance Research Group, a consultancy with a long involvement in the formation of captive insurance companies. Nearly 200 pages of appendices include relevant legislation from the most important captive domiciles and a list of major corporations and their captives.

3.37.21 Directories

Best's captive directory. Oldwick, New Jersey: A. M. Best. $250. Recent addition to the expanding A. M. Best empire, published in association with the former owners, Tillinghast-Towers Perrin. Lists over 4,000 captives, giving parent/sponsor, domicile and other information. Subsidiary sections list risk retention groups, management companies (with full contact details), investment advisers etc. There's also a parent/sponsor index at the back. Annual.

3.37.31 Periodicals

Captive insurance company review. London: Risk & Insurance Research Group. £340 per year.
Newsletter aimed at an international readership. Contains news and a few shortish articles on captives and related subjects. The subscription package includes three or four separate supplements a year (common to all RIRG newsletters). Recent supplements have included *PCCs & rent-a-captives* and *Risk management options*. Monthly.

Captive review: your essential guide to the captive insurance industry: news, views, interviews and updates from around the globe. London: Pageant Media. £300 per year.
Thick, lavishly produced magazine with a lot of shortish articles on aspects of captives worldwide. Includes special reports on particular domiciles. There's also a regular tabulated survey domicile by domicile and a directory of captives. Quarterly.

3.43 Intermediaries

At the time of writing (2000) there are two kinds of insurance intermediary in the United Kingdom: insurance brokers and 'non-registered' intermediaries. Insurance brokers are firms or individuals registered with the **Insurance Brokers Registration Council** (IBRC) under the terms of the Insurance Brokers (Registration) Act 1976 and thus allowed to call themselves brokers. Non-registered intermediaries are commonly referred to simply as insurance intermediaries as though somehow insurance brokers were not intermediaries, which of course they are. However, it is expected that the 1976 Act will be repealed in 2001 and the IBRC will be disbanded. The term 'insurance broker' may thus cease to be restricted to a particular category. Meanwhile a new **General Insurance Standards Council** has already been set up, regulating on a voluntary basis most intermediaries as well as other distribution channels.

There are two sizeable associations of insurance intermediaries in the United Kingdom, the **British Insurance Brokers' Association** and the **Institute of Insurance Brokers**. There is also the much smaller **Association of Insurance Brokers and Intermediaries**, which includes non-registered intermediaries in its membership. All these organisations regard the provision of information services as an important aspect of their membership package.

One of the functions of the intermediary is to be a source of expert knowledge about the market. There are thus many insurance works – in particular journals – which are aimed primarily but not exclusively at the intermediary. Such works will be found in the general insurance section unless the targeting is quite explicit, and this section concentrates on works *about* intermediaries as such: their administration, the legal regime, details of individual firms and so on.

3.43.03 Textbooks

The law of insurance broking. Henley, Christopher. London: Longman, 1990. 329 p. (Longman insurance law library) £53.
Includes chapters on Lloyd's, broker registration, professional liability and the law of agency in relation to insurance. Also several chapters on the insurance contract, by way of background.

3.43.05 Manuals

Insurance intermediaries: law and regulation. Hodgin, R. W. London: LLP. 1 vol. (looseleaf). £295.
Covers the law of agency, tied agents, independent advisers, Lloyd's brokers, broker registration, the Financial Services Act 1986 and aspects of insurance contract law. Appendices at the end of each chapter provide legislation, case summaries, Lloyd's byelaws and financial services rulebooks. Comprises some 750 pages, updated twice a year by looseleaf amendments.

3.43.16 Company research

See also the electronic services *Best's Insight brokers* (part of the *Best's Insight* service, section 3.00.72) and *Wise broker ratings* (section 3.43.75).

Insurance brokers and intermediaries. Hampton, Middlesex: Schober Direct Marketing. (Business ratio)
Covers around 150 firms, two pages per firm. Financial statistics, ratios, contact details and other information from annual reports and accounts. Annual.

Insurance brokers etc. Middlesbrough: Plimsoll. £295 per issue (main report), £195 per issue (supplement).
Consists of two issues per year, each issue consisting of a main report plus supplement, obtainable separately. Both the main report and the supplement are in two volumes and consist of one-page analyses of individual firms of brokers and other insurance intermediaries. There are around 1,000 firms in the main report and another 1,000 smaller firms in the supplement. The data is based on annual reports, comprising statistics, contact information, names of directors, and so on, as well as Plimsoll's own ratios. There are also comparative tables ranking firms by sales and assets.

Insurance intermediaries (home counties). Dunoon, Argyll: Merlin Scott Associates.
Covers around 350 firms, one page per firm. Financial statistics, ratios, contact details and other information from annual reports and accounts. Plus rankings, comparative tables and graphs. Monthly.

3.43.21 Directories

The list: established under section 4 of the Insurance Brokers (Registration) Act 1977. London: Insurance Brokers Registration Council. £20.
Official list of those UK companies allowed to call themselves insurance brokers under the IBRC regime (see introduction above). Arranged by company name, giving name and address only. Annual – but the 2000 issue is expected to be the last.

The register: established under section 2 of the Insurance Brokers (Registration) Act 1977. London: Insurance Brokers Registration Council. £55.
Official list of UK registered insurance brokers under the IBRC regime. Covers individuals only; for firms see *The list*, above. Gives name, address and date of birth; arranged by surname. An extract is separately available listing those individuals who are 'carrying on business' as insurance brokers, i.e. sole traders and partners. Annual – but like *The list* is unlikely to appear after 2000.

3.43.31 Periodicals

These titles are best regarded as periodicals about insurance aimed exclusively at intermediaries, although they do contain some items about intermediaries, such as management matters. Those aimed at the domestic market focus very much on products, and in this there are clear competitors in the section on general insurance periodicals, 3.00.31.

Insurance brokers' monthly & insurance adviser. Stourbridge, West Midlands: Insurance Publishing & Printing Company. £42 per year.
First published in 1950 and the original format clearly found favour with a good number of loyal readers since it seems to have changed little since. Contains news and several regular columns (e.g. 'Market viewpoint', 'Systems scene'). Includes a useful quarterly survey 'EDI review' – comparative tables for motor and household business showing usage of different electronic trading systems.

The international broker. London: Risk & Insurance Research Group. £330 per year.
Strikingly different from periodicals aimed at the domestic insurance intermediary, a newsletter including market news, some short articles and company results (brokers and insurers). With three or four supplements a year, common to all RIRG newsletters. Monthly.

Professional broking: the management magazine for insurance brokers. London: Timothy Benn. Free to insurance intermediaries (registration required).
From the publishers of *Post magazine*, unashamedly aimed at the broker end of the intermediary market. Market news, product news, short articles – typically on particular kinds of product. Oriented towards domestic non-life business. There's also a web site, see section 3.43.75. Monthly.

3.43.75 Web sites

The insurance mall. [UK]: [Insurance Mall Limited]. http://www.timl.co.uk. Free.
A site that aims to put consumers in touch with insurance intermediaries. Includes some technical information, e.g. 'History of insurance' and 'Types of intermediaries'.

Professional broking online: the management magazine for insurance brokers. [London]: Timothy Benn. http://www.broking.co.uk. Free (some sections subscribers only).
Follows the same pattern as *Post magazine online* (3.00.75): news and features from the latest issue of the printed magazine (3.43.31), a searchable archive of back issues and other material. Some sections, such as jobs, are shared with *Post magazine online*.

Wise broker ratings. [London?]: Wise-Broker? http://www.wise-broker.co.uk. By subscription only.

Service providing ratings for UK insurance intermediaries, including both registered brokers and other firms, based on financial data from published accounts and other sources. Includes up to five years of financial data and analysis for each firm, contact details and other information. You can also create your own ratios and comparisons.

3.50 Management

Insurance management is not a clearly defined subject area, unless the phrase is used in its other sense, to refer to the insurance responsibilities of the risk manager (included within section 3.62). For this reason not much is published at the most general level, although there is a coursebook from the **Chartered Insurance Institute**, *Principles and practice of management in insurance* (935). For details of CII coursebooks see section 3.00.03.

Apart from IT, which has its own section below, the chief areas of specialisation are personnel management, financial management, underwriting management and claims management. There is nothing special about personnel management in insurance, in the sense that there is no need for a large corpus of insurance-specific information. The nearest to an association is the **Training and Development Forum** run by the Chartered Insurance Institute, essentially a series of seminars and similar events linked by a common name.

Financial management in insurance is different in that there is a lot to say about it. Most of this is said by accountants and actuaries and usually in papers or newsletters. Several of the larger firms of accountants produce useful newsletters on insurance accounting and related subjects, in particular **KPMG Peat Marwick McLintock**, **Ernst & Young** and **PricewaterhouseCoopers**. The only UK textbooks are the CII coursebooks, *Accounting and finance for managers in insurance* (940), *Accounting and finance for managers in insurance with special reference to Lloyd's* (941) and *Financial aspects of long-term business* (570).

Underwriting management comprises not only the selection and rating of risks but also the administration of an insurer's risk portfolio, including managing reinsurance placements (sometimes called 'reinsurance management') and ensuring an adequate balance of business. The only significant information source on the whole subject as opposed to material on specific classes of business is the CII coursebook *Underwriting management* (815). Claims management is covered by section 3.68.

3.50.03 Textbooks

A guide to insurance management. Diacon, Stephen, ed. Basingstoke: Macmillan, 1990. 330 p. £65.
A little out of date in certain areas (e.g. supervision, the Single Market) but much of this work is still of value. Consists of 19 chapters by different authors, including contributions on corporate planning, staffing policy, marketing and financial management.

3.50.12 Market research

A useful salary survey is published annually by the consultants **Insurance Personnel Selection**. If you want basic statistics on employment levels these can be found quarterly in *Labour market trends* from the **Central Statistical Office**.

3.53 Information technology

Insurance companies have always been at the forefront of developments in information technology, from the introduction of mainframes in the 1960s to the embracing of e-commerce in the late 1990s and beyond. As IT is a rapidly changing area the main literature tends to be periodical. However, the **Chartered Insurance Institute** in conjunction with the **British Computer Society** has recently introduced a Certificate in IT for Insurance Professionals and a separate coursebook is available. Two related questions arise in assessing sources in this area. Are they aimed at IT professionals working in insurance or at insurance professionals working with IT? And to what extent do they cover IT as a general subject, without reference to insurance? The CII certificate is aimed at the second audience and a large part of the course deals with IT generally. The newsletters listed below tend to aim wide, at all those involved in the IT aspects of insurance, providing all they might want to know in connection with their work.

3.53.31 Periodicals

Insurance technology report: information technology in the insurance industry. London: Incisive Research. £465 per year.
News and short articles focusing fairly tightly on IT developments in insurance. 10 issues a year.

Insurance technology: the authority on insurance systems worldwide. London: Informa.
First published in January 2000, a continuation of the earlier newsletter *Insurance systems bulletin* in a completely different format. This is a glossy magazine with both articles and news that, while focusing on the United

Kingdom, makes a good attempt at international coverage with several articles on IT developments elsewhere.

3.56 Marketing

In methodological terms there is little difference between insurance marketing and the marketing of financial services in general, and the sources in section 1.56 will be very relevant.

3.56.05 Manuals

Marketing on a shoestring: the most comprehensive system to improve your business insurance. Dyer, Nigel. [London]: Edgar Hamilton, 1999– . A marketing guide aimed at insurance intermediaries, to be published over a period of time in 12 separate parts, housed in a ring binder. Each part is formatted like a glossy magazine, covering a particular topic in a populist, punchy style. Titles to date include *Public relations: build a higher profile* and *Shout it out: getting attention for your firm*.

3.56.12 Market research

For market research in insurance generally refer to section 3.00.12. For statistics analysing insurance distribution by channel there are two useful publications from the Association of British Insurers in its *Statistical bulletin* series (3.00.12), *General insurance statistics: sources of premium income* and *Long term insurance: sources of new business*. Individual companies are not identified.

3.56.31 Periodicals

Insurance direct & interactive. London: Evandale. £635 per year. Newsletter on direct marketing and e-commerce in insurance worldwide. Short news items. 24 issues a year.

3.62 Risk management

Risk managers were originally called 'insurance managers' and a large part of their job is still to manage the insurances of their firms. However, risk management has evolved into a discipline in its own right, encompassing risk analysis, risk control, risk financing and risk transfer – insurance being (in theory if not in practice) just one option for the latter. As a mark of this evolution there is now a risk management trade association (the **Association of Insurance and Risk Managers**) and a professional body (the **Institute of Risk Management**). But risk management is also a concern within the insurance industry itself and the larger insurance brokers often offer risk management consultancy as an additional service.

A note of caution: 'risk management' has become an extremely attractive phrase and since its original invention by insurance managers everyone wants to be doing it. Thus today a book on risk management could be on the processes of risk analysis, risk control and risk transfer as outlined above, but could alternatively be a book on accident prevention in industry or a book on the use of derivatives and other hedging mechanisms in financial institutions. This section is confined to risk management in its original sense. For risk management in banks and similar institutions see section 2.50.

From the point of view of risk management, insurance is a subdivision, and most of the sources listed here include substantial coverage of corporate insurance. Conversely, many general insurance sources will include coverage of risk management.

3.62.03 Textbooks

The complete guide to business risk management. Sadgrove, Kit. Aldershot, Hampshire: Gower, 1996. xiii, 224 p. £42.
Includes chapters on particular kinds of risk. Unusually for a textbook on risk management this work contains very little on insurance.

How to manage risk. Bannister, Jim. 2nd ed. London: LLP, 1997. xvi, 304 p. (Practical guides) £82.
Aimed at practitioners, with chapters on particular kinds of risk and much material on commercial insurance cover.

Treasury risk. Bland, David E. 1st ed. London: Witherby, 2000. xvi, 491 p. £50.
A detailed analysis, adopting a very broad interpretation of 'treasury risk' to encompass all hazards affecting financial assets.

3.62.05 Manuals

Croner's Management of business risk. Kingston upon Thames, Surrey: Croner.CCH. 1 vol. (looseleaf).
New looseleaf replacing the long-established *Handbook of risk management* from the same group, except that the present work is less than half the size of its predecessor. Takes a less insurance-oriented approach to the subject than the earlier work, reflecting what the publishers suggest is a change in demand amongst its target audience. With chapters on different aspects of risk management, including "Residual risk financing" and "Managing specific business risks". Comprises several hundred pages and the width of the binder suggests much more to come. Updated regularly and there's also a monthly briefing newsletter.

3.62.31 Periodicals

Foresight: the journal of risk management. London: Risk & Insurance Research Group. £278 per year.
One of the first publications to recognise risk management as a separate discipline, published since 1975. A newsletter including short articles and a regular feature 'Risk management abstracts' – longish summaries of recent articles from the trade press. Fairly international in outlook. Includes three or four supplements a year, common to all RIRG newsletters (e.g. *Risk management options*). Monthly.

International risk management. London: Informa. £85 per year.
Magazine for risk managers with an international flavour. News and shortish articles on risk and insurance. Occasional supplements, e.g. *ART 101: the basics of alternative risk transfer*, and an annual *WinfoLinks* web directory. The latter is also available on the related web site, *The global risk management network*, section 3.00.75. 10 issues a year.

Risk management bulletin. London: Ark. £275 per year.
Modestly described by the publishers as a bulletin, but it's more of a journal. Fairly substantial articles on risk and its management, with some news. Little on insurance. 10 issues a year.

Risk management: an international journal. Leicester: Perpetuity Press. £160 per year.
Each issue is a solid A4 paperback containing longish articles, chiefly non-insurance. Not to be confused with the US journal with the same title. Quarterly.

3.64 Risk financing

Risk financing is one of the main subdivisions of risk management: it's what you do with a risk once you've identified, analysed and controlled it. Traditionally the main form of risk financing has been through insurance policies but increasingly new mechanisms are being devised, including self-insurance, captive insurance companies, derivatives, securitisation and other capital market vehicles. However, one of the main exponents of capital market solutions is the insurance industry itself.

'Risk transfer' is slightly broader than risk financing, in that it can include non-financial solutions (sometimes called 'risk avoidance') like the contractual transfer of risk to another party in building construction. But 'alternative risk transfer' rolls off the tongue more euphoniously than 'alternative risk financing' and ART makes a better acronym than ARF, so 'alternative risk transfer' tends to be the preferred term for these non-insurance mechanisms. Many works on ART or ARF restrict themselves to the more recent capital market solutions.

3.64.12 Market research

Biennial risk financing and insurance survey. London: Aon Risk Services.
A statistical survey of 'the changing risk financing climate and its impact on UK and international organisations'.

3.64.31 Periodicals

In addition to the commercially published titles below, Lloyd's has recently launched a lavishly produced journal *ARTwork* focusing on the whole area of alternative risk financing as well as its own involvement.

Alternative insurance capital. London: LLP. £425 per year. Newsletter with an international flavour, containing news and short articles on alternative risk transfer. Focuses on capital market solutions; doesn't seem to include the older established varieties of ART, for instance self-insurance and captives. Formerly published as *Financial reinsurance & futures newsletter*. Monthly.

Risk financier: a monthly commentary on the convergence of the financial and insurance markets. London: Informa. £545 per year. Fairly substantial newsletter on the use of capital markets in alternative risk transfer. Some news plus quite meaty articles, many from the United States. Monthly.

3.64.75 Web sites

Artemis: the alternative risk transfer portal. [Sussex?]: WIRE. http://www.artemis.bm. Free.
Built around links to selected news items on other sites, a news archive and a directory of ART-related organisations. The archive seems to consist of articles from the *National underwriter* only, from 1996 onwards, but the directory has full contact details as well as links. There's also a useful glossary of ART, although some of the definitions leave a little to be desired if you are unfamiliar with this subject.

3.68 Claims

Insurance companies have claims departments to deal with incoming claims but the detailed investigation of larger claims tends to be outsourced to independent firms of loss adjusters, who have their own professional body, the **Chartered Institute of Loss Adjusters**. CILA publishes a useful range of textbooks and other publications on loss adjusting and related subjects, including its own journal (see below). The claims handling function within insurance companies is often referred to as 'claims management'. Some companies are outsourcing this as well.

Most of the information available on claims tends to relate to a particular class of business (and thus is not covered in this section). In this respect a distinction can be made between insurance claims and claims for damages, but since the latter are usually backed by the former and the insurers will, following the principle of subrogation, step into the shoes of the insureds in defending claims, it is not a distinction of much concern to insurance practitioners.

3.68.03 Textbooks

Effective techniques for managing and handling insurance claims: a practical guide to handling personal and commercial claims. Collins, Fred. London: Thorogood, 1997. 162 p. (A Hawksmere special report). Marketed as a management report but more of a manual of practice. Includes sections on individual kinds of claims but concentrates on the practicalities of claims handling rather than interpretation of policy conditions and so on. Non-life only. Unfortunately some of the material on liability claims will be outdated now because of the Woolf reforms to civil procedure.

Winning strategies for negotiating claims. Quinley, Kevin M. Los Angeles: Marshall & Swift, 1995. vi, 223 p.
Based on US practice but of wider value as a practical guide to this subject.

3.68.05 Manuals

Digest of annual reports and bulletins: 1981–1995. London: Insurance Ombudsman Bureau, [1996]. ca 250 p. in various pagings. £90. Arranged alphabetically by specific topic, e.g. 'backdating cover', 'matching sets' and 'subsidence'. Under each topic there are digests of particular (unidentified) cases dealt with by the bureau, with references to the original record in the annual report. Jointly published with the Chartered Insurance Institute.

Insurance disputes. Mance, Sir Jonathan, Goldrein, Iain and Merkin, Robert, eds. London: LLP. 1 vol. (looseleaf). £275 plus £125 per year for updates.
Outlines the legal principles affecting insurance disputes and sets out the litigation procedures involved in handling particular coverage issues. Covers all branches and reinsurance. About 500 pages, updated by looseleaf amendments.

3.68.12 Market research

Data on individual companies' loss experience can be obtained from their annual returns to the FSA (see section 3.00.16) and aggregated data from some of the sources listed in section 3.00.12. The most up-to-date figures are published by the **Association of British Insurers** in the form of press releases and within its *Statistical bulletin* series (see section 3.00.12). But if you are looking for statistics on money in transit losses suffered by curry houses in Brighton or business interruption losses on Norwegian North Sea drilling rigs do stop and ask, Who's counting? If anyone is counting it will be individual insurance companies and this is not the kind of information they are going to publish. The figures required of insurance companies in their annual returns to the FSA and the data collected by the ABI in its surveys of its membership are at a much broader level.

3.68.31 Periodicals

The loss adjuster: the magazine of the Chartered Institute of Loss Adjusters. London: Chartered Institute of Loss Adjusters. Free (restricted circulation).
Claims-related news and short articles, with some CILA information. Aimed at loss adjusters, brokers and risk managers worldwide, to whom it is available free. Quarterly.

3.69 Reinsurance

Although reinsurance is a distinct subdivision of insurance – essentially the insurance of insurance companies' own risk exposure – its chief exponents are often the same companies. There *are* specialist reinsurance companies but insurance companies also transact reinsurance, often reciprocally. Reinsurance is technically very complex and much of the literature reflects this fact, but information aimed at reinsurers is frequently on two other subjects: insurance, because that is what they are reinsuring, and risk because that's what their reinsureds are insuring. Thus a work ostensibly on 'earthquake reinsurance' will contain much material on earthquakes and earthquake insurance. It may even contain nothing on earthquake reinsurance at all. The biggest specialist reinsurers are among the most important suppliers of information not only on reinsurance but also on insurance more generally; see section 3.00.08. The **International Underwriting Association of London** represents *inter alia* the interests of specialist reinsurers trading on the London market.

3.69.03 Textbooks

The law of reinsurance in England and Bermuda. O'Neill, P. T. and Woloniecki, J. W. London: Sweet & Maxwell, 1998. lix, 822 p. (Insurance practitioners library) £140.
The inclusion of Bermuda seems curious, although there is a thriving insurance and reinsurance industry there. Not surprisingly England tends to outweigh Bermuda in this book, although this is difficult to gauge as the two jurisdictions are not dealt with in entirely separate sections. Cov-

ers reinsurance contracts, reinsurance intermediaries and the law of agency and reinsurance regulation.

The nuts and bolts of reinsurance. Riley, Keith. London: LLP, 1997. xiii, 183 p. (Practical guides) £65.
Aimed at practitioners – both reinsurers and reinsureds. Includes practical exercises, worked examples and 50 pages of specimen contract wordings.

Reinsurance. Carter, R. L. 4th ed. London: Reactions Publishing in association with Guy Carpenter & Company, 1999. xi, 906p. £150.
A comprehensive textbook including some statistics and specimen wordings.

Reinsurance for the beginner. Bellerose, R. Phillipe. 4th ed. London: Witherby, 1998. ix, 189 p. £25.
Lives up to its title. Includes some specimen contract wordings.

3.69.05 Manuals

Reinsurance law. Butler, John S and Merkin, Robert M. London: Kluwer. 2 vols (looseleaf).
Truly massive, as the approximately 1,500 pages include none of the common appendices. Updated by quarterly looseleaf amendments and the newsletter *Kluwer insurance & reinsurance law briefing*. Contents: Principles of reinsurance law – The reinsurance agreement – Losses and claims – General matters [including reinsurance brokers, winding up and conflict of laws].

Reinsurance practice and the law. Barlow Lyde and Gilbert. London: LLP. 1 vol. (looseleaf). £195.
Prepared by the reinsurance and international risk team of one of the most important firms of solicitors specialising in insurance and reinsurance. Comprises ca 600 pages updated by looseleaf amendments twice a year together with the same text on CD-ROM, replaced annually. It's also published as part of the *Electronic insurance law service* CD-ROM (see section 3.10.72).

3.69.07 Source materials

Reinsurance clauses. 2nd ed. London: London Insurance and Reinsurance Market Association, 1992. ca 150 p. £30.
A collection of standard clauses developed by LIRMA. Now published by the successor body, the International Underwriting Association of London.

3.69.08 Technical reports

The AIDA RWP reports. London: LLP Professional.
The Reinsurance Working Party of AIDA (Association Internationale de Droit des Assurances) was set up in 1994 with a membership of insurance lawyers and other experts from many jurisdictions. It aims to produce a collation of comparative reinsurance law, to be built up by questionnaires on particular aspects and published in this series of texts. To date three titles have been published: *What is reinsurance?*, *The proper law of reinsurance contracts* and *Follow the settlements*. Prices are £65 (no. 1) or £60.

3.69.12 Market research

Reinsurance statistics: London reinsurance company market. London: International Underwriting Association of London. £30.
Based on returns from member companies but gives aggregate figures only. Includes premiums and claims analysed by class of business and geographical area and detailed underwriting figures broken down by underwriting year and 'development' year. Annual.

3.69.26 Bibliographies

IBR: international bibliography of reinsurance. München: Bayerische Rückversicherung Aktiengesellschaft.
Issued every three years, each issue cumulative. Lists under broad subject headings both books and articles on all aspects of reinsurance. With author and detailed subject indexes. International.

3.69.31 Periodicals

Global reinsurance. London: Regent. £180 per year.
Fat, glossy magazine with lots of articles on insurance, reinsurance and risk – not too short, typically three to four pages each. International flavour with a slant towards the United States. Seven issues a year, including some special or themed numbers, e.g. 'Bermuda edition', 'Risk manager edition' or 'North American edition'.

The re report. London: Evandale. £895 per year.
A slim newsletter, but respected in the industry and used to have a reputation as a scandal sheet you had to read to make sure you weren't in it. Contains longish news items – essentially company news on both insurers and reinsurers, with some market news as well and some coverage of losses. International. Particularly strong in its coverage of troubled companies and has swallowed up two titles focused on this area: *Troubled insurer alert* and *Reinsurance security insider*. 25 issues a year.

Reactions: the financial magazine for the global insurance market. London: Euromoney Institutional Investor. £210 per year.

Not specifically aimed at reinsurers but the international perspective, the Re in the title and the general nature of the content put it squarely in this category. A magazine containing news, statistics and fairly substantial articles on insurance and reinsurance, with occasional supplements – e.g. a directory of world reinsurers, a world map of catastrophes and political risks. There's also a web site (section 3.69.75). Monthly.

Reinsurance: news & analysis from the world's reinsurance markets. London: Timothy Benn. £149 per year.
Trade magazine with an international flavour. News and fairly substantial articles (often supported by statistics or tables) – including regular market and technical reports and regular US and UK legal features. There's also a web site, *Reinsurance online* (section 3.69.75). Monthly.

The review: worldwide reinsurance. London: Informa. £135 per year. The oldest established UK periodical in this category, first published in 1869. Trade magazine aimed at the reinsurer, with an international flavour. News and articles – sometimes fairly substantial – often with statistics and other supporting data. Country surveys. Monthly. See also the related web site, *The global risk management network*, section 3.00.75.

3.69.75 Web sites

Global reinsurance news service network. London: Regent Publications. http://www.globalreinsurance.com. Free.
Like the printed magazine *Global reinsurance* (3.69.31) this site is aimed at reinsurers rather than being exclusively about reinsurance. Includes international insurance news, an international market directory, assorted papers and articles on insurance and reinsurance and related subjects, annotated links and particularly useful reinsurer profiles. The directory has full contact details, not just web addresses, and covers insurers, intermediaries, consultants and other market services; but although very detailed in some areas it is patchy in others, for instance covers only three insurers for Canada.

NewsRe reinsurance news network. [US?]: ELogic Communications. newsre.com. Free.
International reinsurance-related news with a US bias, browsable by topic, company or region.

Reactions. London: Euromoney Institutional Investor. http://www.reactionsnet.com. Subscribers only (free trial available). Carries the full text of all or most news and features from recent issues of the printed magazine of the same title (3.69.31). Browsable by issue numbers and contents listings.

Reinsurance online: news & analysis from the world's reinsurance markets. [London]: Timothy Benn. http://www.re-world.com. Free (some sections subscribers only).
News and features from the magazine *Reinsurance* (3.69.31), together with a searchable archive of back issues and other reinsurance-related material.

3.71 Commercial insurances

This subject is closely linked to risk management, section 3.62.

3.71.03 Textbooks

The insurance of commercial risks: law and practice. Jess, Digby C. 2nd ed. London: Butterworths, 1993. 431 p. £88.
Primarily a legal textbook, much of which deals with insurance law in general. Includes chapters on different kinds of policy and an appendix containing 50 pages of specimen policies.

3.71.31 Periodicals

Corporate insurance & risk. London: Perspective. £79 per year. Fairly wide-ranging magazine aimed at risk managers and commercial insureds generally. News and short articles. Six issues a year. Articles from May 1999 onwards are also available online to subscribers only from http://www.perspectiveonline.co.uk.

3.73 Construction insurance

In the literature of construction insurance the most important source document is not so much the insurance policy itself but the construction contract – which lays down who is liable for what losses and who should insure what for whose benefit. Works on construction contracts will always give substantial attention to the insurance clauses and works on insurance will always give much attention to the construction contract. Works on 'construction claims' aren't strictly about insurance claims at all but about claims for reparations made by one aggrieved party (e.g. a property developer) against another (e.g. a contractor).

3.73.03 Textbooks

Construction insurance and UK construction contracts. Levine, Marshall and Wood, Jeremy. London: Lloyd's of London Press, 1991. 335 p. £109. Includes chapters on insurance under different construction contracts. Over 100 pages of appendices give contract and policy wordings.

Construction insurance: practice, law, reinsurance and risk management. Wright, John D. London: Witherby, 1997. xiii, 275 p. £50. Includes chapters on risk assessment and risk management.

3.75 Personal insurances

Strictly speaking this subject includes household and private motor insurance as well as life and health cover. In practice the focus tends to be restricted to household and private motor.

3.75.31 Periodicals

Personal insurance digest. London: New Hampshire. £299 per year. New title offering news on household and motor insurance in the United Kingdom from the publishers of a related newsletter *International travel insurance digest*. Includes tabulated listings of insurance company web sites. Fortnightly.

Personal lines insurance. London: LLP. £325 per year.
Newsletter covering household and motor business: mostly market and product news, company and market statistics. Fortnightly. Also available online, by subscription.

3.77 Catastrophe insurance

In insurance a catastrophe is a substantial loss arising from a single event or from a series of events taking place over a short period of time, typically natural disasters like hurricanes and earthquakes. The catastrophe risk is one of the main reasons for the existence of reinsurance, and a lot of the literature on this subject tends to be aimed at the reinsurer.

3.77.31 Periodicals

Catastrophe reinsurance newsletter. London: LLP. £425 per year. News and articles (some quite substantial) on the catastrophe risk and its insurance and reinsurance. Seems to concentrate on natural catastrophes and particularly those of most concern to the insurance industry, e.g. hurricanes off the Atlantic seaboard. Monthly.

3.82 Property insurance

Property insurance is the insurance of property on land against loss or damage. It covers what was originally fire insurance (which itself traditionally included such non-fire risks as storm and water damage) as well as more specialist areas like engineering insurance, household insurance and livestock insurance. Property policies frequently include an element of liability cover and the boundary between the two subjects can be blurred. In the United States in particular 'property-liability' is a distinct division of insurance.

Much of the information required by the property insurer is not insurance information at all and a general source on property insurance will itself include material on such non-insurance subjects as fire prevention and security. Particularly in commercial business insurers take an active interest in loss prevention measures and risk and loss surveying. One of the most important aspects of engineering insurance (which is the insurance of machinery) has traditionally been the periodic visits from the insurance surveyor. There are signs however that more non-insurance specialists are being employed by insurers to deal with these areas. A comparison of the syllabuses of the **Chartered Insurance Institute** from today and the 1960s – when the minutiae of plan drawing and fire extinguishment were exhaustively examined – certainly suggests that the amount of non-insurance technical knowledge required of purely insurance personnel has diminished.

Property damage (excluding transport losses) is both a statutory authorisation class and accounting class in the United Kingdom, which means the annual returns of insurers and the published information derived from them can provide much useful data on property insurance. See sections 3.00.12 and 3.00.16.

3.82.03 Textbooks

Claims and standard fire policies, special extensions and special perils. Walmsley, R. M. London: Chartered Institute of Loss Adjusters, 1993. 237 p. £20.
Covers the standard fire policy in detail, from a claims point of view. Includes substantial appendices: wordings, forms, case summaries. Aimed primarily at students of professional examinations.

Fire insurance: theory and practice. Gamlen, Edwin H and Francis, Harold. 7th ed. London: Buckley Press, 1991. 268 p. £24.95.
'Fire insurance' has become a rather old-fashioned term, partly because the cover provided under a traditional fire policy always covered so much more than the fire risk *per se*. Thus this book includes coverage of the household policy and business interruption insurance. There are also chapters on fire losses and their prevention and appendices include policy wordings. The previous edition was by T. R. Smith and H. W. Francis; the publisher has now been absorbed by the Timothy Benn group.

3.83 Pecuniary insurances

The somewhat archaic term 'pecuniary' lives on in insurance, enshrined as a statutory accounting class (see section 3.00.16) and encompassing disparate forms of cover such as credit insurance and business interruption, which all share the essential feature that the loss insured is purely financial. In terms of the literature business interruption is the most important subdivision. Old books on 'fire insurance' sometimes included coverage of this area since fire was and is the most important event leading to business interruption. Works on 'property insurance' do not usually cover pecuniary insurances.

3.83.03 Textbooks

Business interruption insurance: law and practice. Walmsley, R. M. 1st ed. London: Witherby, 1999. xvi, 552 p. £65.
Conceived as a guide to the practical applications of business interruption insurance, for use by company secretaries, brokers, loss adjusters, claims officials and others. Appendices include policy wordings.

Business interruption insurance: theory and practice. Gamlen, Edwin H and Phillips, John H. P. London: Buckley Press, 1992. 257 p. £32.50. Includes 70 pages of policy wordings and worked examples as appendices. Now published by Timothy Benn.

Claims and loss of profits insurance. Walmsley, R. M. Rev. and updated ed. London: Chartered Institute of Loss Adjusters, 1994. 153 p. £20. Aimed at students of professional examinations; concentrates on policy conditions and claims. Includes 40 pages of appendices giving case summaries, policy wordings and examples of accounts.

Riley on business interruption insurance. Riley, Denis. 8th ed. London: Sweet & Maxwell, 1999. ix, 513 p. £95.
Includes 60 pages of appendices giving specimen policy wordings and worked examples of claims.

3.84 Liability insurance

Works on liability insurance inevitably devote a lot of attention to the underlying basis for this form of cover, the law governing legal liability – in particular, the law of tort, and most especially the tort of negligence. Works on 'liability insurance law' and 'liability insurance claims' are almost exclusively about these strictly non-insurance aspects. The main subdivisions of liability insurance are employer's liability, product liability and professional liability – with environmental (or pollution) liability of growing importance. Liability for motor, marine and aviation accidents tends to be insured in the motor, marine and aviation branches (q.v.) and is excluded from liability insurance as usually defined. This is reflected in the United Kingdom statutory authorisation and accounting classes, which means the sources detailed in section 3.00.12 and 3.00.16 can precisely pinpoint this branch.

3.84.03 Textbooks

Claims and public liability policies. Shaw, J. P. P. [Rev. ed.]. London: Chartered Institute of Loss Adjusters, 1994. 213 p. £20.
Aimed at CILA students. Deals with the policy and civil disputes relevant to liability cover.

Public liability insurance: a Hawksmere report. Collins, Fred. London: Hawksmere, 1999. 166 p. £149.
Includes chapters on the law of liability, public liability cover, product liability, professional negligence, claims and reserving. With some specimen policy wordings.

3.84.31 Periodicals

Liability, risk and insurance. London: LLP. £395 per year.
Legal news, 'Awards and settlements', some short articles, 'Case update' (one paragraph per case), insurance statistics. Mostly on liability rather than its insurance. In newsletter format. Monthly.

3.86 Motor insurance

As with all branches of insurance the extent of the subject is defined by the policy. Motor insurance policies, like those of marine insurance, tend to package together quite disparate risks: physical loss of or damage to the vehicle, personal injuries affecting its occupants, and liability for both property and personal injury losses sustained by others. However, motor insurance doesn't include goods in transit insurance, which is the insurance of goods or liability for goods during transit by road, rail or other means.

The main division of motor insurance is between personal and commercial insurances. The most important aspect of the former is private car insurance and many outside the business might regard this as synonymous with motor insurance. Commercial insurances are often transacted by fleet. There are also special policies for the motor trade.

As always non-insurance subjects tend to feature high in the interests of motor insurers and this is reflected in the information sources ostensibly on 'motor insurance'. Non-insurance subjects of particular interest are the law of tort and road traffic legislation.

3.86.03 Textbooks

Motor insurance: theory and practice. Cannar, Kenneth. 2nd ed. London: Witherby, 1994. xxiii, 440 p. £35.
With nearly 70 pages of appendices including policy wordings and the text of market agreements.

3.86.05 Manuals

Handbook of motor insurance. Collins, F. W., ed. Brentford: Kluwer in association with the British Insurance Brokers' Association. 1 vol. (looseleaf).
Covers motor insurance law and procedures and the motor insurance market. Around 750 pages, updated by looseleaf amendments three times a year.

3.86.12 Market research

Motor insurance: the research report into the world's major markets. 3rd ed. [London]: Tillinghast, 1996. 103 leaves.
Describes market structure, types of cover, distribution and so on in 24 countries, with market statistics at the back.

3.87 Marine insurance

Books on shipping will usually include a chapter or two on marine insurance and books on marine insurance return the compliment. It's frequently difficult to see where one subject ends and the other begins, particularly with borderline areas like the law of salvage or 'general average'. Apart from policies covering yachts and pleasure boats marine insurance in the United Kingdom is mostly conducted through the 'London market' and as such is less prepackaged than, for instance, household insurance. However, certain classes of risk (such as liability) tend to be covered by shipowner mutuals called protection and indemnity clubs.

Marine insurance enjoys two other features that tend to separate it from other classes of business: a large body of standardised policy clauses (the 'institute clauses') and a statute of its own (the Marine Insurance Act 1906), which codified in great detail the interpretation of the marine policy. The so-called 'institute clauses' are named after the **Institute of London Underwriters**, which originally developed them, although they are now the responsibility of a successor body, the **International Underwriting Association of London**. The other UK body with a particular interest in marine insurance is **Lloyd's**. The main subdivisions of marine insurance are cargo insurance and hull insurance.

3.87.03 Textbooks

Arnould's law of marine insurance and average. Arnould, Joseph, Sir. 16th ed. London: Stevens, 1981–1997. 3 vols (434; 1,242; xxxi, 595 p.). (British shipping laws) £395.
The most comprehensive British work on this subject. Volumes 1 and 2 were published in 1981; volume 3 is a supplement, published in 1997. Overall includes around 100 pages of legislation and clauses.

Introduction to marine insurance. Brown, Robert H. 2nd ed. London: Witherby, 1995. ca 150 p. in various pagings. (Training notes for brokers) £14.50.
Includes self-study questions at the end of each chapter.

The law of marine insurance. Bennett, Howard N. Oxford: Clarendon Press, 1996. lxviii, 558 p. £70 (paperback £35).
Aimed at students and practitioners new to the subject. With 100 pages of legislation and clauses as appendices.

Law of marine insurance. Hodges, Susan. London: Cavendish, 1996. xlvii, 647 p. £39.95.
Aimed primarily at postgraduate students but also for practitioners. With appendices: 60 pages of legislation and clauses.

Marine insurance. Brown, Robert H. London: Witherby, 1993–1998. 3 vols (xvii, 408; xvi, 628; xvii, 1,187 p.). £145.
Comprises: volume 1, *Principles and basic practice* (6th ed, 1998); volume 2, *Cargo practice* (5th ed, 1998); volume 3, *Hull practice (2nd ed, 1993)*. Also available separately. Volume 1 includes a substantial list of abbreviations and the text of legislation.

Marine insurance: law and policy. O'May, Donald. London: Sweet and Maxwell, 1993. 660 p. £157.
On the law of marine insurance and the marine insurance policy. Nearly 150 pages of appendices include legislation and clauses.

3.87.07 Source materials

Benedict on admiralty. 7th ed. New York: Matthew Bender. 30 vols (looseleaf).
This massive looseleaf collection includes two volumes (available separately) containing American and British marine insurance clauses (vol. 7), and protection and indemnity club rules and clauses relating to P&I (vol. 7A). Updated irregularly by looseleaf amendments.

Cases and materials on marine insurance law. Hodges, Susan. London: Cavendish, 1999. 1,962 p. £45.
Intended as a companion to her *Law of marine insurance* (3.87.03), but can

stand on its own. Primarily case summaries with commentary, plus legislation and clauses in 150 pages of appendices.

Marine insurance legislation. Merkin, Robert. London: LLP, 2000. xxxix, 311 p. (Essential law) £50.
Presents the main legislation affecting marine insurance in the United Kingdom. Includes the Institute clauses as a substantial appendix of over 100 pages.

Reference book of marine insurance clauses: a reference book containing all institute clauses, also some UK and American clauses and forms printed by Witherby & Co Ltd, including a comprehensive index of American clauses. London: Witherby. £30.
Now in its 71ˢᵗ edition, published annually in October. Around 280 pages per issue. A *Witherby clause revision service* is separately available to provide updates between editions.

Marine report and statistics. [London]: International Underwriting Association of London.
A short survey of the marine insurance market with a review of casualty experience and statistics of losses.

3.87.24 Dictionaries

Dictionary of marine insurance terms and clauses. Brown, Robert H. 5ᵗʰ ed. London: Witherby, 1989. ca 500 p. in various pagings. £25.
A substantial work, larger than any dictionary addressing the whole of insurance. Detailed and authoritative explanations of over 1,000 terms, including many relating to insurance generally and to shipping. Includes abbreviations.

Marine insurance & reinsurance abbreviations in practice. Brown, Robert H. 3ʳᵈ ed. London: Witherby, 1993. 81, 47 p. £9.50.
The first section tells you what abbreviations stand for, the second inverts the first and tells you what the abbreviations are for particular terms.

3.87.31 Periodicals

A merger between some of the LLP titles listed here would seem to be logical. And yet *P&I international* has already absorbed the *Marine insurance report*, also from LLP, only to see the *Marine insurance bulletin* spring up to take its place.

Marine insurance bulletin. London: LLP. £295 per year.
Newsletter covering marine insurance and shipping. News, statistics, company results, country surveys, casualty listings. 10 issues a year.

Maritime risk. London: LLP Professional. £320 per year.
Slim magazine focusing on all aspects of maritime risk, including insurance and law. 10 issues a year.

P&I international: incorporating Marine insurance report. London: LLP.
£345 per year.
Slim journal containing short articles mostly on aspects of shipping (losses and legal) of interest to protection and indemnity clubs – the shipowners' mutuals that traditionally cover most third party and defence risks in shipping. Some items on the clubs themselves. Monthly.

3.87.75 Web sites

IUA of London: International Underwriting Association. London: International Underwriting Association of London. http://www.iua.co.uk.
Free.
As well as information on the IUA this site promises sections on 'Marine, aviation, transport'.

The marine insurance megasite: everything on the Net for ocean marine insurance professionals. Thompson, James. [US?]: James Thompson? http://www.insurance-marine.com. Free.
Unusually extensive personal site charting web-based information on marine insurance, shipping and other related subjects. Includes links to online papers and articles and to some useful online policy wordings as well as an annotated book list, with individual links to Amazon. There's a US bias but some UK material.

3.88 Aviation insurance

Aviation insurance started life as a rather special kind of marine insurance and it still shares many features with that branch. In the United Kingdom it tends to be conducted on the London market. In turn, 'space insurance' has started up as a special kind of aviation insurance, chiefly concerned with the insurance of satellites. A new word 'aerospace' is sometimes used to more properly define the whole area.

3.88.03 Textbooks

Aviation insurance: the law and practice of aviation insurance, including hovercraft and spacecraft insurance. Margo, Rod D. 3rd ed. London: Butterworths, 2000. lxxxiii, 862 p. £200.
Impressively weighty treatise, which surprisingly manages to stick very closely to aviation insurance *per se* through most of its 862 pages rather than digressing at length into the background subject of aviation law. In this it is helped by 300 pages of appendices, reproducing clauses and other wordings.

3.88.07 Source materials

Standard policy forms, proposal forms and clauses, etc. 5th ed. London: Lloyd's Aviation Underwriters' Association. 1 vol. (looseleaf). £80 (including updates until 2002).
Comprises around 200 pages, updated by occasional looseleaf amendments.

3.88.24 Dictionaries

Aviation insurance abbreviations, organisations and institutions.
Spurway, M. J. London: Witherby, 1983. 63 p. £6.95.
Includes a short section on insurance organisations, now a little out of date.

3.88.31 Periodicals

Aerospace risk: serving the aerospace insurance and law professional.
London: LLP. £395 per year.
Newsletter with some short articles. Mostly on legal and technical developments; not much on insurance as such. Monthly.

3.91 Life assurance

The simplest form of life assurance is a term assurance policy, which provides cover for a fixed period of years (typically 10) and pays benefits only if the policyholder dies in that period. This is pure insurance: cover against something that may not happen. But a whole life policy covers you for something that will definitely happen, whenever it does; and an annuity – traditionally provided by life insurers – turns the insurance process on its head and back to front so that the client pays the lump sum and the insurer then makes the regular payments. So right from the start life assurance had as much in common with investment as insurance – hence the continued preference in the United Kingdom for the term 'life assurance' rather than the (synonymous) 'life insurance'. When premium relief on life policies was introduced this situation was heightened, with life insurers developing policies that were essentially investment vehicles with a minimum element of life cover to ensure the contract qualified for tax relief. Premium relief was withdrawn in the United Kingdom in 1984 but too late to stem the convergence with investment, which was confirmed by the Financial Services Act 1986. This act addressed itself primarily to 'investment business' and under this heading were included all forms of life assurance except for term policies.

This convergence with investment has led to a situation whereby life assurance falls within two broader areas. It is a branch of insurance, and it is an important component of the narrower definition of financial services promoted by the Financial Services Act. This means you will find a lot on life assurance in works listed in section 3.00, insurance in general, but also in chapter 1, financial services in general. Indeed, most items covering the marketing of life assurance will be found in there.

To add to the confusion, sources on life assurance frequently cover health insurance as well, particularly in markets like the United States where private health insurance is the normal way of providing for medical expenses. A new term 'protection' is also becoming popular, to define an area that includes health insurance plus the non-investment aspects of life assurance. As well as or instead of including health insurance works on life assurance may cover pensions – logically, since life assurance contracts of some kind typically provide the underpinning for private pensions. Life/health and life/pensions are both included in this section.

There is a UK **Life Insurance Association** but this is essentially an association of financial advisers. Medical experts working for life insurers have their own grouping, the **Assurance Medical Society**. The AMS publishes its own journal and collaborates with the **Chartered Insurance Institute** in the production of a specialist examination paper and associated coursebook.

3.91.03 Textbooks

The law and practice of life assurance contracts. McGee, Andrew. London: Sweet & Maxwell, 1995. xxix, 315 p. £76.
Covers contract law and the law relating to life intermediaries, with one chapter on financial services regulation. Includes a glossary.

Law of life assurance. Houseman, David and Davies, B. P. A. 11th ed. London: Butterworth, 1994. xxxv, 538 p. £85.
A practitioner work, covering the life assurance contract and life assurance taxation, with one chapter (now rather out of date) on financial services regulation.

You sign. O'Halloran, Terence. 2nd ed. London: Witherby, 1992. 93 p. £7.95.
The first edition was designed as a consumer guide to life assurance and called *You sign the little cheque and we sign the big one*. It subsequently proved popular as a training guide for new recruits and hence, presumably, the rather elliptical title of this edition, targeted at both consumers and trainees. Includes a glossary.

3.91.05 Manuals

The facts of life and health insurance. Couchman, Andy. London: Taxbriefs. £35.

Concentrates on health cover and on life assurance as protection. Includes chapters on 'The human body', 'Health and care services' and other background subjects. A looseleaf manual issued in a new edition each year.

Life assurance and pensions handbook. Marshall, Chris. London: Taxbriefs. £47 (1998/99).
Published annually; now in its 14th edition. Casts its net wide, drawing in general taxation, mortgages, non-life insurance investments and financial services regulation. Aimed at both practitioners and students, with a glossary and test questions at the end of each chapter. Comprises approximately 750 pages in a ring binder.

Life assurance law and practice. Hamilton, Peter. London: Sweet & Maxwell. 1 vol. (looseleaf). £245.
As always 'law and practice' tends to mean 'law'. Essentially a legal textbook, covering contract law, tax law, financial service regulation. Comprises some 750 pages, half of them appendices: statutes, extracts from rule books and so on. Updated by looseleaf amendments twice a year.

3.91.12 Market research

The US-based Life Insurance Marketing and Research Association has a European arm, **LIMRA Europe**, with its head office in the United Kingdom. On behalf of its membership of life insurers LIMRA Europe conducts research into the life and related financial services market and regularly publishes its findings. Recent reports include *Stakeholder pensions: the views of consumers, the industry and other influential bodies* (£445 to non-members) and *A view from the top: distribution strategies across Europe* (£350 to non-members). There's also a **Life Assurance Market Research Association**, a grouping of UK life insurers one of whose main functions is to commission research on a syndicated basis. It doesn't publish research itself.

Life 2000. London: Cazalet Financial Consulting, [2000]. 679 p. £650 per year (full reports £15 each, short reports £9.50 each).
Includes background statistics (population, divorce, health, work and pay), market statistics (life, pensions and investment), short sections on individual kinds of product and detailed profiles of around 90 UK life offices (e.g. seven pages on Scottish Widows). Supplementary data is available on the publisher's web site at http://www.cazalet-financial.com. There was a *Life 1998* (the first edition) and a *Life 1999* so there's every sign there will be a *Life 2001*.

3.91.16 Company research

See also *Life 2000*, section 3.91.12

Company profile & financial strength reports. Dorking, Surrey: AKG Actuaries & Consultants. £650 per year (full reports £15 each, short re-

ports £9.50 each).
Separate reports on around 80 UK life offices, some long (typically eight pages), some short (two pages). All reports give statistics, commentary, contact information, key personnel and other company information. The longer reports also provide details of product range, servicing and so on, with AKG ratings. Each report is replaced annually. In a ring binder; about 500 pages.

European life ratings digest. London: Standard & Poor's. £995.
Financial strength ratings and commentary on more than 170 leading life insurers in 13 European countries, together with a detailed survey of the life market in each country and league tables. Annual.

Moody's credit opinions & statistical handbook. UK life insurance. New York; London: Moody's Investors Service.
Covers around 50 UK life insurers: statistics, ratings, commentary, comparative tables etc. Annual.

UK life financial strength digest. London: Standard & Poor's Insurance Ratings.
Reviews around 50 UK life insurers, with financial statistics (from annual returns), ratings and commentary, plus comparative tables. Annual.

UK life office with profits report. Dorking, Surrey: AKG. £600.
Detailed studies on individual life insurers with statistics analysing performance, expenses etc. Annual?

3.91.24 Dictionaries

Insurance dictionary. Watford: LIMRA UK & RI Research, 1993. 68 p.
Gives equivalents for and defines life assurance and related terms in English, French, Greek and Spanish. In four sections, all four definitions repeated in each.

3.91.31 Periodicals

Cover: the protection magazine. London: City Financial Communications. £75 per year.
On health insurance and on life assurance as protection rather than investment, together with two important background subjects: medicine and state benefits. Product news, statistics, shortish articles, some longer product surveys (one per issue) with detailed comparative tables. Regular features include 'Benefit of the month' (e.g. housing benefit), 'Product analysis' (an in-depth look at a particular product from a particular company) and the splendidly titled 'Disease of the month'. See also the web site in section 3.91.75. Monthly.

Life insurance international: the industry bulletin on life, health and pensions. Dublin; London: Lafferty. £649 for 12 issues.

An international newsletter on life assurance including some short articles and occasional market surveys. Particularly strong on developments in distribution patterns. Also available on the Web, with other Lafferty publications (see publisher entry). 10 issues a year.

3.91.75 Web sites

Cover online: an online resource for protection advisors. [London]: [City Financial Communications]. http://www.cover-mag.co.uk. Free. Includes news and features from the printed version of this magazine on life/health cover (section 3.91.31).

3.93 Health insurance

Health insurance is frequently bundled together with life assurance by publishers, either as life/health or as 'protection'. Such works are described in section 3.91. It is less important in the United Kingdom than in many other markets, e.g. the United States, because of the role of the NHS. But its importance as a supplementary provider of cover is growing. The main categories of health insurance are private medical insurance (insurance to pay private medical expenses) and income protection insurance (also known as permanent health insurance and covering loss of income arising from disability). Other kinds of policy are long-term care insurance, critical illness insurance and personal accident insurance.

3.93.12 Market research

Private medical insurance: UK market sector report. London: Laing & Buisson. £280.
Includes survey data on the demand for PMI and an analysis of the market. Annual.

3.93.18 Product research

Kluwer's income protection insurance: the unique annual review. ERC Frankona Reassurance Ltd. Kingston upon Thames, Surrey: Croner.CCH. First published in 1967 under the title *Permanent health insurance*. There are two main sections: a survey of policy conditions company by company (42 UK firms) and a comparison of companies under individual policy conditions and other product features. There are also comparative tables and a short sector summary.

The PMI handbook: the annual review of the private medical insurance market. Green, Andrew K. C. Hurstpierpoint, West Sussex: Craigdallie. £59.
Consists of sections on individual insurers, giving tabulated product

details for each plus contact details. One page per product; around 250 pages per issue. Also available on CD-ROM.

3.93.31 Periodicals

Health insurance: for the professional intermediary. London: Informa. £80 per year.
Narrowly focused magazine including market news, shortish articles, comparative product tables and a detailed review of new products. Monthly.

Healthcare insurance report. Great Rissington, Gloucestershire: Bank House Communications. £295 per year.
Newsletter including some short articles and statistical features, with occasional supplements, e.g. 'The state of the NHS'. Includes much detail on background subjects like private healthcare and state benefits. 10 issues a year.

Chapter 4

Investment funds

This chapter deals with packaged or 'collective' investment schemes, products that invest in a wide spread of securities in order to reduce the risk to private investors. These products are sometimes also referred to as 'managed funds', although this phrase can have other, more specific uses. Even the term 'investment fund' is ambiguous, as it can refer to any large sum of money put aside for investment, for example a pension fund is a kind of investment fund. 'Fund management' is the management of such a fund, and a very different subject from 'investment funds' as construed here.

Collective investment schemes can be based on life assurance policies and these products are covered within chapter 3. They might also be used to provide a pension, and these products are covered within chapter 5. Which leaves a rather small chapter here, covering what might be termed 'pure' investment products.

The main division of this subject relates to the intrinsic structure of the fund and gives us unit trusts and investment trusts, together with the newer open-ended investment companies. There are also onshore and offshore funds, the latter based in tax havens to benefit from a favourable fiscal environment. Many funds invest in a particular sector and this can yield another kind of division, for instance, emerging markets funds, smaller companies funds, Japanese funds. They might also be structured for a particular purpose, such as capital growth funds or high income funds. Or they might be designed to benefit from a particular tax allowance, like personal equity plans (PEPs) or the successor to PEPs, individual savings accounts (ISAs).

4.00 General sources

4.00.01 Consumer guides

Getting started in unit and investment trusts. Cole, Robert C. [UK]: John Wiley, 1997. 256 p. £16.99.
Includes an examination of the different products available, showing investors how to analyse their performance and select the most appropriate.

The Investor's Chronicle guide to investment and unit trusts. Slaughter, Joanna. London: Financial Times Management, 1996. 192 p. (The Inves-

tor's Chronicle series) £15.99.
Explains unit and investment trusts, choice of funds, the risks and the process of buying and selling.

4.00.12 Market research

A lot of the more general market research detailed in chapter 1 will include investment funds within their purview and there are some more specific offerings. Recent management reports from **FT Finance** include *Global tracker funds: the tracker revolution, Alternative investment funds, The future of European institutional mutual funds* and *The future of the UK mutual fund industry*. Under the Reuters Business Insight imprint **Datamonitor** in conjunction with **Reuters** has published *UK tracker funds and passive fund management: the revolution in fund management* and *UK ethical investments: the potential in a new market*; **Market Assessment International** has produced a report *Individual savings accounts 1999*.

4.00.18 Product research

Most product research on investment funds tends to include life assurance policies and personal pensions and such broader-based works will be found in chapter 1.

4.00.31 Periodicals

Fund forum. London: Centaur Communications.
Briefing for investment fund advisers and senior executives, providing international news and analysis, with company profiles. The data comes from the web site of the same name; see section 4.00.75. Quarterly.

4.00.75 Web sites

Fund forum. [UK]: Fund Forum? http://www.fundforum.com. £495 per year.
Designed to keep professionals up to date with developments in the investment fund industry. Includes news, analysis, a market survey and data on market share and fund structures. The subscription also provides access to the Standard & Poor's web site, including performance statistics on offshore funds and links to the web sites of fund managers. Information from the site is also published as a printed magazine (section 4.00.31).

Fund-info.com. [UK?]: Fund-info.com. http://www.fund-info.com. Information on UK investment trusts, US SEC-registered country funds, offshore closed end funds and locally listed closed end funds. Boasts a database of 1,085 funds, each with eight pages of detailed information. Free 'for a limited period, in this site's test phase'. Registration required.

TrustNet Limited: investment funds information service. [London]: TrustNet. http://trustnet.co.uk. Free.

Provides daily updated prices, performance data, charts and detailed background information on UK unit trusts and investment trusts, US closed end funds and offshore closed end funds. Also includes regularly updated data on international indices and exchange rates.

4.02 General sources (international)

4.02.21 Directories

The directory of European fund management. London: Euromoney Institutional Investor. £575.

Lists more than 1,600 European fund management companies in 31 markets with around 8,000 contact names. Includes performance statistics and details of assets under management and investment strategy. Access to a parallel web site is included in the price; this includes the full database and updated information.

4.02.31 Periodicals

Funds international. Dublin: Lafferty. £649 per year.

Newsletter covering the fund management industry worldwide. Provides information on the main players, new products, new locations, marketing strategies and industry trends. A typical issue includes news and analysis, interviews with leading industry professionals and profiles of leading organisations. An online version is also available, with a third option of a combined subscription.

4.72 Unit trusts

Unit trusts are pooled investments in securities provided by unit trust management companies, some of which are subsidiaries of banks or life assurance companies. Structurally they are quite different from the newer open-ended investment companies (OEICs), which could eventually replace unit trusts. Introduced in the United Kingdom under the European UCITS (Undertakings for Collective Investment in Transferable Securities) directive, OEICs are companies rather than funds and in this there is a structural similarity with investment trusts. But in terms of information sources OEICs tend to be found with unit trusts and accordingly are included in this section.

The relevant trade association in the United Kingdom is AUTIF, the **Association of Unit Trusts and Investment Funds**.

4.72.01 Consumer guides

The investor's guide to picking the right unit trust: maximising performance with minimum risk. McWilliams, Bruce G. London: Financial Times Management, 1997. 224 p. £21.99.
Demonstrates investment points with real-life case studies. Includes sections on investing a lump sum insurance benefit, the European Bond Fund and charting portfolio risk.

4.72.03 Textbooks

The legal nature of the unit trust. Sin, Kam Fan. Oxford: Clarendon Press, 1998. 398 p. £55.
Traces the evolution of the unit trust and examines its constitution, the character of unit trust relationships, trusteeship and the nature of units.

4.72.05 Manuals

Collective investment schemes: the law and practice. Cornick, Timothy C., et al. London: Sweet & Maxwell. 2 vols (looseleaf). £450.
Based on an earlier work called *Unit trusts: the law and practice* and still focuses on unit trusts, though with some treatment of open-ended investment companies. Covers regulation, Stock Exchange requirements, taxation and other legal issues. Volume 1 contains commentary, volume 2 legislation, rules and other official documentation. Around 1,500 pages in all, updated two or three times a year.

4.72.18 Product research

Unit trust & OEIC handbook. London: PBI Newmedia. £14.99.
Comprehensive guide listing funds by asset management group and including contact details, company profiles, rankings and other data. Additional sections provide an introductory guide, a glossary and commentary from financial journalists and analysts. The 2000 edition contains 250 pages. Annual.

Unit trust and OEICs year book. London: FT Business. £325.
The main part of this long-established work is a directory of around 1,600 individual funds, giving brief details for each including portfolio distribution and changes in offer prices. This is supplemented by a section on management groups, giving contact details and potted company histories. There are also comparative performance tables from Standard & Poor's Micropal, a market survey and other information. Formerly the *Unit trust year book*, now extended to include open-ended investment companies.

4.72.75 Web sites

Association of Unit Trusts and Investment Funds. [London]: Association of Unit Trusts and Investment Funds. http://www.investmentfunds.org.uk. Free.
Information for beginners and experienced investors on unit trusts and related products. Includes fact sheets, links to member companies' sites and a searchable fund directory.

4.74 Investment trusts

Investment trusts are companies whose function is to invest in other companies for the benefit of their shareholders. As such they are the oldest form of pooled investment, dating back to the 19th century. Structurally they are quite distinct from unit trusts.

The UK trade association for investment trusts is the **Association of Investment Trust Companies**.

4.74.01 Consumer guides

The **Association of Investment Trust Companies** publishes a free information pack on investment trusts, including a short product directory, and a range of free fact sheets, also available on the Association's web site (section 4.74.75).

4.74.18 Product research

The investment trust handbook. London: PBI Newmedia. £14.99. Provides contact details, rankings and other data for each fund, listed by management group. Also includes an overview of the investment year, a sector-by-sector review, a glossary and an introductory guide. The 2000 edition contains 250 pages. Annual?

Investors update. London: AITC Services. £20 per year.
Quarterly newsletter on investment trusts from the industry's trade association.

ITS statistics: a monthly information service from the Association of Investment Trust Companies. London: Association of Investment Trust Companies.
Contains comparative information on individual trusts in tabulated form, showing key features, managers etc., together with a detailed statistical section covering portfolio distribution, prices and other data. Monthly. To be made available on the AITC web site in the near future.

4.74.31 Periodicals

Investment trusts. Woodford Green, Essex: Flaxdale. £3.50 per issue. Magazine featuring short articles on different aspects of investment trusts, studies of individual firms, performance statistics, summaries of company reports, a news round-up and detailed statistics plotting recent changes in corporate stakes in particular trusts. Quarterly.

Investment trusts newsletter. Bristol: McHattie Group. £79.90 per year. Aims to provide private investors with independent advice on 'how to buy the right trusts at the right time'. Includes analysis of public announcements, comments on directors' dealings, summaries of stockbroker research and news.

4.74.75 Web sites

Investment trusts: the easy way to invest in the stock market. [London]: AITC Services. http://itsonline.co.uk. Free.
From the Association of Investment Trust Companies. Includes a step-by-step guide to choosing an investment trust, performance statistics on individual products, recent news and a search engine for locating detailed information about particular trusts or management groups.

4.77 Offshore funds

Offshore funds or 'offshore trusts' are investment and unit trusts based in tax havens in order to benefit from relaxed tax conditions.

4.77.03 Textbooks

Butterworths taxation of offshore trusts and funds. Fraser, R. D. A. and Wood, J. R. 3rd ed. London: Butterworths, 1998. £75.
Provides guidance and advice on the investment management of offshore trusts and funds. Includes sections on residence and domicile, income tax, inheritance tax and capital gains tax.

The Trident practical guide to offshore trusts. International Trident Trust Group. [UK]: Chancellor Publications, 1999. 250 p. £95.
Analyses legislation in 14 international trust jurisdictions. Includes coverage of general trust law, trust deeds, administration and taxation.

4.77.18 Product research

Standard & Poor's Micropal guide to offshore investment funds. London: Standard & Poor's Micropal. £99.95.
Provides wide coverage of offshore vehicles, including mutual funds, unit trusts, open-ended investment companies and closed end funds, with guidance for those new to the area as well as detailed fund analysis.

Includes performance statistics on over 6,000 funds, detailed profiles of the top 350 and a review of the tax situation in Australia, Canada, Japan, the United Kingdom and the United States.

4.77.31 Periodicals

International money marketing: for the distributors of international financial products. London: Centaur Communications.
International version of the weekly newspaper *Money marketing*, concentrating on offshore investments and related products. Includes surveys of particular national markets and regular product statistics. Monthly.

Portfolio international: the professional's guide to investment worldwide. London: Southern Magazines. £120 per year.
Tabloid-style monthly magazine focusing on offshore investment funds, with background data on investment conditions internationally. Includes news on marketing, distribution, products, providers, investment and offshore centres together with some short articles and special features on particular offshore centres or product categories. With a tabulated offshore fund directory and some special supplements, e.g. *Alternative investment: an essential guide for IFAs*.

4.78 Emerging markets

Emerging markets funds are products investing in developing economies like those of South America and Asia.

4.78.18 Product research

Micropal directory of emerging market funds. London: Standard & Poor's Micropal. £1,120.
Gives contact details for several thousand portfolio managers worldwide, indexed by equity / debt split, geographical investment sector, fund name and portfolio manager. Covers global funds, Asia, Latin America, central and eastern Europe, Africa and the Middle East. Annual.

Micropal emerging markets fund monitor. London: Standard & Poor's Micropal. £1,115 per year.
Contains performance data for equity and debt funds, open and closed end, reviewing around 2,000 funds worldwide. Includes rankings, sector averages, capital movement and cash flow analysis, breakdown of fund asset allocation and editorial commentary. Monthly.

Chapter 5

Pensions

The earliest occupational pensions were provided by benevolent employers and financed 'unfunded' from general assets. But in the 1920s the first insured pensions emerged in the United Kingdom (following a slightly earlier trend in the United States), financed by the employer but backed by the greater security of an insurance contract. Thus began the involvement of the financial services industry in the provision of retirement benefits. In the United Kingdom this development faltered – for better or worse – with the extension of state retirement pensions after the second world war, only to receive a boost with the government's active encouragement of personal pension schemes in the 1980s. The pensions misselling episode that followed was a major setback to private sector involvement but – as the industry gears itself up to deliver the new 'stakeholder' pensions – it seems to be a setback only and the financial services industry is poised to become the main provider of retirement benefits in the new century.

Pensions are essentially of two types – state and private – and the latter admits of two subdivisions, group and individual. Individual pensions include self-employed and executive contracts as well as 'personal pensions' as such. To further complicate the situation, pensions are frequently subsumed within the somewhat broader area of 'employee benefits', particularly outside the United Kingdom where the provision of private medical insurance through employers can be every bit as important as the provision of private pensions.

Pensions information is aimed at a disparate audience. There is information on pension scheme rules, government requirements on 'approved' tax status, pensions case law and so on. This information is typically of interest to the in-house pensions administrator as well as pensions consultants. Then there is product information on the different pensions contracts available, typically aimed at the pensions consultant or (particularly for personal pensions) the broader-based independent financial adviser. Finally there is information aimed at the investor of pensions funds, whether in-house or based in an insurance company or other financial institution.

In addition to commercial publishers an important source of pensions information are a few consultancies specialising in pensions and other employee benefits. Of particular note in this respect are **Bacon & Woodrow**,

William M. Mercer and **Watson Wyatt**. Much published information is also available from the **National Association of Pension Funds**, which represents the employers (and others), and there is also a specialist professional body, the **Pensions Management Institute**, although the **Chartered Insurance Institute** and the **Chartered Institute of Bankers** also hold examinations on pensions.

Because of the nature of private sector pensions several other chapters will also contain much material of relevance. Many of the sources in chapter 1 (financial services in general) aimed at the independent financial adviser – for instance web sites providing product data – will cover pensions, in particular personal pensions and other individual contracts. And because the basis of most private pensions is some kind of insurance contract, chapter 3 (insurance) – and in particular section 3.91 (life assurance) – will contain much that is relevant as well. Note that many textbooks and other sources take as their subject matter 'life and pensions' and these items will be found listed in section 3.91 and not here.

5.00 General sources

5.00.01 Consumer guides

The **Pensions Advisory Service** is a charitable organisation, which exists to provide advice and assistance on pensions matters to members of the public. The **Association of British Insurers** also provides consumer information on pensions.

The Which? guide to pensions. Lowe, Jonquil. 3rd ed. London: Which? Books: distributed by the Penguin Group, 1999. 335 p. (Which? consumer guides) £9.99.
Commissioned and researched by the Consumers' Association. With useful addresses and a glossary.

5.00.03 Textbooks

Coursebooks on pensions are published by the **Chartered Institute of Bankers**, the **Chartered Insurance Institute** and the **Pensions Management Institute**.

The Allied Dunbar pensions handbook. London: Pearson Education. £24.99.
Guide for business owners, company directors, the self-employed and professional pensions planners. Annual.

Pension schemes and pension funds in the United Kingdom. Blake, David. Oxford: Oxford University Press, 1995. xxii, 607 p. £65.
Substantial academic work looking at the past, present and future of pensions in the United Kingdom – from a mid-1990s perspective.

Pensions: a practical guide. Seres, J. S. D. 4th ed. London: FT Law & Tax, 1997. xxxix, 468 p. £53.
Guides practitioners through the procedures to be followed in the establishment, alteration and administration of a pension scheme. Includes a glossary.

Understanding occupational pension schemes. Oldfield, Maurice. 5th ed. Croydon: Tolley, 1994. xviii, 133 p.
Basic guide aimed at trustees, administrators, members and other beneficiaries. Includes a short glossary and specimen wordings for standard documents.

5.00.05 Manuals

Croner's pensions compliance service. Kingston upon Thames, Surrey: Croner. 1 vol. (looseleaf).
Successor to the long-established *Handbook on pensions* covering all aspects of pensions and providing both commentary and legislation. It's not about the work of a pensions compliance officer; rather, it aims to provide everything you need to know to ensure compliance – i.e., with legal and technical requirements. Updated by looseleaf amendments quarterly, plus a newsletter *Pensions compliance briefing* and an online service.

The pensions factbook. Gaines, Robert, ed. London: Gee. 2 vols (looseleaf).
Primarily a reference book for practitioners, with a lot of lists and so on. Covers all aspects of pensions. Around 1,000 pages in all, updated by quarterly looseleaf amendments and a newsletter *Pensions news*.

Pensions pocket book. Henley-on-Thames, Oxfordshire: NTC Publications in association with Bacon & Woodrow. £22.
Compendium of useful facts on pensions together with the economic and demographic background and social security. Includes statistics, legal summaries, a list of legislation, a chronology of recent events, a glossary and a directory. Chiefly limited to the UK although there is a short section on benefits overseas. Annual.

Pensions: law and practice. Ellison, Robin. London: Sweet & Maxwell. 3 vols (looseleaf). £299.
Guide to the law, administration and taxation of pension schemes in the United Kingdom. Comprises over 2,000 pages in all, including several hundred pages of forms, precedents and official documents. Updated by looseleaf amendments twice a year plus a bulletin.

Tolley's Pensions administration. Croydon: Tolley. 1 vol. (looseleaf). £125.
Practical guide to the daily administration of a pension scheme. Includes sample forms and other precedents and member benefit calculations. Also includes the full text on CD-ROM – or you can subscribe instead to *Tolley's Pensions law link* on CD-ROM (5.10.72), which includes the text of *Pensions*

administration as well as other information. Updated by quarterly looseleaf amendments, quarterly disks and six bulletins a year.

5.00.07 Source materials

Practical pensions precedents. Cunliffe, John, ed. London: Gee. 1 vol. (looseleaf). £250.
Extensive range of precedents to support occupational pensions administration. Includes trust deeds, pensions act forms and optional rules, with commentary. Updated by looseleaf amendments twice a year.

5.00.08 Technical reports

Analysis: benefits research. Epsom, Surrey: Bacon & Woodrow. Free.
Ad hoc series of briefings on topical issues, typically five or six titles a year of two to four pages each. Recent briefings include *Income drawdown flexibility: much ado about nothing?* and *Low inflation: pensions through the pain barrier*.

5.00.12 Market research

Datamonitor has recently produced *UK corporate pensions and employee benefits 1999* (£795) and **FT Finance** has published *Pensions: new routes to market* (£395, or £650 including four supplements to be published over two years). Other firms producing occasional research on pensions include **Market Assessment** and **Mintel**.

Annual survey of occupational pension schemes. London: National Association of Pension Funds.
Aggregate statistics derived from information provided by over 500 organisations. Coverage includes scheme rules, topical issues and investment. Annual.

Facts & figures.. Epsom, Surrey: Bacon & Woodrow. Free.
Useful compilation of background statistics including retail prices, financial markets, interest rates and national insurance. Gives figures for a wide range of years. Annual, updated by monthly bulletins.

Second tier pension provision. [London]: Department of Social Security. £15.
Contains statistical analyses of contracted-out salary-related schemes, contracted-out money purchase schemes, 'appropriate' personal pensions and people belonging to the state earnings related pension scheme (SERPS). Compiled by the Analytical Services Division of the Department of Social Security from a 1 per cent sample of national insurance records. Includes breakdown by age, area and earnings. Annual, in two volumes.

5.00.18 Product research

Executives' & directors' and top up pensions. Budden, Rob. London: FT Business. £60.
Covers executive pension plans, additional voluntary contributions and free-standing additional voluntary contributions. Comprises sections on individual products, a directory, comparative tables and market commentary. Annual.

5.00.21 Directories

NAPF year book: a guide to the National Association of Pension Funds Limited. London: National Association of Pension Funds.
Essentially a directory of members, but because of the nature of the NAPF's membership this is a useful reference work in its own right. Divided into sections by kind of organisation. Lists 1,100 pension funds and 350 consultants, insurers etc. Entries are fairly detailed, those for pension funds including value of contributions, number of members and names of advisers. Annual.

Pension funds and their advisers. London: AP Information Services. £95.
Gives detailed information on over 2,000 UK pension funds and around 350 advisers as well as international listings and some articles. Entries are fairly detailed, including advisers, contribution information, number of members. Comes with a pocket-sized contacts directory, *Pensions: the pocket blue book*. Also on CD-ROM. Annual.

Professional pensions yearbook. London: MSM International.
Separate sections on investment managers, insurance companies, consultants, solicitors, IFAs, software providers and other kinds of organisation providing pensions-related services. Gives contact details plus brief description. Distributed free to subscribers to *Professional pensions* (5.00.36). Annual.

5.00.24 Dictionaries

See the free online *Plain English Campaign's A to Z of pensions* in section 5.00.75.

Pensions terminology: a glossary for pension schemes. 5th ed. London: Pensions Management Institute, 1997. 124 p.
Short definitions of over 600 terms, with a separate listing of common abbreviations.

5.00.31 Periodicals

In addition to the commercially published titles listed here there are some often quite substantial newsletters issued by benefits consultants, in particular **Watson Wyatt**, **William M. Mercer** and **Bacon & Woodrow**.

Journal of pensions management: an international journal. London: Henry Stewart. £180 per year (institutions), £105 per year (individuals). Substantial articles by a wide range of authors including lawyers, actuaries and academics. Each issue includes an international section. Quarterly.

Occupational pensions. London: Eclipse. £170 per year.
Newsletter including fairly substantial articles, surveys of practice, case studies and news, aimed at scheme administrators, trustees and advisers. Monthly.

Pensions age. London: Perspective. £94 per year.
Trade magazine aimed at pensions advisers and product providers. News and short articles. Monthly.

Pensions management: the magazine for pensions professionals. London: Financial Times Business. £69 per year.
Thick, glossy magazine similar to the *Money management* title from the same stable. News, fairly substantial articles – often with comparative product tables – and regular product performance statistics. Includes some ad hoc supplements, e.g. *Stakeholder administration systems for the 21st century*. Monthly.

Pensions week: first for pensions news. London: Financial Times Business. £112 per year.
Weekly news magazine with occasional in-depth surveys, e.g. 'Local government pensions funding'.

Pensions world. Cheam, Surrey: Butterworths Tolley. £70 per year. Notwithstanding its title, focuses squarely on pensions in the United Kingdom. Mostly articles, some quite substantial. Published independently but also distributed to members of the National Association of Pension Funds as the official journal of the association. Wide ranging in coverage, not primarily product-oriented although there are some comparative surveys.

5.00.36 Newspapers

Professional pensions. London: MSM International. £135 per year. Tabloid-style paper containing news, some short articles and lots of advertising. Occasional special supplements provide more in-depth coverage, e.g. *UK investment managers 1999, Local authority pensions 1999*. There's also a web site: see section 5.00.75.

5.00.72 CD-ROMs

The pension schemes database UK & Europe. London: Financial Times Business.
Searchable database containing contact details and fund information on over 3,100 of the UK's largest occupational pension schemes, details on over 1,400 of Europe's top pension funds and profiles of the leading pensions service and product providers in the United Kingdom and Europe. Updated monthly.

5.00.75 Web sites

There is a lot of pensions information aimed at the consumer on the ABI web site, section 3.00.75

Aries: a website for the UK pensions industry from Aries Pensions and Insurance Systems Ltd. London: Aries Pensions and Insurance Systems. http://www.ariesps.co.uk. Free (some sections members only). Includes news and articles on pensions and related subjects, links and a good selection of statistics covering state pensions, RPI, national insurance, tax bands, contribution limits and so on. Further news, articles and technical information is promised behind an 'Aries members' button.

Bacon & Woodrow online! [UK]: Bacon & Woodrow. http://www.bacon-woodrow.com. By subscription only.
Provides comprehensive information on pensions and employee benefits, including briefings on individual topics, legislation and other data.

Impartial information about pensions. Bristol: DSS Pensions. http://www.dss.gov.uk/pen. Free.
Contains the text of eight DSS leaflets produced to help people make informed decisions about their pensions. Includes leaflets on personal pensions, pensions for the self-employed and pensions for women.

OPRA online. Brighton: Occupational Pensions Regulatory Authority. http://www.opra.gov.uk. Free.
Offers extensive collection of online texts on different aspects of occupational pensions aimed at consumers, scheme members, trustees and pensions professionals. Includes factsheets, technical guides and case reports.

Paul Smith Associates. Colchester: Paul Smith Associates. http://www.psa-pensions.co.uk. £54.99 per year.
A 'comprehensive pension guide' includes company reports, charging projections and fund performance data. Site also offers a pension report writer and a section on compliance.

Pensions & social insurance. London: Centre for Pensions and Social Insurance, Birkbeck College. http://www.econ.bbk.ac.uk/pi/pi.html.

Free.

Provides information about the Centre for Pensions and Social Insurance plus a list of publications (a few downloadable in PDF format), a glossary and research summaries. Also offers a 'virtual library' – lists, summaries and reviews of publications on pensions and social insurance – and an extensive directory of related web sites.

The Pensions Advisory Service. London: Pensions Advisory Service. http://www.opas.org.uk. Free.
Includes a series of online leaflets on different aspects of personal and occupational pensions together with case studies and annual reports.

Plain English Campaign's A to Z of pensions. [UK]: Plain English Campaign. http://www.plainenglish.co.uk/pensions.html. Free.
Extensive glossary aimed at the non-specialist.

Professional pensions: the pension site. London: MSM International. http://www.thepensionsite.co.uk. Free.
News, views and jobs from the weekly newspaper *Professional pensions* (5.00.36).

5.02 General sources (international)

International sources on pensions frequently focus on the wider area of employee benefits and this can include state benefits like social security.

5.02.03 Textbooks

Pension funds: retirement-income security and capital markets: an international perspective. Davis, E. Philip. Oxford: Oxford University Press, 1997. xii, 337 p. £15.
Assesses the major economic issues raised by occupational pension funds, focusing on 12 OECD countries.

5.02.12 Market research

See also the life and benefits series of country reports from Axco: *Insurance market report*, section 3.02.12.

IBIS briefing service. Chicago: International Benefits Information Service. £875 per year.
In-depth research on employee benefits internationally, including IBIS profiles on particular countries.

International benefit guidelines. Leatherhead, Surrey: William M. Mercer.
Country-by-country guide to mandatory and private benefits practices in 60 countries. Over 300 pages per issue. Annual.

International benefits yearbook. London: Sweet & Maxwell. £150.
Covers nearly 50 jurisdictions with details on pensions, social security, supplementary plans and taxation. Arranged by country. Annual.

5.02.24 Dictionaries

Dictionary of international benefits terminology. Jackson, Brian, ed. London: National Association of Pension Funds, 1998. 92 p. £15 (NAPF members £10).
Often quite substantial definitions of around 400 benefits-related terms taken from all over the world. Includes some foreign language words and abbreviations. Published in association with William M. Mercer.

5.02.31 Periodicals

Benefits & compensation international: total remuneration and pension investment. London: Pensions Publications. £275 per year.
Wide ranging in subject matter and geographical coverage, covering all forms of remuneration and employee benefits as well as pensions, although this tends to be a focal consideration. Fairly substantial articles plus some news and other features. 10 issues a year.

European pensions news. London: Financial Times Business. £495 per year.
Newsletter with some short articles as well as news as such. Covers all aspects of pensions throughout Europe. With occasional special supplements, e.g. on global custody. Fortnightly.

IBIS review. Chicago: International Benefits Information Service. $125 per year.
Monthly magazine on employee benefits internationally.

IBIS online!: access to international employee benefits information. Chicago: International Benefits Information Service. £840 per year.
Coverage includes employee benefits, pensions, remuneration, social security, labour agreements and so on, with monthly briefings covering more than 80 countries and profiles for selected countries. 'Disseminated electronically under agreement between Charles D. Spencer Associates, Chicago, and Bacon & Woodrow, London.' Also available as part of the *Bacon & Woodrow online!* service (5.00.75).

5.10 Law and regulation

Pensions law is of particular concern to the personnel manager, the pensions adviser and specialist solicitors. It is an extensive and complex area and has its own association in the United Kingdom, the **Association of Pensions Lawyers**, which publishes its own journal, *Pensions lawyer*

(5.10.31). The regulator is the **Occupational Pensions Regulatory Authority**.

5.10.03 Textbooks

Pension disputes: prevention and resolution. Marshall, Jane, ed. Bristol: Jordans, 1998. xx, 161 p. £40.
Explains how disputes arise, how they can be avoided and how best they can be resolved.

Pensions law and practice. Chatterton, David A. London: Cavendish, 1998. xxiv, 180 p. £39.95.
Targeted at legal practitioners and students.

5.10.05 Manuals

Sweet & Maxwell's Law of pension schemes. Inglis-Jones, Nigel. London: Sweet & Maxwell. 2 vols (looseleaf). £290.
Comprehensive account, including sections on contracting out and personal pensions. With transcripts of the judgements from important cases and the text of relevant EU directives. Comprises some 1,500 pages in all, updated two or three times a year by looseleaf amendments.

Tolley's pensions law. Croydon, Surrey: Butterworths Tolley. 1 vol. (looseleaf). £125.
New looseleaf providing guidance on all aspects of law and practice relating to pensions, aimed at both lawyers and pensions practitioners. Includes a digest of pensions case law. Updated three times a year.

5.10.07 Source materials

NAPF pensions legislation service. London: Tolley. 3 vols (looseleaf). £250.
Collects together the text of statutes, statutory instruments and EU directives affecting pensions, together with Inland Revenue materials and other official documentation. Comprises around 3,000 pages in all, updated by looseleaf amendments four times a year. There's also an accompanying CD-ROM (also updated) called *Pensions legislation plus*, which contains statutes and statutory instruments in parallel with the looseleaf, together with additional Inland Revenue guidance manuals and case summaries.

Occupational pensions law reports. London: Eclipse. £310 per year.
Sets out the full transcript and judgement for all significant English cases on pensions, with additional summaries. Includes a cumulative subject and case index. Approximately 24 issues a year.

5.10.31 Periodicals

Pension lawyer: the journal of the Association of Pension Lawyers. London: Association of Pension Lawyers. £40 per year (free to members). Fairly substantial articles on pensions law and related subjects, plus case notes and some legal news. Formerly *British pension lawyer*. Six issues a year.

5.10.72 CD-ROMs

Tolley's Pensions law link. Croydon, Surrey: Tolley. £149 plus VAT (single user), £199 plus VAT (2–5 users), plus updates.
Includes the text of *Tolley's Pensions administration* (5.00.05). Updated quarterly.

5.17 Taxation

In the United Kingdom 'approved pensions'– those that meet Inland Revenue requirements – enjoy substantial tax benefits, hence the importance of taxation in this area. The Inland Revenue's responsibilities are discharged by the **Pension Schemes Office**.

5.17.03 Textbooks

Taxation of pension schemes. Woodhouse, Stephen, Eden, Sandra and Lippiatt, Stuart. London: Sweet and Maxwell, 1996. xxiv, 364 p. £89. Covers both approved and unapproved schemes and includes a comparison of pensions with other investment media. With glossary.

Tolley's Taxation of pension benefits. Ure, Alec. Croydon: Tolley, 1998. £85.
Sets out current provisions relating to tax reliefs and liabilities throughout the United Kingdom together with related overseas provisions.

5.17.07 Source materials

Practice notes on approval of occupational pension schemes. Nottingham: Pension Schemes Office. 1 vol. (looseleaf).
Practice guidelines relating to 'schemes for which approval is sought under the exercise of the board's discretion'. Updated by looseleaf amendments as necessary. Includes the same text on diskette.

5.46 Trustees

Pensions trustees are non-specialists with specialist responsibilities and accordingly there is a lot of literature aimed at explaining to them the intricacies of occupational pensions and their own rights and obligations.

5.46.03 Textbooks

The pension fund trustee handbook. Self, Roger. 5th ed. Croydon, Surrey: Tolley, 1999. x, 220 p.
Detailed, practical guide. Includes extensive appendices containing background information etc.

The pension trustee's handbook: the definitive guide to practical pension fund trusteeship. Ellison, Robin. 2nd ed. London: Thorogood, 1997. xi, 226 p. £25.
Targeted at trustees and their advisers. With extensive appendices including a glossary, statistics and case summaries.

Pensions and trusteeship: a specially commissioned report. Arthur, Hugh. London: Sweet & Maxwell, 1998. xxxvii, 360 p. £125.
Detailed guide aimed at pensions lawyers and other pensions professionals. Particularly concerned with highlighting the changes brought about by the Pensions Act 1995.

The role of the pension fund trustee. Cunliffe, John. 4th ed. London: FT Law & Tax, 1997. ix, 250 p. £25.
A handbook for the non-specialist who has been appointed as a trustee. Published in conjunction with the National Association of Pension Funds.

5.54 Accounting

Works on pensions accounting tend to be aimed at the employer and the accountant. The **Institute of Chartered Accountants in England and Wales** is the most important institutional source of information.

5.54.03 Textbooks

Accounts and audit of pension schemes. Mascarenhas, Amyas and McIntyre, Mary-Ann. 3rd ed. London: Butterworths, 1997. xxviii, 377 p. £55.
Outlines the legal and accounting requirements that apply to the preparation and audit of pension scheme accounts. Includes tabulated summaries, worked examples, a model annual report and a checklist of disclosure requirements.

Pension schemes: an industry accounting and auditing guide. Rowley, Peter and Tarshis, Sondra. 2nd ed. Central Milton Keynes: Accountancy Books, 1997. xvii, 616 p. £50.

Incorporates the requirements of the Pensions Act 1995 as well as other standards and guidelines. Includes extracts from some official documents.

5.77 Personal pensions

Personal pensions were introduced in the United Kingdom by the Social Security Act 1986. They are not the only kind of individual pension arrangements, which also include executive pension schemes and self-employed pensions. The providers are typically life assurance companies.

5.77.18 Product research

Group personal pensions. Battersby, Mark. London: FT Business. £60.
A company-by-guide to product details with commentary on key features and the state of the market. Covers over 60 products, both with-profits and unit-linked. Includes comparative tables. Annual.

Personal pensions. Walford, Janet. London: FT Business.
Aims to cover 'every plan currently on the market which may be purchased by the general public'. Comprises a company-by-company sequence giving product details, together with comparative tables and market commentary. Annual.

Chapter 6

Publishers

3d Consulting Ltd

28 Grosvenor Street
London
W1X 9FE
Tel: *020 7917 9648*
Fax: *020 7917 6002*
Email: *ddd@cix.co.uk*

Entries

Insurance company law handbook for Windows 3.10.72

A. M. Best Company, Inc.

Ambest Road
Oldwick
New Jersey 08858
United States
Tel: *+1 908 439 2200*
Fax: *+1 908 439 3296*
Web site: *http://www.ambest.com*

Entries

Best's insurance reports 3.02.16
A M Best Company: the insurance information source 3.02.75
Best's captive directory 3.37.21

A. M. Best International, Ltd

264 Northfield Avenue
London
W5 4UB
Tel: *020 8579 1091*
Web site: *http://www.ambest.com/sales/global*

Entries

Best's UK insurance security analysis service: ISAS 3.00.16

Best's Insight 3.00.72
Best's Insight global 3.02.72
Best's key rating guide international 3.02.72
Best's guide to Lloyd's market results & prospects 3.25.16
Best's Marksman 4: the Lloyd's market analysis system 3.25.72

A. T. Kearney, Inc.

222 West Adams Street
Chicago
IL 60606
United States
Tel: *+1 312 648 0111*
Web site: *http://www.atkearney.com*

Entries

Global investment banking strategy: insights from industry leaders 2.37.12

AA Insurance Services

PO Box 74
Basingstoke
Hampshire
RG21 1LF
Tel: *01256 20123*
Email: *customer.services@theaa.co.uk*
Web site: *http://www.theaa.co.uk/insuranceandfinance*

Entries

British insurance premium index 3.00.12

Academic Press

Harcourt Place
32 Jamestown Road
London
NW1 7BY
Tel: *020 7424 4200*
Fax: *020 7483 2293/020 7485 4752*
Email: *apbcs@harcourtbrace.com*
Web site: *http://www.apnet.com*

Entries

EU and US banking in the 1990s 2.02.03
Digital cash: commerce on the net 2.72.03

Accountancy Books

PO Box 21375
London
WC1N 1QP
Tel: *020 7920 8991*
Fax: *020 7920 8992*
Email: *info@accountancybooks.co.uk*
Web site: *http://www.accountancybooks.co.uk*

Entries

Banking: an industry accounting and auditing guide 2.50.03
Pension schemes: an industry accounting and auditing guide 5.54.03

Advanced Media Group

167 Wardour Street
London
W1V 3TA
Tel: *020 7287 6771*
Fax: *020 7468 3488*

Entries

*Lamont's glossary: the definitive plain English money and investment diction-
ary for the finance professional and money-minded consumer* 1.00.24

Age Concern Books

Age Concern
Knowsley Community Services Centre
Lathom Road
Huyton
Merseyside
L36 9XZ
Tel: *0151 480 4632*
Fax: *0151 449 3537*
Email: *contact@acknowsley.fsnet.co.uk*
Web site: *http://acknowsley.fsnet.co.uk*

Entries

Your taxes and savings 2000–2001: a guide for older people 1.00.01

AITC Services

See Association of Investment Trust Companies.

AKG Actuaries & Consultants

Anderton House
92 South Street
Dorking
Surrey
RH4 2EW
Tel: *01306 876439*
Fax: *01306 885325*
Email: *AKGactuaries@compuserve.com*

Entries

UK life office with profits report 3.91.16
Company profile & financial strength reports 3.91.16

American Bankers Association

1120 Connecticut Avenue NW
Washington
DC 20036
United States
Tel: *+1 202 663 5087*
Email: *custserv@aba.com*
Web site: *http://www.aba.com/*

Entries

Global banking 2.02.03
Internet sources for Bankers: a selective guide to web sites 2.02.26
ABA banking journal 2.02.31
American Bankers Association 2.02.75

Aon Risk Services Companies, Inc

2 World Trade Center
New York
NY 10048
United States
Tel: *+1 212 441 1000*
Fax: *+1 212 479 6905*
Web site: *http://www.aon.com/about/busi_desc/companies/ARS*

Entries

Biennial risk financing and insurance survey 3.64.12

AP Information Services

Roman House
296 Golders Green Rd
London
NW11 9PZ
Tel: *020 8455 4550*
Fax: *020 8455 6381*
Email: *ap_inform@compuserve.com*
Web site: *http://www.ap_info.co.uk*

Entries

Crawford's directory of City connections 1.00.21
Pension funds and their advisers 5.00.21

Ark Publishing

352–354 Fulham Road
London
SW10 9UH
Tel: *020 7795 1234*
Fax: *020 7376 3776*

Entries

Risk management bulletin 3.62.31

Arrow

Random House
20 Vauxhall Bridge Road
London
Tel: *020 7840 8400*
Fax: *020 7828 6681*
A division of Random House Group.

Entries

Perfect insurance: all you need to get it right first time 3.00.01

Ashgate Publishing Group

Gower House
Croft Road
Aldershot
Hampshire
Tel: *01252 331551*
Fax: *01252 344405*

Entries

The single market in insurance: breaking down the barriers 3.10.03

Assecuranz Compass

Avenue Molière 256
1060 Brussels
Belgium
Tel: *+32 (0) 2 345 90 70*
Fax: *+32 (0) 2 347 33 40*
Email: *info@assecuranz.com*
Web site: *http://www.kompass.be*

Entries

Assecuranz-compass: the worldwide insurance directory 3.02.21

Associated New Media

60 Charlotte Street
London
W1H 1PH
Tel: *020 7209 1234*
Fax: *020 7209 1235*
Email: *information@associated.co.uk*
Web site: *http://www.associated.co.uk*

Entries

This is money: your personal financial adviser: from the Daily Mail, Mail on Sunday, & Evening Standard 1.00.75

Association for Payment Clearing Services

Mercury House
14 Finsbury Square
London
EC2A 1BR
Tel: *020 7711 6200*
Fax: *020 7711 6276*
Email: *publicaffairs@APACS.org.uk*
Web site: *http://www.apacs.org.uk*

Entries

Introduction to chapter 2
Introduction to section 2.15
Introduction to section 2.72

Association Internationale de Droit des Assurances

C/o Colin V. Croly
Secretary General
Barlow Lyde & Gilbert
Beaufort House
15 St Botolph Street
London
EC3A 7NJ
Tel: *020 7643 8657*
Fax: *020 7643 8509*
Email: *ccroly@blg.co.uk*

Entries

Insurance contract law 3.10.05
International encyclopaedia of laws. [Insurance law] 3.10.05
The international journal of insurance law 3.10.31
The AIDA RWP reports 3.69.08
Introduction to section 3.10

Association Internationale des Sociétés d'Assurance Mutuelle

114 rue la Boétie
75008 Paris
France
Tel: *+33 (0) 1 42 25 84 86*

Entries

Mutuality 3.36.31

Association Internationale pour l'Etude de l'Economie de l'Assurance

18 chemin Rieu
1208 Geneva
Switzerland
Tel: *+41 22 347 09 38*
Fax: *+41 22 347 20 78*
Email: *geneva.association@vtx.ch*
Web site: *http://www.genevaassociation.org*

Also known as the Geneva Association.

Entries

The Geneva papers on risk and insurance theory 1.07.31
Etudes et dossiers 3.00.08
The Geneva papers on risk and insurance, issues and practice 3.00.31

Association of British Insurers

51 Gresham Street
London
EC2V 7HQ
Tel: *020 7600 3333*
Fax: *020 7696 8999*
Email: *info@abi.org.uk*
Web site: *http://www.abi.org.uk*

Entries

General insurance research report 3.00.08
Occasional paper 3.00.08
Insurance statistics yearbook 3.00.12
Insurance: facts, figures and trends 3.00.12
Statistical bulletin 3.00.12
Daily press summary 3.00.26
Media contact directory 3.00.26
Insurance trends: quarterly statistics and research review 3.00.31
Association of British Insurers 3.00.75
Introduction to chapter 3
Introduction to section 3.00.01
Introduction to section 3.00.02
Introduction to section 3.00.07
Introduction to section 3.00.12
Introduction to section 3.00.31
Introduction to section 3.02

Association of Insurance and Risk Managers

6 Lloyd's Avenue
London
EC3N 3AX
Tel: *020 7480 7610*
Fax: *020 7702 3752*
Email: *enquiries@airmic.co.uk*
Web site: *http://www.airmic.com*

Entries

Introduction to section 3.62

Association of Investment Trust Companies

Durrant House
8–13 Chiswell Street
London
EC1Y 4YY
Tel: *020 7282 5555*
Fax: *020 7282 5556*
Email: *info@aitc.co.uk*
Web site: *http://aitc.co.uk*

Entries

Investors update 4.74.18
ITS statistics: a monthly information service from the Association of Investment Trust Companies 4.74.18
Investment trusts: the easy way to invest in the stock market 4.74.75
Introduction to section 4.74
Introduction to section 4.74.01

Association of Lloyd's Members

16 St Mary at Hill
London
EC3R 8EE
Tel: *020 7283 4026*

Entries

Introduction to section 3.25

Association of Pension Lawyers

C/o Susan J. Andrews
Eversheds
Senator House
85 Queen Victoria Street
London
EC4V 4JL
Tel: *020 7919 4500*

Entries

Pension lawyer: the journal of the Association of Pension Lawyers 5.10.31
Introduction to section 5.10

Association of Unit Trusts and Investment Funds

65 Kingsway
London
WC2B 6TD
Tel: *020 7831 0898*
Fax: *020 7831 9975*
Email: *Publications@investmentfunds.org.uk*
Web site: *http://www.investmentfunds.org.uk*

Entries

Association of Unit Trusts and Investment Funds 4.72.75
Introduction to section 4.72

Assurance Medical Society

Lettsom House
11 Chandos Street
London
W1M 0EB
Tel: 020 7636 6308

Entries

Introduction to section 3.91

Axco Insurance Information Services Ltd

Forum House
15–18 Lime Street
London
EC3M 7AP
Tel: *020 7623 9828*
Fax: *020 7623 9003*
Email: *axco@axcoinfo.com*
Web site: *http://axcoinfo.com*

Entries

Insurance market report 3.02.12

Bacon & Woodrow

Parkside House
Ashley Road
Epsom
Surrey

KT18 5BS
Tel: *01372 733700*
Fax: *01372 733991*
Web site: *http://www.bandw.co.uk*

Entries

Pensions pocket book 5.00.05
Analysis: benefits research 5.00.08
Facts & figures. 5.00.12
Bacon & Woodrow online! 5.00.75
Introduction to chapter 5
Introduction to section 5.00.31

Bank for International Settlements

CH-4002
Basel
Switzerland
Tel: *+41 61 280 80 80*
Fax: *+41 61 280 91 00/+41 61 280 81 00*
Email: *emailmaster@bis.org*
Web site: *http://www.bis.org*

Entries

Introduction to section 2.15
Introduction to section 2.02.09
Introduction to section 2.72

Bank House Communications Limited

Bank House
Great Rissington
Gloucestershire
GL54 2LP
Tel: *01451 821982*
Fax: *01451 821972*
Email: *AndyCouchman@Compuserve.com*

Entries

Healthcare insurance report 3.93.31

Bank of England

Threadneedle Street
London
EC2R 8AH

Tel: *020 7601 4444*
Fax: *020 7601 4771*
Web site: *http://www.bankofengland.co.uk*

Entries

The City handbook 1.00.75
Financial stability review 1.10.31
Practical issues arising from the euro 2.39.08
Inflation report 2.39.12
Bank of England quarterly bulletin 2.39.31
Bank of England 2.39.75
Introduction to section 2.39

Bankers Books

See Chartered Institute of Bankers.

Banking Ombudsman Scheme

Financial Ombudsman Service
PO Box 4
South Quay Plaza
183 Marsh Wall
London
E14 9SR
Tel: *020 7404 9944*
Fax: *020 7405 5052*
Email: *banking.ombudsman@financial-ombudsman.org.uk*
Web site: *http://www.obo.org.uk*

Entries

Introduction to section 2.33.01

Banks and Building Societies National Training Organisation

See Financial Services National Training Organisation.

Barlow Lyde & Gilbert

Beaufort House
15 St Botolph Street
London
EC3A 7NJ
Tel: *020 7247 2277*
Fax: *020 7643 8500*

Email: *mwood@blg.co.uk*
Web site: *http://www.blg.co.uk*

Entries

Reinsurance practice and the law 3.69.05
Introduction to section 3.10.31

Baron's Educational Series Inc.

250 Wireless Boulevard
Hauppauge
NY 11788
United States
Tel: *+1 800 645 3476*
Fax: *+1 631 434 3723*
Email: *webmaster@barronseduc.com*
Web site: *http://www.barronseduc.com*

Entries

Dictionary of banking terms 2.00.24

Basle Committee on Banking Supervision

See Bank for International Settlements.

Bayerische Rückversicherung Aktiengesellschaft

Sederanger 4–6
D-80538 Munich
Germany
Fax: *+49 89 38 44 22 79*
Email: *info@bayerischeruck.com*

Entries

IBR: international bibliography of reinsurance 3.69.26

BBA

See British Bankers' Association.

Best (A. M.) Company, Inc.

See A. M. Best Company, Inc.

Best (A. M.) International, Ltd

See A. M. Best International, Ltd.

Blackstone Press

Aldine Place
London
W12 8AA
Tel: *020 8740 2277*
Fax: *020 8743 2292*
Email: *sales@blackstone.demon.co.uk*
Web site: *http://www.blackstonepress.co.uk*

Entries

Practical banking and building society law 2.10.03
Blackstone's guide to the Bank of England Act 1998 2.39.03

Blackwell Publishers

108 Cowley Road
Oxford
OX4 1JF
Tel: *01865 791100*
Fax: *01865 791347*
Web site: *http://www.blackwellpublishers.co.uk*

Entries

World banking abstracts 2.02.26
The Geneva papers on risk and insurance, issues and practice 3.00.31

Blue Moon Publishing

3rd Floor
84 Tooley Street
London
SE1 2TF
Tel: *020 74074700*
Fax: *020 7407 4704*
Email: *credittoday@compuserve.com*

Entries

Credit today 2.78.31

BPP Publishing Ltd

Aldine House
Aldine Place
142–144 Uxbridge Road
Shepherd's Bush Green
London
Tel: *020 8740 2222*
Fax: *020 8740 1184*
Email: *sales@bpp-pub.co.uk*
Web site: *http://www.bpp.co.uk*

Entries

Introduction to section 1.00.03

British Bankers' Association

Pinners Hall
105–108 Old Broad Street
London
EC2N 1EX
Tel: *020 7216 8800*
Fax: *020 7216 8811*
Web site: *http://www.bba.org.uk*

Entries

The banking year ahead 1999/2000: a survey sponsored by the BBA and the Financial Times 2.00.12
British Bankers' Association 2.00.75
Introduction to chapter 2
Introduction to section 2.15
Introduction to section 2.33.01
Introduction to section 2.33.12
Introduction to section 2.50

British Insurance Brokers' Association

BIIBA House
14 Bevis Marks
London
EC3A 7NT
Tel: *020 7623 9043*
Fax: *020 7626 9676*
Web site: *http://www.biiba.org.uk*

Has recently reverted back to its original name after many years as British Insurance and Investment Brokers' Association.

Entries

Introduction to section 3.43

British Insurance Law Association

C/o Alison Potts
20 Aldermanbury
London
EC2V 7HY
Tel: *020 7417 4780*
Fax: *020 7726 0131*
Email: *bila@cii.co.uk*
Web site: *http://www.bila.org.uk*

Entries

Journal 3.10.31
Introduction to section 3.10

British Insurers' European Committee

51 Gresham Street
London
EC2V 7HQ
Tel: *020 7216 7630*
Fax: *020 7696 8997*

Entries

Bulletin 3.10.31
Introduction to section 3.02

British Invisibles

Windsor House
39 King Street
London
EC2V 8DQ
Tel: 020 7600 1198
Fax: *020 7606 4248*

Entries

International financial markets in the UK 1.00.12
The 'City' table 1.00.12

Buckley Press

See Timothy Benn Publishing.

Building Societies Association

3 Savile Row
London
W1X 1AF
Tel: *020 7437 0655*
Fax: *020 7734 6416*
Web site: *http://www.bsa.org.uk*

Entries

Building Societies Act 1986: a BSA summary 2.10.03
The Building Societies Act 1986: practice manual 2.10.05
Taxation of building society interest 2.35.01
Going for it 2.35.02
Building society annual accounts manual 2.35.05
Investment manual 2.35.05
BSA monthly statistics digest 2.35.16
Economics of mutuality and the future of building societies: series of research papers 2.35.16
Building society news 2.35.26
Library bulletin 2.35.26
Introduction to chapter 2
Introduction to section 2.15
Introduction to section 2.35
Introduction to section 2.35.01
Introduction to section 2.35.16

Building Societies Commission

See Financial Services Authority.

Butterworth Heinemann

Linacre House
Jordan Hill
Oxford
OX2 8DP
Tel: *01865 310366*
Email: *bhuk.orders@repp.co.uk*
Web site: *http://www.bh.com*

Entries
Marketing financial services 2.56.03

Butterworths

Halsbury House
35 Chancery Lane
London
WC2A 1EL
Tel: *020 7400 2500*
Fax: *020 7400 2842*
Web site: *http://ww.butterworths.co.uk*

Entries

Personal financial planning manual 1.00.05
Financial services law and practice 1.10.07
Financial regulations service 1.10.72
Banking and financial services regulation 2.10.03
Banking law in Scotland 2.10.03
Butterworths banking law handbook 2.10.03
Butterworths international guide to money laundering: law and practice 2.10.03
Paget's law of banking 2.10.03
Encyclopaedia of banking law 2.10.21
Butterworths journal of international banking and financial law 2.10.31
Butterworths banking law direct 2.10.75
General principles of insurance law 3.10.03
Butterworths insurance law handbook 3.10.07
Legal decisions affecting insurance 1729–1991 3.10.07
Insurance law service 3.10.72
Taxation of insurance business 3.17.03
The insurance of commercial risks: law and practice 3.71.03
Aviation insurance: the law and practice of aviation insurance, including hover-craft and spacecraft insurance 3.88.03
Law of life assurance 3.91.03
Butterworths taxation of offshore trusts and funds 4.77.03
Accounts and audit of pension schemes 5.54.03

Butterworths Tolley

2 Addiscombe Road
Croydon
Surrey
CR9 5AF
Tel: *020 8662 2000*
Fax: *020 8662 2012*

Entries

Tolley's Insurance handbook 3.10.03
Understanding occupational pension schemes 5.00.03
Tolley's Pensions administration 5.00.05
Pensions world 5.00.31
Tolley's Pensions law 5.10.05
NAPF pensions legislation service 5.10.07
Tolley's Pensions law link 5.10.72
Tolley's Taxation of pension benefits 5.17.03
The pension fund trustee handbook 5.46.03

BZW Research

Ebbgate House
2 Swan Lane
London
EC4R 3TS
Tel: *020 7623 2323*

Entries

Introduction to section 3.00.16

C&M Publications

3A Market Place
Uppingham
Leicestershire
LE15 9QH
Tel: *01572 820088*
Fax: *01572 820099*
Email: *enquiries@candmpubs.com*
Web site: *http://www.candmpubs.com/*

Entries

Card world independent 2.72.31

Cambridge Market Intelligence

The Quadrangle
49 Atalanta Street
London
SW6 6TR
Tel: *020 7565 7900*
Fax: *020 7565 7938*
Email: *marketing@cmi.co.uk*

Web site: *http://www.cmi.co.uk/*

Entries

The inside careers guide to actuaries 1.07.02
The inside careers guide to insurance 3.00.02

Carlton Laws

See Turpin Distribution Services Ltd.

Cartermill Publishing

Maple House
149 Tottenham Court Road
London
W1P 9LL
Tel: *020 7806 2412*
Fax: *020 7896 2449*
Email: *colleenk@pearson-pro.com*

Entries

Onscreen insurance terms 3.00.72

Cavendish

The Glass House
Wharton Street
London
WC1X 9PX
Tel: *020 7278 8000*
Fax: *020 7278 8080*
Email: *info@cavendishpublishing.com*
Web site: *http://www.cavendishpublishing.com*

Entries

Insurance law: text and materials 3.10.07
Law of marine insurance 3.87.03
Cases and materials on marine insurance law 3.87.07
Pensions law and practice 5.10.03

Cazalet Financial Consulting

37–39 York Street
Twickenham
Middlesex
TW1 3LP

Tel: *020 8296 0562*
Fax: *020 8892 8162*
Web site: *http://www.cazalet-financial.com*

Entries

Life 2000 3.91.12

Centaur Communications Ltd

St Giles House
50 Poland Street
London
W1V 4AX
Tel: *020 7970 4000*
Fax: *020 7970 4898*

Entries

Fund forum 4.00.31
International money marketing: for the distributors of international financial products 4.77.31

Central Banking Publications Ltd

6 Langley Street
London
WC2H 9JA
Tel: *020 7836 3607*
Fax: *020 7836 3608*
Email: *info@centralbanking.co.uk*
Web site: *http://www.centralbanking.co.uk*

Entries

How countries supervise their banks, insurers and securities markets 1.10.21
Flemings who's who in central banking 1999 2.02.12
Morgan Stanley Dean Witter central bank directory 2000 2.02.12
Central banking 2.02.31
The emerging framework of financial regulation 2.15.03
Who's who in financial regulation 2.15.21
The financial regulator 2.15.31

Central Statistical Office

See Office for National Statistics.

Centre for Central Banking Studies

See Bank of England.

Centre for Economic Policy Research

25–28 Old Burlington Street
London
W1X 1LB
Tel: *020 7878 2900*
Fax: *020 7878 2999*
Email: *cepr@cepr.org*
Web site: *http://www.econ.bbk.ac.uk/lmig/cepr.html*

Entries

The future of European banking 2.00.03

Centre for Risk and Insurance Studies

See University of Nottingham Centre for Risk and Insurance Studies.

Centre for the Study of Financial Innovation

18 Curzon Street
London
W1Y 7AD
Tel: *020 7493 0173*
Fax: *info@csfi.demon.co.uk*

Entries

The Internet and financial services: a CSFI report 2.33.03
Europe's new banks: the "non-bank" phenomenon 2.33.12
Mutuality for the twenty-first century 2.35.03
Introduction to section 2.00.12

Ceuterick SA

Brusselsestraat 153
B-3000 Leuven
Belgium
Fax: *+32 (0) 16 204533*
Email: *info@ceuterick.be*

Entries

The ASTIN bulletin: the journal of the ASTIN and AFIR sections of the International Actuarial Association 1.07.31

Chancellor Publications

20 Woodland Rise
London
N10 3UG
Tel: *020 8444 0235*
Fax: *020 8444 0235*

Entries

The Trident practical guide to offshore trusts 4.77.03

Chartered Institute of Bankers

Emmanuel House
4–9 Burgate Lane
Canterbury
Kent
CT1 2XJ
Tel: *01227 818603*
Fax: *01227 763788*
Email: *bbooks@cib.org.uk*
Web site: *http://www.cib.org.uk*

Entries

Getting into financial services 1.00.02
International dictionary of banking and finance 1.02.24
Introduction to the financial services environment 2.00.03
The business of banking: an introduction to the modern financial services indus-
try 2.00.03
The monetary and financial system 2.00.03
The CIB directory of corporate banking in the UK 2.00.21
Dictionary of banking terms and finance terms 2.00.24
CIB news 2.00.31
Financial world 2.00.31
The Chartered Institute of Bankers 2.00.75
Law relating to financial services 2.10.03
Introduction to law in the financial services 2.10.03
Introduction to building society operations 2.35.03
Building society operations: the uniqueness of mutual societies and their role in
the modern financial services industry 2.35.03
Banking operations: regulation, practice and treasury management 2.50.03
Management in the financial services industry: thriving on organisational change
2.50.03
Managing information: understanding the impact of IT on the financial services
2.50.03

Treasury management 2.50.03
Customer services: marketing and the competitive environment 2.56.03
Introduction to marketing, customer service and sales 2.56.03
Introduction to money transmission 2.72.03
Banking operations: UK lending and international business 2.78.03
Residential lending and property law 2.78.03
Dictionary of insurance and finance terms 3.00.24
Introduction to chapter 2
Introduction to section 1.00.03
Introduction to section 2.00.02
Introduction to section 2.00.12
Introduction to section 2.50.03
Introduction to section 2.78.03
Introduction to chapter 5
Introduction to section 5.00.03

Chartered Institute of Loss Adjusters

36 Monument Street
London
EC3R 8LJ
Tel: *020 7337 9960*
Fax: *020 7929 3082*
Email: *info@cila.co.uk*
Web site: *http://www.cila.co.uk*

Entries

The loss adjuster: the magazine of the Chartered Institute of Loss Adjusters
3.68.31
Claims and standard fire policies, special extensions and special perils 3.82.03
Claims and loss of profits insurance 3.83.03
Claims and public liability policies 3.84.03
Introduction to section 3.68

Chartered Insurance Institute

20 Aldermanbury
London
EC2V 7HY
Tel: *020 8989 8464*
Fax: *020 7726 0131*
Email: *info@cii.co.uk*
Web site: *http://www.cii.co.uk*

Entries

The inside careers guide to insurance 3.00.02
Glossary of insurance terms 3.00.24
Insurance research & practice 3.00.31
Journal 3.00.31
CII Library online 3.00.75
The Chartered Insurance Institute 3.00.75
Digest of annual reports and bulletins: 1981–1995 3.68.05
Introduction to chapter 3
Introduction to section 3.53
Introduction to section 1.00.03
Introduction to section 1.00.12
Introduction to section 1.00.72
Introduction to section 3.00.02
Introduction to section 3.00.03
Introduction to section 3.00.08
Introduction to section 3.00.26
Introduction to section 3.00.72
Introduction to chapter 5
Introduction to section 5.00.03

Charterhouse Communications plc

Arnold House
36–41 Holywell Lane
London
EC2A 3SF
Tel: *020 7827 5484*

Entries

The official CML yearbook 99 2.78.21
Mortgage finance gazette 2.78.31
What mortgage 2.78.31

Charterhouse Securities Ltd

PO Box 66
Royal Liver Building
Pier Head
Liverpool
L69 3RJ
Tel: *0151 472 5555*

Entries

Introduction to section 3.00.16

Chatset

PO Box 661
London
SW1
Tel: *020 7823 6980*

Entries

Directory of Lloyd's & London insurance market 3.25.21

CIB

See Chartered Institute of Bankers.

CIB Publishing

See Chartered Institute of Bankers.

City Financial Communications

7 Air Street
London
W1R 5RJ
Tel: *020 7439 3050*
Fax: *020 7439 3070*
Email: *editorial@invweek.co.uk*

Entries

Bloomberg money 1.00.31
Investment week: the premier publication for professional advisers 1.00.36
IFA online 1.00.75
Global adviser.com 1.02.75
Mortgage solutions 2.78.31
Cover: the protection magazine 3.91.31
Cover online: an online resource for protection advisors 3.91.75

City University Department of Actuarial Science and Statistics

Northampton Square
London
EC1V 0HB
Tel: *020 7477 8472*
Fax: *020 7477 8838*

Entries

Actuarial research paper 1.07.12

Clarendon Press

See Oxford University Press.

CML

See Council of Mortgage Lenders.

Collins & Brown Ltd

London House
Great Eastern Wharf
Parkgate Road
London
SW11 4NQ
Tel: *020 7924 2575*
Fax: *020 7924 7725*
Email: *info@collins-and-brown.co.uk*
Web site: *http://www.collins-and-brown.co.uk*

Entries

The art of marketing mortgages 2.56.03

Comité Européen des Assurances

3 bis, rue de la Chaussée d'Antin
F75009 Paris
France
Tel: *+33 (0) 1 44 83 11 83*
Fax: *+33 (0) 1 47 70 03 75*
Web site: *http://www.cea.assur.org*

Entries

European insurance in figures 3.02.12
CEA doc 3.02.26
Single licence vademecum for operators 3.10.05
Introduction to section 3.02.12

Companies House

Crown Way
Cardiff
CF14 3UZ

Tel: *029 20388588*
Fax: *029 20380900*
Web site: *http://www.companies-house.gov.uk*

Entries

Introduction to section 3.00.16

Compliance Register

Enterprise House
PO Box 843
Greenlys
Milton Keynes
Bucks MK12 6YZ
Tel: *01908 322450*
Fax: *01908 220213*
Email: *Compliance.Register@btinternet.com*
Web site: *http://www.compliance-register.com*

Entries

The compliance digest: quarterly journal of the Compliance Register 1.10.31
*The Compliance Register: the international organisation for compliance profes-
sionals and senior managers in the financial services industry* 1.10.75 *Fax*:

Consumers' Association

See Which? Books.

Corporation of Lloyd's

1 Lime Street
London
EC3M 7HA
Tel: *020 7327 6256*
Fax: *020 7327 6233*
Web site: *http://www.lloyds.com*

Entries

An introduction to Lloyd's 3.25.03
Statistics relating to Lloyd's 3.25.12
Lloyd's 3.25.75
Introduction to section 3.25

Council of Mortgage Lenders

3 Savile Row
London

W1X 1AF
Tel: *020 7437 0075*
Fax: *020 7434 3791*
Email: *info@cml.org.uk*
Web site: *http://www.cml.org.uk*

Entries

Mortgage law and practice manual 2.10.05
A regional analysis of mortgage possessions: causes, trends and future prospects
2.78.03
EMU and the UK housing and mortgage markets 2.78.03
Compendium of housing finance statistics 1997 2.78.12
CML directory of members 2.78.21
The official CML yearbook 99 2.78.21
CML market briefing 2.78.31
CML news & views 2.78.31
European mortgage review 2.78.31
Housing finance 2.78.31
Introduction to chapter 2
Introduction to section 2.35
Introduction to section 2.78
Introduction to section 2.78.01
Introduction to section 2.78.12

Craigdallie Publishing

East Wing
Naldretts
Mill Lane
Hurstpierpoint
West Sussex BN6 9HL
Tel: *01273 834732*

Entries

The PMI handbook: the annual review of the private medical insurance market
3.93.18

Credit Suisse First Boston

1 Cabot Square
London
E14 4QJ
Tel: *020 7888 8888*
Fax: *020 7888 1600*
Web site: *http://www.csfb.com*

Entries

Introduction to section 3.00.16

Croner.CCH Group

Croner House
London Road
Kingston upon Thames
Surrey
KT2 6SR
Tel: *020 8547 3333*
Fax: *020 8547 2638*
Email: *info@croner.co.uk*
Web site: *http://croner.co.uk*

Entries

Consumer protection in financial services 2.15.03
Handbook of insurance 3.00.05
The insurance buyer's guide: a guide to schemes, packages and unusual risks
3.00.18
The insurance register 3.00.21
Insuring foreign risks: a guide to regulations world-wide 3.02.12
Insurance contract law 3.10.05
Regulation of insurance in the United Kingdom and Ireland 3.15.05
Croner's Management of business risk 3.62.05
Reinsurance law 3.69.05
Handbook of motor insurance 3.86.05
Kluwer's Income protection insurance: the unique annual review 3.93.18
Croner's pensions compliance service 5.00.05

CSC Financial Services Group

423 London Road
Camberley
Surrey
GU15 3QP
Tel: *01276 686838*
Fax: *01276 411799*

Entries

Introduction to section 1.53.12

Datamonitor plc

106 Baker Street

London
W1M 1LA
Tel: *020 7316 0001*
Fax: *020 7675 7410*
Email: *pssales@datamonitor.com*
Web site: *http://www.datamonitor.com*

Entries

The insurance competitor intelligence service 3.00.16
Global finbase insurance 3.00.72
Introduction to section 1.00.12
Introduction to section 2.00.12
Introduction to section 2.02.12
Introduction to section 2.33.12
Introduction to section 2.75.12
Introduction to section 2.78.12
Introduction to section 3.00.12
Introduction to section 3.00.16
Introduction to section 3.02.12
Introduction to section 4.00.12
Introduction to section 5.00.12

Deloitte & Touche

Hill House
1 Little New Street
London
EC4A 3TR
Tel: *020 7936 3000*
Web site: *http://www.deloitte-touche.co.uk*

Entries

Introduction to section 3.15

Demos

The Mezzanine
Elizabeth House
39 York Road
London
SE1 7NQ
Tel: *020 7401 5330*
Fax: *020 7401 5331*
Email: *mail@demos.co.uk*
Web site: *http://www.demos.co.uk*

Entries

To our mutual advantage 2.35.03

Department of Social Security

Richmond House
79 Whitehall
London
SW1A 2NS
Tel: *020 7210 3000*
Web site: *http://www.dss.gov.uk*

Entries

Second tier pension provision 5.00.12

Dryden Press

Harcourt Publishers
Foots Cray High Street
Sidcup
Kent
DA14 5HP
Tel: *020 8308 5700*
Fax: *020 8308 5702*
Email: *cservice@harcourt.com*
Web site: *http://www.harcourt-international.com*

Entries

Bank management 2.50.03
Financial services marketing: a reader 2.56.03

Eclipse Group

18–20 Highbury Place
London
N5 1QP
Tel: *020 7354 6742*
Fax: *020 7226 8618*
Email: *publications@irseclipse.co.uk*
Web site: *http://www.irseclipse.co.uk*

Entries

Occupational pensions 5.00.31
Occupational pensions law reports 5.10.07

Economist Intelligence Unit

15 Regent Street
London
SW1Y 4LR
Tel: *020 7830 1007*
Fax: *020 7830 1023*
Email: *london@eiu.com*
Web site: *http://www.eiu.com*

Entries

Creating tomorrow's leading retail bank 2.33.12
Global investment banking strategy: insights from industry leaders 2.37.12

Economist Newspaper Ltd

25 St James' St
London
SW1A 1HG
Tel: *020 7830 7000*
Fax: *020 7839 2968*
Web site: *http://www.economist.com*

Entries

The economist 2.00.36

Edgar Hamilton & Wellard

City Reach
5 Greenwich View Place
Millharbour
London
E14 9NN
Tel: *020 7712 6000*
Fax: *020 7712 6001*

Entries

Marketing on a shoestring: the most comprehensive system to improve your business insurance 3.56.05

Edward Elgar Publishing Limited

Glensanda House
Montpellier Parade
Cheltenham
Gloucestershire

GL50 1UA
Tel: *01242 226934*
Fax: *01242 262111*
Email: *info@e-elgar.co.uk*
Web site: *http://www.e-elgar.co.uk*

Entries

An introduction to actuarial studies 1.07.03
Handbook of banking regulation and supervision in the United Kingdom 2.15.03

Elsevier Science Publishers BV

The Boulevard
Langford Lane
Kidlington
Oxford
Tel: *00 44 1865 843000*
Fax: *01865 843010*
Email: *niinfo-f@elsevier.nil*
Web site: *http://www.elsevier.com*

Entries

Journal of banking and finance 2.00.31
Elsevier's dictionary of insurance and risk prevention: in English, French, Spanish, German and Portuguese 3.02.24
Insurance: mathematics & economics 3.07.31
Advances in international banking and finance. Vol 3 2.02.03

Ernst & Young

Rolls House
7 Rolls Buildings
Fetter Lane
London
EC4A 1NH
Tel: *020 7928 2000*
Web site: *http://www.ernsty.co.uk*

Entries

Introduction to section 3.50

Euromoney Books

Nestor House
Playhouse Yard
London

EC4V 5EX
Tel: *020 7779 8544*
Fax: *020 7779 8541*
Email: *books@euromoneyplc.com*
Web site: *http://www.euromoneybooks.com*

Entries

Financial products: a survival guide 1.00.03
Investment banking: theory and practice 2.37.03
Understanding volatility and liquidity in the financial markets: building a comprehensive system of risk management 2.50.03

Euromoney Institutional Investor PLC

Nestor House
Playhouse Yard
Oakfield House
London
EC4V 5EX
Tel: *020 7779 8888*
Fax: *020 7 779 8407*
Email: *editor@euromoneyplc.com*
Web site: *http://www.euromoney.com*

Entries

Euromoney 2.02.31
Reinsurance 3.69.03
Reactions: the financial magazine for the global insurance market 3.69.31
Reactions 3.69.75
The directory of European fund management 4.02.21

European Central Bank

Postfach 16 03 19
D-60066 Frankfurt am Main
Germany
Tel: *+49 69 1344 0*
Fax: *+49 69 1344 6000*
Web site: *http://www.ecb.int*

Entries

Introduction to section 2.02.09

European Insurance Committee

See Comité Européen des Assurances.

European Mortgage Federation

14/2 avenue de la Joyeuse Entrée
1040 Brussels
Belgium
Tel: *+32 2 285 40 30*
Fax: *+32 2 285 40 31*
Email: *emfinfo@hypo.org*
Web site: *http://www.hypo.org*

Entries

Mortgage info 2.78.31
Quarterly figures 2000 2.78.31
Introduction to section 2.78.12

Evandale Publishing Ltd

Holborn Tower
137 High Holborn
London
WC1V 6PL
Tel: *020 7242 2500*
Fax: *020 7242 2526*
Email: *evandale@compuserve.com*

Entries

Retail finance direct 1.56.31
Virtual finance international 2.50.31
Evandale's London insurance market directory 3.00.21
Evandale insurance online 3.00.75
Evandale's directory of world underwriters 3.02.21
Insurance direct & interactive 3.56.31
The re report 3.69.31

Faculty of Actuaries

Maclaurin House
18 Dublin Street
Edinburgh
EH1 3PP
Tel: *0131 240 1300*
Fax: *0131 240 1313*
Email: *faculty@actuaries.org.uk*
Web site: *http://www.actuaries.org.uk*

Entries

The inside careers guide to actuaries 1.07.02
British actuarial journal: incorporating Journal of the Institute of Actuaries and Transactions of the Faculty of Actuaries 1.07.31
Introduction to section 1.07
Introduction to section 1.07.12
Introduction to section 3.00.16

Financial Ombudsman Service

See Banking Ombudsman Scheme; Insurance Ombudsman Bureau.

Financial Regulatory Briefing

2 Clifton Villas
London
W9 2PH
Tel: *020 7289 9784*
Fax: *020 7266 1991*
Web site: *http://www.frb.co.uk*

Entries

Financial regulatory briefing: the monthly digest of official pronouncements 1.10.31
Financial regulatory briefing 1.10.75

Financial Services Authority

25 North Colonnade
Canary Wharf
London
E14 5HS
Tel: *020 7676 3292*
Fax: *020 7676 1017*
Web site: *http://www.fsa.gov.uk*

Entries

FSA occasional paper 1.00.08
Consumer research 1.00.12
Financial Services Authority 1.10.75
Directory of consumer information and enquiry services in personal finance 2.00.21
Banking supervisory policy 2.15.05
A cost-benefit analysis of statutory regulation of mortgage advice 2.78.09
Introduction to section 1.10

Introduction to section 2.15
Introduction to section 3.15
Introduction to section 2.35.16
Introduction to section 2.78.01

Financial Services National Training Organisation

27–32 Poultry
London
EC2P 2BX
Tel: *020 7260 3742*
Fax: *020 7260 7272*
Web site: *http://www.fsnto.org*

Entries

Introduction to section 2.00.02

Financial Times

See also under FT.

Financial Times Business Limited

Maple House
149 Tottenham Court Road
London
W1P 9LL
Tel: *020 7896 2326*
Fax: *020 7896 2172*

Entries

Money management: the professional's independent adviser 1.00.31
Financial adviser 1.00.36
Daily adviser 1.00.78
The banker 2.00.31
Global insurance directory 3.02.21
Unit trust and OEICs year book 4.72.18
Executives' & directors' and top up pensions 5.00.18
Pensions management: the magazine for pensions professionals 5.00.31
Pensions week: first for pensions news 5.00.31
The pension schemes database UK & Europe 5.00.72
European pensions news 5.02.31
Group personal pensions 5.77.18
Personal pensions 5.77.18

Financial Times Limited

1 Southwark Bridge
London
SE1 9HL
Tel: *020 7873 3000*
Fax: *020 7407 5700*
Web site: *http://www.ft.com*
See also under FT.

Entries

FT Quicken: UK personal finance 1.00.75
Online banking: effective strategies for success 2.33.12
Financial Times 2.33.75

Financial Times Management

128 Long Acre
London
WC2E 9AN
Tel: *020 7447 2000*
Fax: *020 7240 5771*
Web site: *http://www.ftmanagement.com*

Entries

The Financial Times guide to using the financial pages 1.00.03
The Investor's Chronicle guide to investment and unit trusts 4.00.01
The investor's guide to picking the right unit trust: maximising performance with minimum risk 4.72.01

Financial Times Pitman

See Financial Times Management.

Fitch IBCA Limited

Eldon House
2 Eldon Street
London
EC2M 7UA
Tel: *020 7417 4222*
Fax: *020 7417 4242*
Web site: *http://www.fitchibca.com*

Entries

Market analysis of insurance companies: UK property/casualty & UK reinsurers 3.00.16

Flaxdale Printers Ltd

5 Malvern Drive
Woodford Green
Essex
IG8 0JR
Tel: *020 8504 6862*

Entries

Investment trusts 4.74.31

Fox-Pitt Kelton

35 Wilson Street
London
EC2M 2SI
Tel: *020 7377 8929*

Entries

Introduction to section 3.02.16

FT

See also under Financial Times.

FT Business

See Financial Times Business Limited.

FT Finance

Maple House
149 Tottenham Court Road
London
W1P 9LL
Tel: *020 7896 2279*
Fax: *020 7896 2274*
Email: *info.finance@ft.com*
Web site: *http://www.finance.ft.com*

Entries

FT virtual finance report 1.53.31

Online retail financial services 2.33.12
The future of the building society movement: a vibrant sector or a spent force?
2.35.12
Branding in retail financial services: capitalising on untapped value 2.56.12
Marketing strategies in retail banks: current trends and future prospects 2.56.12
The future of marketing retail financial services 2.56.12
Retail credit and banking fraud: fraud risk exposure in the retail credit industry
2.78.03
Introduction to section 1.00.12
Introduction to section 2.02.12
Introduction to section 3.00.12
Introduction to section 3.02.12
Introduction to section 4.00.12
Introduction to section 4.00.18
Introduction to section 5.00.12

FT Law & Tax

21–27 Lambs Conduit Street
London
WC1N 3NJ

Entries

Pensions: a practical guide 5.00.03
The role of the pension fund trustee 5.46.03

Fundaçion Mapfre Estudios

Monte del Pilar
s/n 28023
El Plantio
Madrid
Spain

Entries

Catalogo de obras de seguros y seguridad 3.02.26

GDP

See Gilmour Drummond Publishing.

Gee Publishing Limited

100 Avenue Road
Swiss Cottage
London

NW3 3PG
Tel: *020 7393 7400*
Fax: *020 7393 7463*

Entries

The financial adviser's factbook 1.00.05
The pensions factbook 5.00.05
Practical pensions precedents 5.00.07

General Insurance Market Research Association

C/o Derek Gibbens
AXA Provincial
Meridian Gate
Bute Terrace
Cardiff
CF1 2XA
Tel: *029 20239239*
Fax: *029 20238238*

Entries

Introduction to section 3.00.12

General Insurance Standards Council

Bankside Business Centre
3rd Floor
107–112 Leadenhall
London
EC3A 4AH
Tel: *020 7891 2558*
Fax: *020 7891 2559*
Web site: *http://www.gisc.co.uk*

Entries

Introduction to section 3.43

Geneva Association

See Association Internationale pour l'Etude de l'Economie de l'Assurance.

Gilmour Drummond Publishing

PO Box 187
Cambridge
CB1 4TL

Tel: *01223 508059*
Fax: *01223 511357*
Email: *ram21@dial.pipex.com*

Entries

Back office and beyond: a guide to procedures, settlements and risk in financial markets 2.50.03

Glenlake Publishing

1261 West Glenlake
Chicago
ILL 60660
United States
Email: *glenlake@ix.netcom.com*

Entries

International dictionary of banking and finance 1.02.24
Information technology and financial services: the new partnership 2.50.03
Managing the new bank technology: an executive blueprint for the future 2.50.03

Gower Publishing Limited

Gower House
Croft Road
Aldershot
Hampshire
Tel: *01252 331551*
Fax: *01252 344405*

Entries

Credit management handbook 2.78.03
The complete guide to business risk management 3.62.03

Gresham Books

PO Box 61
Henley-on-Thames
Oxfordshire RG9 3LQ
Tel: *01189 403 789*
Fax: *01189 403 789*
Email: *greshambks@aol.com*

Entries

Managing banking risks 2.50.03

Guardian Magazines

119 Farringdon Road
London
EC1R 3ER
Tel: *0870 870 1324*
Fax: *020 8289 7959*
Email: *money.observer@publishing-power.co.uk*

Entries

Money observer 1.00.31

Halifax plc

Trinity Road
Halifax
West Yorkshire
HX1 2RG
Tel: *01422 333333*
Web site: *http://www.halifax.co.uk*

Entries

Introduction to section 2.78

HarperCollins Publishers

77–85 Fulham Palace Road
Hammersmith
London
Tel: *020 8741 7070*
Fax: *020 8307 4440*

Entries

The Sunday Times personal finance guide to tax free savings: how to make your money work harder for you 1.00.01
The Sunday Times personal finance guide to the protection game: a straightforward guide to insurance 3.00.01

Harrington

International Centre
Spindle Way
Crawley
West Sussex
RH10 1TG
Tel: *01293 537003*

Fax: *01293 531105*

Entries

Prospect: for the professional financial adviser 1.00.31

Hart Publishing Ltd

Salter's Boatyard
Oxford
OX1 4LB
Tel: *01865 245533*
Fax: *01865 794882*
Email: *mail@hartpub.co.uk*

Entries

Insurance law: doctrines and principles 3.10.03

Hastie Publishing Ltd

6 Elder Street
London
E1 6BT
Tel: *020 7375 1226*
Fax: *020 7375 0689*
Email: *editor@theinsider.co.uk*
Web site: *http://www.theinsider.co.uk*

Entries

The insurance insider: insight and intelligence on the London insurance market 3.00.31

Hawksmere

12–18 Grosvenor Gardens
London
SW1W 0DH
Tel: *020 7824 8257*
Web site: *http://www.hawksmere.co.uk*

Entries

Public liability insurance: a Hawksmere report 3.84.03

Henry Stewart Publications

Russell House
28–30 Little Russell St

London
WC1A 2HN
Tel: *020 7404 3040*
Fax: *020 7404 2081*
Web site: *http://henrystewart.co.uk*

Entries

Journal of financial regulation and compliance: an international journal 1.10.31
Journal of financial services marketing 1.56.31
Derivatives use, trading & regulation 2.00.31
Journal of pensions management: an international journal 5.00.31

HMSO

See Stationery Office.

How To Books

3 Newtec Place
Magdalen Road
Oxford
Tel: *01865 793806*
Fax: *01865 248780*
Email: *info@howtobooks.co.uk*
Web site: *http://www.howtobooks.co.uk*

Entries

Saving and investing: how to achieve financial security and make your money grow 1.00.01
Getting into banking and finance: how to launch a rewarding career 2.00.02
Dealing with your bank: how to assert yourself as a paying customer 2.33.01
Money-saving mortgages: how to take years off a mortgage and save thousands of pounds 2.78.01
Arranging insurance: how to manage policies and claims for everyday personal and business purposes 3.00.01

IBC Business Publishing Ltd

69–77 Paul Street
London
EC2A 4LQ
Tel: *020 7553 1000*
Fax: *020 7553 1593*

Entries

Electronic banking and the law 2.10.03

Banking technology 2.50.31

IFA Association

41–43 Praed Street
London
W2 1NR
Tel: *020 7839 5152*
Fax: *020 7262 2675*
Web site: *http://ifaa.org.uk*

Entries

IFA contact: the official yearbook of the IFA magazine 1.00.18
The IFA magazine: the official magazine of the IFA Association 1.00.31

Incisive Research

39 Earlham Street
Covent Garden
London
WC2H 9LD
Tel: *020 7306 7117*
Fax: *020 7306 7112*

Entries

Financial marketing: strategic marketing across financial services 1.56.31
New media financial marketing: interactive marketing across financial services
1.56.31
Financial IT 2.50.31
Insurance technology report: information technology in the insurance industry
3.53.31

Industrial Society

Quadrant Court
49 Calthorpe Road
Edgbaston
Birmingham
B15 1TH
Tel: *0121 410 3000*
Fax: *0121 410 3333*
Email: *customercentre@indsoc.co.uk*
Web site: *http://www.indsoc.co.uk*

Entries

Banking and the City 2.00.02

Informa Publishing Group

Customer Services
Sheepen Place
Colchester
Essex
CO3 3LP
Tel: *01206 772277*
Fax: *01206 772771*

Entries

Planned savings: the business magazine for financial advisers 1.00.31
Financial technology bulletin 2.02.31
Financial regulation report 2.15.31
Insurance age: first choice of the insurance professional 3.00.31
The journal 3.00.31
Insurance day 3.00.36
Insurance age electronic 3.00.75
Insurance technology: the authority on insurance systems worldwide 3.53.31
International risk management 3.62.31
Risk financier: a monthly commentary on the convergence of the financial and insurance markets 3.64.31
The review: worldwide reinsurance 3.69.31
Health insurance: for the professional intermediary 3.93.31
Introduction to section 1.00.12
Introduction to section 2.33.12
Introduction to section 2.56.12
Introduction to section 2.72.12
Introduction to section 3.00.12

Institute for Fiscal Studies

7 Ridgmount Street
London
WC1E 7AE
Tel: *020 7291 4800*
Fax: *020 7323 4780*
Email: *mailbox@ifs.org.uk*
Web site: *http://www.ifs.org.uk*

Entries

Household saving in the UK 1.00.12

Institute of Actuaries

Staple Inn

High Holborn
London
WC1V 7QJ
Tel: *020 7632 2100*
Fax: *020 7632 2111*
Email: *institute@actuaries.org.uk*
Web site: *http://www.actuaries.org.uk*

Entries

The inside careers guide to actuaries 1.07.02
British actuarial journal: incorporating Journal of the Institute of Actuaries and Transactions of the Faculty of Actuaries 1.07.31
Introduction to section 1.07
Introduction to section 1.07.02
Introduction to section 1.07.12

Institute of Chartered Accountants in England and Wales

Chartered Accountants' Hall
PO Box 433
London
EC2P 2BJ
Tel: *020 7920 8100*
Fax: *020 7920 8547*
Web site: *http://www.icaew.co.uk/*

Entries

Introduction to section 5.54

Institute of Credit Management

The Water Mill
Station Road
South Luffenham
Oakham
Leicestershire
LE15 8NB
Tel: *01780 722900*
Web site: *http://www.icm.org.uk*

Entries

Journal of credit management 2.78.31

Institute of Financial Services

See Chartered Institute of Bankers.

Institute of London Underwriters

See International Underwriting Association of London.

Institute of Risk Management

Lloyd's Avenue House
6 Lloyd's Avenue
London
EC3N 3AX
Tel: *020 7709 9808*
Fax: *020 7709 0716*
Email: *irm@figtree.co.uk*
Web site: *http://www.figtree.co.uk/irm*

Entries

Introduction to section 3.62

Insurance Brokers Registration Council

Higham Business Centre
Midland Road
Higham Ferrers
Northamptonshire
NN10 8DW
Tel: *01933 359083*
Fax: *01933 359077*

Entries

*The list: established under section 4 of the Insurance Brokers (Registration) Act
1977* 3.43.21
*The register: established under section 2 of the Insurance Brokers (Registration)
Act 1977* 3.43.21
Introduction to section 3.43

Insurance Institute of London

20 Aldermanbury
London
EC2V 7HY
Tel: *020 7600 1343*
Fax: *020 7600 6857*

Web site: *http://www.iilondon.co.uk*

Entries

The Insurance Institute of London 3.00.75
Introduction to section 3.00.08

Insurance Ombudsman Bureau

South Quay Plaza
183 Marsh Wall
London
E14 9SR
Tel: *020 7964 1400*
Fax: *020 7964 0459*
Email: *technical.advice@financial-ombudsman.org.uk*
Web site: *http://www.theiob.org.uk*

Now part of the new Financial Ombudsman Service.

Entries

Digest of annual reports and bulletins: 1981–1995 3.68.05

Insurance Personnel Selection

Lloyd's Avenue House
6 Lloyd's Avenue
London
EC3N 3ES
Tel: *020 7481 8111*
Fax: *020 7481 0994*
Email: *enquiries@ipsgroup.co.uk*
Web site: *http://ipsgroup.co.uk*

Entries

Introduction to section 3.50.12

Insurance Publishing & Printing Company

7 Stourbridge Road
Lye
Stourbridge
West Midlands
DY9 7DG
Tel: *01384 895228*
Fax: *01384 893666*

Entries

The insurance manual 3.00.05
Insurance brokers' monthly & insurance adviser 3.43.31

Insurance Research & Publishing Ltd

9 High Beech Road
Loughton
Essex
IG10 4BN
Tel: *020 8508 8088*
Fax: *020 8502 5201*
Email: *info@insurance-research.com*
Web site: *http://www.insurance-research.com*

Entries

Introduction to section 3.00.12

Insurance Tax Review

Cobwebs
West Hill
Elstead
Godalming
Surrey
GU8 6DQ
Tel: *01252 702758/0976 749253*
Fax: *01252 703908*

Entries

Insurance tax review 3.17.31

International Benefits Information Service

250 S Wacker Drive
Suite 600
Chicago
IL60606-5834
United States
Tel: *+1 312 993 7900*
Fax: *+1 312 993 7910*
Email: *ibisnet@mindspring.com*
Web site: *http://ibisnews.com*

Entries

IBIS briefing service 5.02.12
IBIS review 5.02.31
IBIS online!: access to international employee benefits information 5.02.75

International Monetary Fund

700 19th Street NW
Washington
DC20431
United States
Tel: *+1 202 623 7000*
Fax: *+1 202 623 4661*
Web site: *http://www.imf.org*

Entries

Bank soundness and macroeconomic policy 2.02.09
Banking soundness and monetary policy: issues and experiences in the global economy 2.02.09
Systemic bank restructuring and macroeconomic policy: papers presented at the seventh Seminar on Central Banking, Washington DC, January 27–31 1997 2.02.09
International financial statistics 2.02.31
Introduction to section 2.02.09

International Research Services

PO Box 455
Lake Forest
Illinois 60045
United States
Tel: *+1 847 234 4762*
Fax: *+1 847 295 2608*
Email: *irl@isn-inc.com*

Entries

Insurance research letter 3.02.31

International Thomson Business Press

Berkshire House
168–173 High Holborn
London
WC1V 7AA
Tel: *020 7497 1422*

Fax: *020 7497 1426*
Email: *itbp@itpuk.co.uk*
Web site: *http://www.itbp.com*

Entries

The virtual banking revolution: the customer, the bank and the future 2.33.03

International Underwriting Association of London

London Underwriting Centre
3 Minister Court
Mincing Lane
London
EC3R 7DD
Tel: *020 7617 4444*
Fax: *020 7617 4440*
Email: *info@iua.co.uk*
Web site: *http://www.iua.co.uk*

Entries

Reinsurance clauses 3.69.07
Reinsurance clauses 3.69.07
Reinsurance statistics: London reinsurance company market 3.69.12
Marine report and statistics 3.87.12
IUA of London: International Underwriting Association 3.87.75
Introduction to section 3.00.07
Introduction to section 3.69
Introduction to section 3.87
Introduction to section 3.91

Internet Handbooks

Unit 5
Dolphin Building
Queen Anne's Battery
Plymouth
PL4 0LP
Tel: *01752 262626*
Fax: *01752 262641*
Email: *post@internet-handbooks.co.uk*
Web site: *http://www.internet-handbooks.co.uk*

Entries

Personal finance on the Internet: a practical guide to savings, banking, investment, loans, insurance, pensions and tax 2.00.01

JAI Press

See Elsevier Science Publishers BV.

Jim Bannister Developments

Bridge House
181 Queen Victoria Street
London
EC4V 4DD
Tel: *020 7248 1084*
Fax: *020 7248 1082*
Web site: *http://www.jbdltd.co.uk*

Entries

UK non life insurance industry: results... 3.00.16
The Jim Bannister report: covers all that matters in insurance 3.00.31

John Murray (Publishers) Ltd

50 Albemarle Street
London
W1
Tel: *020 7493 4361*
Fax: *020 7499 1792*

Entries

Success in investment 1.00.03

John Wiley & Sons Ltd

Baffins Lane
Chichester
West Sussex
PO19 1UD
Tel: *01243 779777*
Fax: *01243 770144*
Email: *ctownley@wiley.co.uk; ferris@wiley.co.uk*

Entries

Modern banking in theory and practice 2.00.03
Risk management in banking 2.50.03

Getting started in unit and investment trusts 4.00.01

Joint Money Laundering Steering Group

Pinners Hall
105–108 Old Broad Street
London
EC2N 1EX
Tel: *020 7216 8863*
Fax: *020 7216 8908*

Entries

Money laundering: guidance notes for the financial sector 2.10.03

Jordans

21 St Thomas Street
Bristol
BS1 6JS
Tel: *0117 923 0600*
Fax: *0117 925 0486*
Email: *customerservice@jordanpublishing.co.uk*
Web site: *http://www.jordanpublishing.co.uk*

Entries

Pension disputes: prevention and resolution 5.10.03

Key Note Publications

Field House
72 Oldfield Road
Hampton
Middlesex
TW12 2HQ
Tel: *020 8481 8750*
Fax: *020 8783 0049*
Web site: *http://www.keynote.co.uk*

Entries

Introduction to section 1.00.12
Introduction to section 2.33.12
Introduction to section 2.78.12
Introduction to section 3.00.12

Kluwer

For looseleafs see Croner.CCH Group.

Kluwer Academic Publishers Group

Spuiboulevard 50
PO Box 989
3300 AZ Dordrecht
Netherlands
Tel: *00 31 78 6392392*
Fax: *00 31 78 6183273*

Entries

Journal of financial services research 1.00.31
The Geneva papers on risk and insurance theory 1.07.31
Proceedings of the International Conference on Risk Management and Regulation in Banking (1997) 2.02.03

Kluwer Law International

Sterling House
66 Winton Road
London
SW1V 1DE
Tel: *020 7233 5729*
Fax: *020 7233 5723*
Email: *enquiries@kluwerlaw.co.uk*
Web site: *http://www.kluwerlaw.com*

Entries

Financial services and EC law: materials and cases 1.10.07
European financial services law 1.10.31
Journal of international insurance 3.02.31
Insurance and EC law: commentary 3.10.05
International encyclopaedia of laws. Insurance law 3.10.05

Kogan Page

120 Pentonville Road
London
N1 9JN
Tel: *020 7278 0433*
Fax: *020 7837 6348*
Email: *kpinfo@kogan-page.co.uk*

Entries

The Daily Telegraph guide to lump sum investment 1.00.01
An A-Z of finance: a jargon-free guide to investment and the City 1.00.24
Careers in banking and finance 2.00.02
The rise and fall of the merchant bank: the evolution of the global investment bank 2.37.03
Slash your mortgage 2.78.01

KPMG Peat Marwick McLintock

Distribution Centre
Unit 2, Odhams Trading Estate
St Albans Road
Watford, Herts
WD2 5RE
Tel: *01923 214 805*
Web site: *http://www.kpmg.co.uk*

Entries

Introduction to section 3.50

Lafferty Publications

IDA Tower
Pearse Street
Dublin 2
Ireland
Tel: *00 353 1 671 8022*
Fax: *00 353 1 671 8240*
Email: *cuserv@lafferty.ie*
Web site: *http://www.lafferty.co.uk*

Entries

Financial services distribution 1.56.31
E-commerce@lafferty.com 1.56.75
European banker 2.00.31
Retail banker international 2.33.31
Bank marketing international 2.56.31
Cards international 2.72.31
Electronic payments international 2.72.31
Life insurance international: the industry bulletin on life, health and pensions 3.91.31
Funds international 4.02.31
Introduction to section 1.00.12
Introduction to section 2.00.12

Introduction to section 2.02.12
Introduction to section 2.33.12
Introduction to section 2.56.12
Introduction to section 2.75.12
Introduction to section 3.02.12

Laing & Buisson Publications Ltd

29 Angel Gate
City Road
London
EC1V 2PT
Tel: *020 7833 9123*
Fax: *020 7833 9129*

Entries

Private medical insurance: UK market sector report 3.93.12

Life Assurance Market Research Association

C/o Chris Found
Friends Provident Life Office
Warner House
Castle Street
Salisbury
Wiltshire SP1 3SH
Tel: *01722 311617*

Entries

Introduction to section 3.91.12

Life Insurance Association

Citadel House
Chorleywood
Rickmansworth
Herts
WD3 5PF
Tel: *01923 285333*
Fax: *01923 285 395*
Web site: *http://www.lia.co.uk*

Entries

Prospect: for the professional financial adviser 1.00.31

Life Insurance Marketing and Research Association European Region

See LIMRA Europe Ltd.

LIMRA Europe Ltd

34 Claredon Road
Watford
WD1 1JJ
Tel: *01923 226178*
Fax: *01923 236561*

Entries

Insurance dictionary 3.91.24
Introduction to section 3.91.12

Lipper

The Towers
Park Green
Macclesfield
Cheshire
SK11 7NG
Tel: *01625 511311*
Fax: *01625 616616*
Email: *media.relations@lipper.reuters.com*
Web site: *http://www.lipper.reuters.com*

Entries

Statspack 1.00.18
Hindsight 1.00.72

Lloyd's

See Corporation of Lloyd's.

Lloyd's Aviation Underwriters' Association

Room 662
1 Lime Street
London
EC3M 7HA
Tel: *020 7327 4045*
Fax: *020 7327 4711*

Entries

Standard policy forms, proposal forms and clauses, etc 3.88.07

Lloyd's of London Press

See LLP Professional Publishing.

Lloyd's Underwriters' Non-Marine Association Limited

Suite 732
1 Lime Steet
London
EC3M 7DQ
Tel: *020 7327 4931*
Fax: *020 7623 9390*

Entries

UK & overseas policy forms 3.00.07
USA & Canada policy forms 3.00.07
Introduction to section 3.00.07
Introduction to section 3.25

LLP Professional Publishing

Customer Services
Sheepen Place
Colchester
Essex
CO3 3LP
Tel: *01206 772277*
Fax: *01206 772771*
Web site: *http://www.llplimited.com*

Entries

Banks and remedies 2.10.03
Introduction to insurance 3.00.03
Financial Times world insurance policy guide 3.00.18
London market newsletter 3.00.31
LLP 3.00.75
International insurance directory 3.02.21
European insurance market 3.02.31
World insurance report 3.02.31
The law of insurance contracts 3.10.03
Compendium of insurance law 3.10.07

EC insurance directives 3.10.07
Lloyd's law reports. Insurance & reinsurance 3.10.07
The international journal of insurance law 3.10.31
The electronic insurance law service 3.10.72
Insurance M&A report 3.22.31
Insurance security watch 3.23.31
Lloyd's acts, byelaws and regulations 3.25.07
Insurance intermediaries: law and regulation 3.43.05
How to manage risk 3.62.03
Alternative insurance capital 3.64.31
Insurance disputes 3.68.05
The nuts and bolts of reinsurance 3.69.03
Reinsurance practice and the law 3.69.05
The AIDA RWP reports 3.69.08
Construction insurance and UK construction contracts 3.73.03
Personal lines insurance 3.75.31
Catastrophe reinsurance newsletter 3.77.31
Liability, risk and insurance 3.84.31
Marine insurance legislation 3.87.07
Marine insurance bulletin 3.87.31
P&I international: incorporating Marine insurance report 3.87.31
Maritime risk 3.87.31
Aerospace risk: serving the aerospace insurance and law professional 3.88.31
Introduction to section 3.25

Lodge Information Services

Slough Lane
Danbury
Essex
CM3 4LX
Tel: *01245 227828*
Fax: *01245 227019*
Email: *WIN@LISLtd.co.uk*

Entries

Weekly insurance news 3.00.31

London Financial News Publishing Ltd

29 Scrutton Street
London
EC2
Tel: *020 7739 7523*

Entries

Financial news 2.37.36

London Insurance and Reinsurance Market Association

See International Underwriting Association of London.

London International Insurance and Reinsurance Market Association

See International Underwriting Association of London.

Longman Group UK Ltd

Longman House
Burnt Mill
Harlow
Essex
Tel: *01279 426721*

Entries

EC insurance law 3.10.03
The law of insurance broking 3.43.03

Macmillan Press Ltd

25 Eccleston Place
London
SW1W 9NF
Tel: 020 7881 8000
Fax: 020 7881 8001

Entries

An introduction to global financial markets 1.00.03
Finance and financial markets 1.00.03
Who's who in the City: incorporating Beckett's directory 1.00.21
The recent evolution of financial systems 2.00.03
The big four British banks 2.33.03
Leadership in financial services: lessons for the future 2.50.03
The commercial banking handbook: strategic planning for growth in the new decade 2.50.03
Marketing financial services 2.56.03
A guide to insurance management 3.50.03

Manchester University Press

Oxford Road
Manchester
M13 9NR
Tel: *0161 273 5539*
Fax: *0161 274 3346*
Email: *mup@man.ac.uk*
Web site: *http://www.manchesteruniversitypress.co.uk*

Entries

The UK financial system: theory and practice 2.00.03

Market Assessment International

Field House
72 Oldfield Road
Hampton
TW12 2HQ
Tel: *020 8481 8710*
Fax: *020 8783 0310*

Entries

Introduction to section 1.00.12
Introduction to section 2.00.12
Introduction to section 2.02.12
Introduction to section 2.33.16
Introduction to section 2.35.12
Introduction to section 4.00.12
Introduction to section 5.00.12

Marshall & Swift

39A Southampton Road
Ringwood
Hampshire
BH24 1HE

Entries

Winning strategies for negotiating claims 3.68.03

Matrix-Data Ltd

Gossard House
7–8 Savile Row
London

W1X 1AF
Tel: *020 7734 8334*
Fax: *020 7734 8324*

Entries

The Matrix directory of independent financial advisers 1.43.21

Matthew Bender & Co, Inc.

1275 Broadway
Albany
NY 12204-2694
United States
Tel: *+1 800 833 9844*
Fax: *+1 518 487 3584*
Web site: *http://www.bender.coms*

Entries

Benedict on admiralty 3.87.07

McGraw-Hill

McGraw-Hill House
Shoppenhangers Road
Maidenhead
Berkshire
SL6 2QL
Tel: *01628 502500*
Fax: *01628 770224*
Web site: *http://www.mcgraw-hill.co.uk*

Entries

Global capital markets and banking 2.02.03
Fundamentals of financial institutions management 2.50.03

McHattie Group

Clifton Heights
Triangle West
Bristol
BS8 1EJ
Tel: *0117 925 8882*
Fax: *0117 925 4441*
Email: *mchattie@tipsheets.co.uk*

Entries

Investment trusts newsletter 4.74.31

Merlin Scott Associates

Dunselma Castle
Strone
Dunoon
Argyll
PA23 8RU
Tel: *01369 840643*

Entries

Insurance intermediaries (home counties) 3.43.16

Merrill Lynch & Co.

20 Farringdon Road
London
EC1M 3NH
Tel: *020 7867 2676*

Entries

Introduction to section 3.00.16

Micropal

See Standard & Poor's Micropal.

Millennium Group

Dolphin House
St Peter Street
Winchester
SO23 8BW
Tel: *01962 829729*
Fax: *01962 842388*
Email: *admin@millenn.co.uk*

Entries

Introduction to section 1.00.12

Mintel International Group Limited

18–19 Long Lane
London

EC1A 9HE
Tel: *020 7606 6000*
Fax: *020 7606 5932*
Email: *enquiries@mintel.co.uk*
Web site: *http://www.mintel.co.uk*

Entries

Introduction to section 1.00.12
Introduction to section 2.33.12
Introduction to section 2.56.12
Introduction to section 2.75.12
Introduction to section 2.78.12
Introduction to section 3.00.12
Introduction to section 5.00.12

Mitre House Publishing

The Clifton Centre
110 Clifton Street
London
EC2A 4HD
Tel: *020 7729 6644*

Entries

IFA review: the magazine for the professional adviser 1.00.31
Financial systems 1.53.31
General insurance 3.00.31
Insurance international 3.02.31

Money Marketing

50 Poland Street
London
W1V 4AX
Tel: *020 7943 8000*
Fax: *020 7970 4397*
Email: *moneym@dial.pipex.com*
Web site: *http://www.moneymarketing.co.uk*
Part of Centaur Communications Ltd.

Entries

Money marketing focus: the professional adviser's guide 1.00.31
Money marketing: first for the professional financial adviser 1.00.36
IFAresearcher 1.00.72
Money marketing on-line 1.00.75

Moneyfacts

Moneyfacts House
66–70 Thorpe Road
Norwich
Norfolk
NR1 1BJ
Tel: *01603 476476*
Fax: *01603 476477*
Email: *Mfacts@dircon.co.uk*
Web site: *http://www.mfacts.dircon.co.uk*

Entries

Life & pensions & unit trusts moneyfacts: the monthly manual of life, pensions and collective investments 1.00.18

Monitor Press

Monitor Press
Suffolk House
Church Field Road
Sudbury
Suffolk
CO10 2YA
Tel: *01787 378607*
Fax: *01787 880201*
Email: *enquiries@monitorpress.co.uk*
Web site: *http://www.monitorpress.co.uk*

Entries

Insurance law monthly 3.10.31

Moody's Investors Service, Inc.

2 Minster Court
Mincing Lane
London
EC3R 7XB
Web site: *http://www.moodys.com*

Entries

Moody's credit opinions. Insurance: insurance holding companies, life & health insurers, property & casualty insurers... 3.02.16
Moody's Investors Service. Insurance 3.02.75
Moody's Lloyd's syndicate rating guide 3.25.16
Moody's credit opinions & statistical handbook. UK life insurance 3.91.16

Introduction to section 3.02.16

MSM International Ltd

Thames House
18 Park Street
London
SE1 9ER
Tel: *020 7378 7131*
Fax: *020 7234 0702*

Entries

Insurance times: the general insurance industry's largest circulating weekly news-paper 3.00.36
Professional pensions yearbook 5.00.21
Professional pensions 5.00.36
Professional pensions: the pension site 5.00.75

Munich Reinsurance Company

107 Königstrasse
D-80791 München
Germany
Tel: *+49 89 38 91 0*
Fax: *+49 89 39 90 56*
Email: *info@munichre.com*
Web site: *http://munichre.com*

Entries

Introduction to section 3.00.08

MWD Administration

Technical Services
Lloyd's Policy Signing Office
Gun Wharf
Chatham
Kent
ME4 4TU
Tel: *01634 392000*
Fax: *01634 830275*

Entries

Market wordings database 3.00.72

National Association of Pension Funds Ltd

12–18 Grosvenor Gardens
London
SW1W 0DH
Tel: *020 7730 0585*
Fax: *020 7730 2595*
Web site: *http://www.napf.co.uk*

Entries

Annual survey of occupational pension schemes 5.00.12
NAPF year book: a guide to the National Association of Pension Funds Limited
5.00.21
Pensions world 5.00.31
Dictionary of international benefits terminology 5.02.24
Introduction to chapter 5

National Consumer Council

20 Grosvenor Gardens
London
SW1W ODH
Tel: *020 7730 3469*
Fax: *020 7730 0191*
Email: *info@ncc.org.uk*
Web site: *http://www.ncc.org.uk*

Entries

Savings and investments for low-income consumers 2.75.12
Introduction to section 2.33.01

Nationwide Building Society

Nationwide Building Society
Nationwide House
Pipers Way
Swindon
SN38 1NW
Tel: *457 30 20 10*
Email: *customer.services@nationwide.co.uk*

Entries

Introduction to section 2.78

New Hampshire Publishing

Kemp House
152–160 City Road
London
EC1V 2NX
Tel: *020 7588 5887*
Fax: *020 7256 6663*

Entries

Personal insurance digest 3.75.31

Non-Marine Association

See Lloyd's Underwriters' Non-Marine Association Limited.

Northern Rock plc

Northern Rock House
Gosforth
Newcastle-upon-Tyne
NE3 4PL
Tel: *019 285 7191*
Web site: *http://www.nrock.co.uk*

Entries

Introduction to section 2.78

NTC Publications Limited

PO Box 69
Henley-on-Thames
Oxfordshire
RG9 1GB
Tel: *01491 574671*
Fax: *01491 571188*

Entries

The financial services pocket book 1.00.12
Insurance pocket book 3.00.12
Pensions pocket book 5.00.05

Oak Tree Press

Oak Tree Press
Merrion Building

Lower Merrion Street
Dublin 2
Tel: *+353 1 676 1600*
Fax: *+353 1 676 1644*
Email: *oaktreep@iol.ie*
Web site: *http://www.oaktreepress.com*

Entries

Internal controls in banking 2.50.03

Ocarina Publishing

Bridge House
181 Queen Victoria Street
London
EC4V 4DD
Tel: *020 7248 5959*
Fax: *020 7248 6633*

Entries

Digest of Lloyd's news: the monthly review of news for members of Lloyd's and their advisers 3.25.31

Occupational Pensions Regulatory Authority

Invicta House
Trafalgar Place
Brighton
BN1 4DW
Tel: *01273 627600*
Fax: *01273 627688*
Email: *helpdesk@opra.gov.uk*
Web site: *http://www.opra.gov.uk*

Entries

OPRA online 5.00.75
Introduction to section 5.10

Oceana Publications, Inc.

75 Main St
Dobbs Ferry
NY 10522
United States
Tel: *+1 914 693 8100*
Fax: *+1 914 693 0402*

Email: *info@oceanalaw.com*
Web site: *http://www.oceanalaw.com*

Entries

International insurance law and regulation 3.10.05

OECD Publications

2 rue André-Pascal
75775 Paris
Cedex 16
France
In the UK OECD publications can be ordered from the Stationery Office,
q.v.

Entries

Bank profitability: financial statements of banks 1999 2.02.09
Insurance statistics yearbook 3.02.12
Introduction to section 2.02.09

Office for National Statistics

1 Drummond Gate
London
SW1V 2QQ
Tel: *020 7533 6363*
Fax: *020 7533 5719*
Web site: *http://www.ons.gov.uk*

Entries

Insurance companies', pension funds' and trusts' investments 3.00.12
Introduction to section 3.50.12

Office for Official Publications of the European Communities

2 rue Mercier
2985 Luxembourg
Luxembourg
Tel: *+352 499281*
Fax: *+352 488573*
Email: *info-info-opoce@cec.eu.int*
Web site: *http://www.eur-op.eu.int*
For UK agents see Stationery Office.

Entries

Banking in Europe: data 1994–1997 2.00.09

Office of Fair Trading

Fleetbank House
2–6 Salisbury Square
London
EC4Y 8JX
Tel: *0870 6060 321*
Fax: *020 7211 8800*
Email: *enquiries@oft.gov.uk*
Web site: *http://www.ons.gov.uk*

Entries

Mortgage repayment methods: a report by the Office of Fair Trading 2.78.09
Introduction to section 2.78.01

Old Bailey Press

200 Greyhound Road
London
W14
Tel: *020 7385 3377*
Fax: *020 7381 3377*
Email: *OBP@HLTpublications.co.uk*

Entries

Introduction to financial services: the giving of financial advice 1.43.03

Organisation for Economic Co-operation and Development

See OECD Publications.

Oxford University Press

Great Clarendon Street
Oxford OX2 6DP
Tel: *01865 556767*
Fax: *01865 556646*
Email: *enquiry@oup.co.uk*
Web site: *http://www.oup.co.uk*

Entries

A dictionary of finance and banking 1.00.24
The review of financial studies 1.00.31
The handbook of international financial terms 1.02.24
Global banking 2.02.03
Universal banking: international comparisons and theoretical perspectives 2.02.03
Virtual money: understanding the power and risks of money's high-speed journey into electronic space 2.72.03
Policies and perceptions of insurance: an introduction to insurance law 3.10.03
The law of marine insurance 3.87.03
The legal nature of the unit trust 4.72.03
Pension schemes and pension funds in the United Kingdom 5.00.03
Pension funds: retirement-income security and capital markets: an international perspective 5.02.03

Pageant Media Limited

35–37 William Road
London
NW1 3ER
Tel: *020 7388 4444*
Fax: *020 7388 3277*
Email: *info@pageantmedia.com*

Entries

Captive review: your essential guide to the captive insurance industry: news, views, interviews and updates from around the globe 3.37.31

PBI Newmedia Ltd

Arnold House
36–41 Holywell Lane
London
EC2A 3SF
Tel: *020 7827 5484*

Entries

Mortgage introducer 2.78.31
Unit trust & OEIC handbook 4.72.18
The investment trust handbook 4.74.18

Pearson Education

128 Long Acre

London
WC2E 9AN
Tel: *020 7379 7383*
Fax: *020 7240 5771*
Email: *customer.enquiries@pearsoned-ema.com*
Web site: *http://www.pearsoned-ema.com*

Entries

Financial services marketing 1.56.03
Directory of financial sites on the Internet 2.00.24
Dictionary of banking 2.00.24
The banking revolution: salvation or slaughter?: how technology is creating winners and losers 2.50.03
Dictionary of insurance 3.00.24
The Allied Dunbar pensions handbook 5.00.03

Peat Marwick McLintock

See KPMG Peat Marwick McLintock.

Penguin Books Ltd

27 Wrights Lane
London
W8 5TZ
Tel: *020 7416 3000*
Fax: *020 7416 3099*

Entries

Be your own financial adviser 1.00.01
The money machine: how the City works 1.00.03
All that glitters: the fall of Barings 2.37.03

Pension Schemes Office

Yorke House
PO Box 62
Castle Meadow Road
Nottingham
NG1 1BG
Tel: *0115 974 0000*
Fax: *0115 974 1480*

Entries

Practice notes on approval of occupational pension schemes 5.17.07
Introduction to section 5.17

Pensions Management Institute

PMI House
4–10 Artillery Lane
London
E1 7LS
Tel: *020 7247 1452*
Fax: *020 7375 0603*
Email: *enquiries@pensions-pmi.org.uk*
Web site: *http://www.pensions-pmi.org.uk*

Entries

Pensions terminology: a glossary for pension schemes 5.00.24
Introduction to chapter 5
Introduction to section 5.00.03

Pensions Publications Ltd

East Wing
4th Floor
Hope House
45 Great Peter Street
London
SW1P 3LT
Tel: *020 7222 0288*
Fax: *020 7799 2163*
Email: *subscriptions@benecompintl.com*
Web site: *http://www.benecompintl.com*

Entries

Benefits & compensation international: total remuneration and pension invest-
ment 5.02.31

Perpetuity Press

PO Box 376
Leicester
LE2 3ZZ
Tel: *0116 270 4186*
Fax: *0116 270 7742*
Email: *info@perpetuitypress.co.uk*
Web site: *http://www.perpetuitypress.co.uk*

Entries

Risk management: an international journal 3.62.31

Perspective Publishing

408 Fruit & Wool Exchange
Brushfield Street
London
E1 6EP
Tel: *020 7426 0101*
Fax: *020 7426 0123*

Entries

Financial sector technology 2.50.31
Corporate insurance & risk 3.71.31
Pensions age 5.00.31

Peter Collins Publishing

1 Cambridge Road
Teddington
Middlesex
Tel: *020 8943 3386*

Entries

Dictionary of banking and finance 2.00.24

Pitman Publishing

See Pearson Education.

Plimsoll Publishing Ltd

The Vanguard Suite
Broadcasting House
Middlesbrough
TS1 5JA
Tel: *01642 257800*
Fax: *01642 257806*
Email: *plimsoll@dial.pipex.com*
Web site: *http://www.plimsoll.co.uk*

Entries

Insurance 3.00.16
Insurance brokers etc 3.43.16

Pressfactory

1–1a Brockley Cross Business Centre

96 Endwell Road
London
SE4 2PD
Tel: *020 7635 8886*
Fax: *020 7277 6911*

Entries

IT professional in finance 1.53.31

PricewaterhouseCoopers

Southwark Towers
32 London Bridge Street
London
SE1 9SY
Tel: *020 7804 7083*
Web site: *http://www.pwcglobal.com*

Entries

Financial services survey 1.00.12
Creating tomorrow's leading retail bank 2.33.12
Introduction to section 2.33
Introduction to section 3.15
Introduction to section 3.18
Introduction to section 3.50

Professional & Business Information Publishing

5th Floor
12–18 Paul Street
London
EC2A 4NX

Entries

Building societies yearbook 2.35.21

Professional Briefing

187 Baslow Road
Totley
Sheffield
S17 4DT
Tel: *0114 235 1347*
Fax: *0114 235 0878*

Email: *info@probrief.com*
Web site: *http://www.probrief.com*

Entries

Professional Briefing: briefing pack 1.00.05

Profile Books

58a Hatton Garden
London
EC1N 8LX
Tel: *020 7404 3001*
Fax: *020 7404 3003*
Web site: *http://www.profilebooks.co.uk*

Entries

International dictionary of finance 1.02.24

RD Publications Ltd

11 Westferry Circus
London
E14 4HE
Tel: *020 7715 8000*
Web site: *http://www.readersdigest.co.uk*

Entries

Moneywise: Britain's best-selling personal finance magazine 1.00.31
Moneywise personal finance 1.00.75

Reactions

See Euromoney Institutional Investor PLC.

Readers Digest

See RD Publications Ltd.

Reed Business Information

Quadrant House
The Quadrant
Sutton
Surrey
SM2 5AS
Tel: *020 8652 3152*
Fax: *020 8652 8932*

Web site: *http://www.reedinfo.co.uk*

Entries

The bankers' almanac 2.00.21
UK clearings directory: a directory of offices of banks and other financial institutions participating in the payment clearings operations under the auspices of APACS 2.33.21

Reed Information Services

East Grinstead House
East Grinstead
West Sussex
RH19 1XA
Tel: *01342 335 671*
Fax: *01342 335 612*

Entries

Bankers almanac world ranking 2000 2.02.12
Bank sorting code numbers 1999 2.33.12

Regent Publications Limited

30 Cannon Street
London
EC4M 6YJ
Tel: *020 7618 3456*
Fax: *020 7618 3420*
Email: *info@globalreinsurance.com*
Web site: *http://www.globalreinsurance.com*

Entries

Global reinsurance 3.69.31
Global reinsurance news service network 3.69.75

Research Department Limited

Financial Research Centre
Haddenham Aerodrome
Haddenham
Nr Aylesbury
HP17 8LJ
Tel: *01844 295454*
Fax: *01844 295555*
Email: *enquiries@trd.co.uk*
Web site: *http://www.trd.co.uk*

Entries

The savings market 1.00.18
Policygen 3.00.72

Reuters Group PLC

85 Fleet Street
London
EC4P 4AJ
Tel: *020 7250 1122*
Web site: *http://www.reuters.com*

Entries

Reuters 2.50.75
Reuters insurance briefing 3.00.78
Introduction to section 1.00.12
Introduction to section 1.00.78
Introduction to section 2.00.12
Introduction to section 3.00.12
Introduction to section 3.02.12
Introduction to section 4.00.12

Rhine Re

London Underwriting Centre
3 Minster Court
Mincing Lane
London
EC3R 7DD
Tel: *020 7617 6150*
Fax: *020 7617 6151*

Entries

UK non life insurance industry: results... 3.00.16

Risk & Insurance Research Group

44 Maiden Lane
Covent Garden
London
WC2E 7LJ
Tel: *020 7836 0614*
Fax: *020 7379 6355/8335*
Email: *rirg@rirg.co.uk*

Entries

Global insurance bulletin: incorporating Worldwide insurance abstracts 3.02.31
Captive insurance company review 3.37.31
The international broker 3.43.31
Foresight: the journal of risk management 3.62.31

Risk Books

Risk Books
Haymarket House
28–29 Haymarket
London
SW1Y 4RX
Tel: *020 74849700*
Web site: *http://www.riskbooks.com*

Entries

Credit risk: models and management 2.78.03
Internal credit risk models: capital allocation and performance measurement 2.78.03
Credit 2.78.31
Introduction to section 2.50.03

Routledge

11 New Fetter Lane
London
EC4P 4EE
Tel: *020 75839855*
Email: *info@routledge.co.uk*
Web site: *http://www.routledge.co.uk*

Entries

Applied financial economics 2.00.31

Royal & SunAlliance

1 Bartholomew Lane
London
EC2N 2AB
Tel: *020 7588 2345*
Fax: *020 7826 1159*
Web site: *http://www.royal-and-sunalliance.com*

Entries

Global insurance directory 3.02.12
Global insurance directory 3.02.75

Salomon Smith Barney Inc.

UK Office
111 Buckingham Palace Road
London
SW1
Tel: *020 7721 2000*
Web site: *http://www.smithbarney.com*

Entries

UK banks: u-shaped, v-shaped or pear shaped? 2.00.12
Tenth annual global banking conference: conference themes, presentation summaries 2.02.12
Tearing down the walls: changing bank distribution 2.33.12

SBW Insurance Research

12th Floor
25 Old Broad Street
London
EC2N 1HQ
Tel: *020 7342 4050*
Fax: *020 7342 4003*

Entries

Syndicate profiles 3.25.16

Schober Direct Marketing Ltd

Field House
72 Oldfield Road
Hampton
Middlesex
TW12 2HQ
Tel: *020 8481 8720*
Fax: *020 8783 1940*

Entries

The insurance industry 3.00.16
Insurance brokers and intermediaries 3.43.16

SCOR

Immeuble SCOR
92074 Paris
La Défense Cedex
France
Tel: *+33 (0) 1 46 98 74 24*
Fax: *+33 (0) 1 46 98 77 92*
Email: *scor@scor.com*
Web site: *http://www.scor.com*

Entries

SCOR tech 3.00.08

SEP l'Assurance Française

55 rue de Châteaudun
75009 Paris
France

Entries

Lexicon: risk, insurance, reinsurance: French-English/American, English/American-French: including abbreviations, initials and tables 3.02.24

Silkscreen Publications

PO Box 1882
Brentwood
Essex
CM15 0GA
Tel: *07010 701129*
Fax: *07010 701131*
Email: *publications@countermoneylaundering.com*
Web site: *http://www.countermoneylaundering.com*

Entries

How not to be a money launderer 2.10.03

Society of Financial Advisers

20 Aldermanbury
London
EC2V 7HT
Tel: *020 8989 8464*
Fax: *020 7726 0131*
Web site: *http://www.sofa.org*

Entries

Technical adviser: the technical newsletter of the Society of Financial Advisers 1.00.31
The Society of Financial Advisers 1.00.75
Introduction to section 1.00.12

Southern Magazines

30 Cannon Street
London
EC4M 6YJ
Tel: *020 7618 3456*
Fax: *020 7618 3499*

Entries

Portfolio international: the professional's guide to investment worldwide 4.77.31

Special Libraries Association Insurance and Employee Benefits Division

C/o Paula Grande
1301 Avenue of the Americas
New York
NY 10019
United States
Tel: *+1 212 259 3229*
Fax: *+1 212 259 1310*

Entries

Insurance and employee benefits literature 3.02.26

Standard & Poor's Micropal

Commonwealth House
2 Chalkhill Road
London
W6 8DW
Tel: *020 8938 7100*
Fax: *020 8741 0929*
Email: *info@Micropal.com*
Web site: *http://www.micropal.com*

Entries

Micropal workstation 1.00.72
Standard & Poor's Micropal fund expert 1.00.72

Micropal.com 1.02.75
Standard & Poor's Micropal guide to offshore investment funds 4.77.18
Micropal directory of emerging market funds 4.78.18
Micropal emerging markets fund monitor 4.78.18

Standard & Poor's Thesys

226 Sheen Lane
London
SW14 8LD
Tel: *01473 735 959*
Fax: *01473 735 960*
Email: *info@thesys.co.uk*

Entries

Synthesys 3.00.72
EuroThesys life & non-life 3.02.72

Standard & Poor's United Kingdom

Garden House
18 Finsbury Circus
London
EC2M 7NJ
Tel: *020 7826 3800*
Fax: *020 7826 3890*

Entries

Standard & Poor's UK insurer ratings service 3.00.16
Standard & Poor's Insurance Solvency International market profiles 3.02.12
Classic ratings database 3.02.72
Standard & Poor's Lloyd's syndicate performance measures 3.25.16
European life ratings digest 3.91.16
UK life financial strength digest 3.91.16

Staple Inn Actuarial Society

Staple Inn
High Holborn
London
WC1V 7QJ
Tel: *020 7632 2100*
Fax: *020 7632 2111*

Entries

The actuary 1.07.31

Stationery Office

Publications Centre
PO Box 276
London
SW8 5DT
Tel: *0870 600 5522*
Fax: *0870 600 5533*

Entries

Competition in UK banking: report to the Chancellor of the Exchequer 2.00.09
Economic trends 2.00.31
Mortgage arrears and possessions: perspectives from borrowers, lenders and the court 2.78.09
Insurance: annual report 3.15.09

Stevens & Sons

100 Avenue Road
Swiss Cottage
London
Tel: *020 7393 7000*
Fax: *020 7393 7010*
Email: *Francine.Barsam@smlawpub.co.uk*
Web site: *http://www.smlawpub.co.uk*
Now an imprint of Sweet & Maxwell.

Entries

Arnould's Law of marine insurance and average 3.87.03

Sweet & Maxwell Ltd

100 Avenue Road
Swiss Cottage
London
Tel: *020 7393 7000*
Fax: *020 7393 7010*
Email: *sharonchong@smlawpub.co.uk*
Web site: *http://www.smlawpub.co.uk*

Entries

How the City of London works: an introduction to its financial markets 1.00.03
Moneyguide: the handbook of personal finance 1.00.05
Financial journals index 1.00.72
Encyclopedia of financial services law 1.10.07
The journal of international banking law 2.10.31

The payment system in the European Union: law and practice 2.72.03
Colinvaux's Law of insurance 3.10.03
Modern insurance law 3.10.03
MacGillivray on insurance law: relating to all risks other than marine 3.10.03
Encyclopedia of insurance law 3.10.07
The law of reinsurance in England and Bermuda 3.69.03
Riley on business interruption insurance 3.83.03
Marine insurance: law and policy 3.87.03
The law and practice of life assurance contracts 3.91.03
Life assurance law and practice 3.91.05
Collective investment schemes: the law and practice 4.72.05
Pensions: law and practice 5.00.05
International benefits yearbook 5.02.12
Sweet & Maxwell's Law of pension schemes 5.10.05
Taxation of pension schemes 5.17.03
Pensions and trusteeship: a specially commissioned report 5.46.03

Swiss Reinsurance Company

Mythenquai 50/60
PO Box 8022
Zurich
Switzerland

Swiss Reinsurance Company (UK) Limited
71–77 Leadenhall Street
London
EC3A 2PQ

Tel: *+41 1 285 21 21 (Zurich); 020 7623 3456 (London)*
Fax: *+41 1 285 29 99 (Zurich); 020 7929 4282 (London)*
Web site: *http://www.swissre.com*

Entries

The insurance report 3.00.12
Sigma 3.02.12
Swiss Re 3.02.75
Introduction to section 3.00.08

Taxbriefs

193 St John Street
London
EC1V 4QA
Tel: *020 7250 0967*

Fax: *020 7251 8867*
Email: *info@taxbriefs.co.uk*
Web site: *http://www.taxbriefs.co.uk*

Entries

The professional adviser's factfile 1.00.05
Taxbriefs report planner 1.00.07
Financial timesaver: the essential monthly newsletter for the busy financial adviser 1.00.31
Life assurance and pensions handbook 3.91.05
The facts of life and health insurance 3.91.05
Introduction to section 1.00.03

Technical Indexes Ltd

Willoughby Road
Bracknell
Berkshire
RG12 8DW
Tel: *01344 426311*
Fax: *01344 424971*
Email: *mktg@techindex.co.uk*
Web site: *http://www.techindex.co.uk*

Entries

Financial services compliance data 1.10.72

Tekron Publications Limited

PO Box 4329
Walton-on-the-Naze
Essex
CO14 8HS
Tel: *020 8597 1455*
Fax: *020 8597 1455*
Email: *norkett@tekron.co.uk*
Web site: *http://www.tekron.co.uk*

Entries

Britain's largest insurers 3.00.16

Thedata

Clinton House
142 Whitehouse Loan
Edinburgh

EH9 2AN
Tel: *0131 447 2951*
Web site: *http://www.thedata.co.uk*

Entries

Introduction to section 2.35.16
Introduction to section 2.78.16

Thesys

See Standard & Poor's Thesys.

Thomson Financial

Corporate Communications
22 Thomson Place
Boston
MA 02210
United States
Tel: *+1 617 8564 636*
Email: *tfinfo@tfn.com*
Web site: *http://www.thomsonfinancial.com*

Entries

Thomson global banking resource 2.02.72
ISIS: insurance information and statistics 3.02.72
Search2 3.02.72

Thomson Financial Insurance Solutions

Aldgate House
33 Aldgate High Street
London
EC3N 1DL
Tel: *020 7377 3456*
Fax: *020 7481 5311*
Formerly the Sedgwick Information Exchange.

Entries

Insurance M&A weekly 3.22.31
Lloyd's syndicate results: also known as Limelight 3.25.72

Thorogood Ltd

12–18 Grosvenor Gardens
London

SW1
Tel: *020 7824 8257*
Fax: *020 7730 4293*

Entries

*Effective techniques for managing and handling insurance claims: a practical
guide to handling personal and commercial claims* 3.68.03
*The pension trustee's handbook: the definitive guide to practical pension fund
trusteeship* 5.46.03

Tillinghast-Towers Perrin

Publications
Financial Centre
Suite 600
695 East Main Street
Stamford
CT 06901-2138
United States

Castlewood House
77–91 New Oxford Street
London
WC1A 1PX

Tel: *+1 203 326 5468 (US), 020 7872 0537 (UK)*
Fax: *+1 203 326 5498 (US), 020 7872 0556 (UK)*

Entries

Insurance pocket book 3.00.12
Best's captive directory 3.37.21
Motor insurance: the research report into the world's major markets 3.86.12

Timothy Benn Publishing

39 Earlham Street
Covent Garden
London
WC2H 9LD
Tel: *020 7306 7000*
Fax: *020 7306 7122*

Entries

*Post index: UK general insurance market analysis: insurers, brokers, loss adjust-
ers* 3.00.16

Special risks: the UK's comprehensive guide to specialist and bespoke policies 3.00.18
The insurance directory: the definitive guide to the insurance industry 3.00.21
Post magazine & insurance week 3.00.31
ID.se@rch gold: the insurance database on CD-ROM 3.00.72
Post magazine online: insurance information for insurance professionals 3.00.75
Professional broking: the management magazine for insurance brokers 3.43.31
Professional broking online: the management magazine for insurance brokers 3.43.75
Reinsurance: news & analysis from the world's reinsurance markets 3.69.31
Reinsurance online: news & analysis from the world's reinsurance markets 3.69.75
Fire insurance: theory and practice 3.82.03
Fire insurance: theory and practice 3.82.03
Business interruption insurance: theory and practice 3.83.03
Business interruption insurance: theory and practice 3.83.03

Tolley Publishing Co.

See Butterworths Tolley.

Training and Development Forum

C/o Chartered Insurance Institute
20 Aldermanbury
London
EC2V 7HT
Tel: *020 8989 8464*
Fax: *020 7726 0131*

Entries

Introduction to section 3.50

Turpin Distribution Services Ltd

Blackhorse Road
Letchworth
Herts
SG6 1HN
Tel: *01462 672555*
Fax: *01462 480947*

Entries

The regulation of banking in Europe 2.15.03

Unicorn Training Partnership Ltd

1 West Hill Place

Bournemouth
Dorset
BH2 5NX
Tel: *01202 316643*
Fax: *01202 316642*
Email: *info@ciitt.co.uk*
Web site: *http://www.ciitt.co.uk*

Entries

Introduction to section 1.00.72
Introduction to section 3.00.72

University of Insurance & Banking

C/o Professor Miroslaw Zdanowski
Ul Modlinska 51
03-199 Warsaw
Poland

Entries

Journal of European financial services 1.02.31

University of Nottingham Centre for Risk and Insurance Studies

School of Management and Finance
Nottingham
NG7 2RD
Tel: *0115 951 5269*
Web site: *http://www.nottingham.ac.uk/unbs/cris*

Entries

Insurance company performance: a statistical summary of the top 200 UK insurers 3.00.16
UK insurance premiums 3.00.16
Centre for Risk and Insurance Studies 3.00.75
Centre for Risk and Insurance Studies 3.00.75

Van Nostrand Reinhold

115 Fifth Avenue
New York
NY 10003
United States
Tel: *+1 212 2543232*

Entries

Banking and finance on the Internet 2.50.03

Verlag Versicherungswirtschaft GmbH

Klosestrasse 22
76137 Karlsruhe
Germany
Tel: *0721 35090*
Fax: *0721 31833*
Web site: *http://www.vvw.de*

Entries

Insurance dictionary 3.02.24
Insurance contract law 3.10.05

Warburg Dillon Read

1 Finsbury Avenue
London
EC2M 2PA
Tel: *020 7567 8000*
Fax: *020 7568 4800*
Web site: *http://www.wdr.com*
The investment banking division of UBS AG.

Entries

Introduction to section 3.00.16

Watson Wyatt

London Road
Reigate
Surrey
RH2 9PQ
Tel: *01737 241144*
Fax: *01737 241496*

Entries

Introduction to chapter 5
Introduction to section 5.00.31

Weidenfeld & Nicolson

Orion House
5 Upper St Martins Lane

London
WC2H 9EA
Tel: *020 7240 3444*
Fax: *020 7240 4822*
Email: *nac@orionbooks.co.uk*

Entries

The world's banker: the history of the house of Rothschild 2.37.03

Which? Books

2 Marylebone Road
London
NW1 4DF
Email: *books@which.net*
Web site: *http://www.which.net*

Entries

Which? way to save and invest 2001 1.00.01
Be your own financial adviser 1.00.01
The Which? guide to insurance 3.00.01
The Which? guide to pensions 5.00.01
Introduction to section 1.00.01

Wiley

Baffins Lane
Chichester
West Sussex
PO19 1UD
Tel: *01243 779777/770671*
Fax: *01243 770144*
Email: *sprice@wiley.co.uk; ferris@wiley.co.uk*

Entries

The business of investment banking 2.37.03

William M. Mercer

Telford House
14 Tothill Street
London
SW1H 9WB
Tel: *020 7222 9121*
Fax: *020 7802 3786*
Web site: *http://www.wmmercer.com*

Entries

International benefit guidelines 5.02.12
Dictionary of international benefits terminology 5.02.24
Introduction to chapter 5
Introduction to section 5.00.31

Witherby & Co. Ltd

32–36 Aylesbury Street
London
EC1R 0ET
Tel: *020 7251 5341*
Fax: *020 7251 1296*
Email: *info@witherbys.com*
Web site: *http://witherbys.com*

Entries

Insurance non-marine: an introduction 3.00.03
Witherby's dictionary of insurance 3.00.24
Captive insurance companies: establishment, operation and management 3.37.03
Treasury risk 3.62.03
Reinsurance for the beginner 3.69.03
Construction insurance: practice, law, reinsurance and risk management 3.73.03
Business interruption insurance: law and practice 3.83.03
Motor insurance: theory and practice 3.86.03
Introduction to marine insurance 3.87.03
Marine insurance 3.87.03
Reference book of marine insurance clauses: a reference book containing all institute clauses, also some UK and American clauses and forms printed by Witherby & Co Ltd, including a comprehensive index of American clauses 3.87.07
Dictionary of marine insurance terms and clauses 3.87.24
Marine insurance & reinsurance abbreviations in practice 3.87.24
Aviation insurance abbreviations, organisations and institutions 3.88.24
You sign 3.91.03

Woodhead Publishing

Woodhead Publishing Ltd
Abington Hall
Abington
Cambridge
CB1 6AH
Tel: *01223 891358*
Fax: *01223 893694*
Email: *WP@woodhead-publishing.com*

Web site: *http://www.woodhead-publishing.com*

Entries

Achieving transformation and renewal in financial services 2.50.03

World Bank

1818 H Street NW
Washington
DC 20433
United States
Tel: *+1 202 477 1234*
Web site: *http://www.worldbank.org*

Entries

Analyzing banking risk: a framework for assessing corporate governance and financial risk management 2.02.09
Introduction to section 2.02.09

Youngman, Ian

Pinewood Lodge
Grove Lane
Tasburgh
Norwich
Norfolk
NR15 1LR
Tel: *01508 470079*
Fax: *01508 471269*

Entries

Introduction to section 3.00.16

Chapter 7

Libraries

This chapter focuses on specialist libraries in the United Kingdom that are available to the public, whether free or on payment of a fee. You may not need to visit these organisations; frequently they will provide some services by post, telephone, fax, email or via a web site, although to obtain maximum benefit you may wish to visit.

There are also more general libraries that may be able to offer the information you need.

The **British Library** in London includes a **Business Information Service**, which benefits from the copyright deposit laws whereby a copy of each printed item published in the United Kingdom must be deposited with the BL. This means that in theory even the most expensive market research report will be available for reference. In practice it may well arrive too late to be of much use to you, and may never arrive at all. The BIS reading room is open to anyone needing access to business information, but all users will need first to obtain a readers' pass from the BL admissions office. You can consult the catalogue at http://blpc.bl.uk.

There are also some very large university libraries to which you may be able to gain access, possibly on payment of a fee. Some of these enjoy the same legal deposit privileges as the British Library and others are attached to universities that run financial services courses. Their catalogues may be available on the Web. The library of the **London Business School** for example has a good collection of financial services material.

In addition some large public library services run specialist business information services. The **City Business Library** in the City of London is one such example, but before attempting to contact such libraries, as opposed to visiting them, bear in mind that they are funded locally for the benefit of the local business and residential community and may be reluctant to help you over the phone or in writing.

But don't confuse business with financial services, which – in terms of the stock of such libraries – is a surprisingly small area. Many of the most useful information sources in this area are either very expensive or of a 'fugitive', semi-published nature and may well be absent from the largest business library. The specialist libraries listed below aim for depth rather than breadth and if you use them you will also benefit from staff familiar with the information sources covered by this book.

Bank of England Information Centre

Threadneedle Street
London EC2R 8AH
Tel: *020 7601 4846/4715*
Web site: *http://www.bankofengland.co.uk*
Email: *library@bankofengland.co.uk*
Hours: *9 a.m. to 5 p.m. Monday to Friday*

Availablity: *The objective of the Information Centre (IC) is to serve the staff of the Bank. However, reference facilities for research workers are available by prior arrangement with the IC Manager (when material is not readily available elsewhere). Application to use the IC must be in writing stating clearly the identity of the applicant, the nature of the research and the materials required. Please note that undergraduates are not admitted.*

The Information Centre has extensive holdings of central banks' publications from around the world, including annual reports. It has strong holdings in the history of banking and central banking as well as a collection of UK and overseas banking and finance statistics. One of the Information Centre's major strengths lies in its collection of economics and finance monographs and journals. Special collections include UK economics tracts from the 17th to the 19th centuries and 19th century government reports on banking and finance. The IC also holds a set of *The course of the Exchange* (Castaing, Shergold, Lutyens & Wetenhall) from 1698 to 1898. A collection of the Bank's own publications is also maintained.

Building Societies Association/Council of Mortgage Lenders Library

3 Savile Row
London
W1X 1AF
Tel: *020 7437 0655 (BSA); 020 7437 0075 (CML)*
Web site: *http://www.bsa.org.uk (BSA); http://www.cml.org.uk (CML)*
Email: *Simon.Rex@bsa.org.uk*
Hours: *9 a.m. to 5 p.m. Monday to Friday*

Availability: *CML and BSA members, post-graduate students and researchers by appointment only. Enquiries via telephone, post or email.*

A joint library and information service for the BSA and CML providing a comprehensive coverage of material on the building society sector, savings market, housing and mortgage markets. Also included is a collection of building society historical material and a substantial international collection (including publications from the European Mortgage Federation). Contains 200 serials, 3,000 reports and books and a BSA and CML archive of guidance, newsletters and press releases.

Services include self-service photocopying and use of the library's OPAC containing bibliographic details of books and journal articles (with abstracts) using an in-house designed thesaurus of key words. The library produces a monthly *Library bulletin* providing bibliographic details of books and journal articles, arranged by subject. Both the BSA and CML web sites contain a substantial amount of full text material such as press releases and fact sheets.

The Chartered Institute of Bankers Library and Information Service

90 Bishopsgate
London
EC2N 4DQ
Tel: *020 7444 7100*
Fax: *020 7444 7109*
Web site: *http://www.ifsis.org.uk*
Hours: *9 a.m. to 5 p.m. Monday, Wednesday and Friday; 9 a.m. to 6 p.m. Tuesday and Thursday*

Availability: *The library is open to members of the CIB using the library for personal use, members of the Association of Corporate Treasurers and members of the Securities Institute. Companies, small businesses and consultants can gain access to the library by taking out a subscription to the Business Research and Information Service (BRIS). Visitors who wish to use the library for the day can do so for a daily fee.*

The Chartered Institute of Bankers Library is a specialist banking and financial library based in the heart of the City. It holds over 30,000 books on topics such as economics, lending, financial services law, marketing and management. It contains over 200 journals on issues relating to the financial services industry, bank annual reports and a law collection.

A suite of CD-ROMs is available in the library, which include the *Financial times*, two article databases and a company information database. Self-service photocopying is available. The library's catalogue is accessible via the web site.

Chartered Insurance Institute Library

20 Aldermanbury
London
EC2V 7HY
Tel: *020 7417 4415/4416*
Fax: *020 7972 0110*
Email: *library@cii.co.uk*
Web site: *http://www.ciilo.org*
Hours: *9 a.m. to 5 p.m. Monday, Tuesday and Thursday; 10 a.m. to 5 p.m. Wednesday; 9 a.m. to 4.45 p.m. Friday*

Availability: *Open to all, admission charges payable by non-members.*

Dedicated to insurance, risk and related financial services and one of the largest libraries of its kind in the world. Subjects covered include all branches of insurance, risk management, loss prevention, civil liability, shipping, aviation, pensions, investment and other financial services. The collection is international, with extensive holdings from all parts of the world in addition to a definitive collection of UK material, which includes virtually everything ever published in the United Kingdom on insurance. There are around 20,000 monographs and over 2,000 serial titles.

Services include lending (including a postal service covering the whole of Europe), photocopying (self-service and orders) and a research and enquiry service. Lending is restricted to CII members and subscribing libraries but any individual can join the CII and any library or information unit can subscribe directly to the library. These services are supported by an extensive database, which combines a catalogue of holdings with the detailed indexing of journal articles and web sites and other web-based documents. Within the library there are several PCs providing public access to the database and to a wide range of CD-ROMs, computer-based training programs and the Internet.

The library also maintains a web service *CII Library online*, which includes full access to the database and a range of full text material; see section 3.00.75.

Institute and Faculty of Actuaries Library Services

Norwich Library
Institute of Actuaries
Napier House
4 Worcester Street

Oxford
OX1 2AW

Historical collection
Institute of Actuaries
Staple Inn Hall
High Holborn
London
WC1V 7QJ

Ross Library
Faculty of Actuaries
Maclaurin House
18 Dublin Street
Edinburgh
EH1 3PP

Tel: *01865 268 206/208 (Norwich Library); 020 7632 2114 (historical collection); 0131 240 1311 (Ross Library)*

Fax: *01865 268 211 (Norwich Library); 020 7632 2111 (historical collection); 0131 240 1313 (Ross Library)*

Email: *libraries@actuaries.org.uk*

Web site: *http://www.actuaries.org.uk*

Hours: *9 a.m. to 5 p.m. Mondays to Fridays*

Availability: *Members of the Institute and Faculty of Actuaries; non-members by arrangement.*

The combined libraries of the Institute and Faculty of Actuaries aim to serve all members of the UK actuarial profession, those studying actuarial science in UK universities, members of overseas actuarial bodies working in the United Kingdom and others undertaking research in actuarial topics. In addition to actuarial science as such and the traditional areas of life assurance and pensions, the library covers health care, corporate finance, banking and personal finance. The collection is international. The Norwich Library in Oxford houses the current collection, including reports, life tables, demographic and economic statistics, market data, journals and CD-ROMs. The library at Staple Inn in London holds a reference collection comprising the publications of the Institute and Faculty, demographic journals, European journals and a special collection of antiquarian and rare books. The Ross Library in Edinburgh comprises some 6,000 volumes, 100 serials and a small collection of antiquarian books.

The libraries provide a lending service to members and other approved borrowers, by post if required. Other services include photocopying and enquiries. A database is maintained of the holdings of the libraries together with selected journal articles. Select printouts can be provided and longer reading lists are available for purchase. The libraries intend to make the database available on the Web soon.

Subject index

Form index

Consumer guides—Banks and building societies—Building societies 2.35.01
Consumer guides—Banks and building societies—Lending 2.78.01
Consumer guides—Banks and building societies—Retail banks 2.33.01
Consumer guides—Financial services in general 1.00.01
Consumer guides—Insurance 3.00.01
Consumer guides—Investment funds 4.00.01
Consumer guides—Investment funds—Investment trusts 4.74.01
Consumer guides—Investment funds—Unit trusts 4.72.01
Consumer guides—Pensions 5.00.01
Dictionaries—Banks and building societies 2.00.24
Dictionaries—Banks and building societies—International 2.02.24
Dictionaries—Financial services in general 1.00.24
Dictionaries—Financial services in general—International 1.02.24
Dictionaries—Insurance 3.00.24
Dictionaries—Insurance—Aviation insurance 3.88.24
Dictionaries—Insurance—International 3.02.24
Dictionaries—Insurance—Life assurance 3.91.24
Dictionaries—Insurance—Marine insurance 3.87.24
Dictionaries—Pensions 5.00.24
Dictionaries—Pensions—International 5.02.24
Directories—Banks and building societies 2.00.21
Directories—Banks and building societies—Building societies 2.35.21
Directories—Banks and building societies—Law 2.10.21
Directories—Banks and building societies—Lending 2.78.21
Directories—Banks and building societies—Regulation 2.15.21
Directories—Banks and building societies—Retail banks 2.33.21
Directories—Financial services in general 1.00.21
Directories—Financial services in general—Intermediaries 1.43.21
Directories—Financial services in general—Law and regulation 1.10.21
Directories—Insurance 3.00.21
Directories—Insurance—Captive insurers 3.37.21
Directories—Insurance—Intermediaries 3.43.21
Directories—Insurance—International 3.02.21
Directories—Insurance—Lloyd's 3.25.21
Directories—Investment funds—International 4.02.21
Directories—Pensions 5.00.21
Journals—*see* Periodicals
Legislation—*see* Source materials
Looseleafs—*see* Manuals
Manuals—Banks and building societies—Building societies 2.35.05
Manuals—Banks and building societies—Law 2.10.05
Manuals—Banks and building societies—Lending 2.78.05
Manuals—Banks and building societies—Regulation 2.15.05
Manuals—Financial services in general 1.00.05

Author index

Clark, John *International dictionary of banking and finance* 1.02.24

Clark, John O. E. *Dictionary of banking terms and finance terms* 2.00.24

Clark, John O. E. *Dictionary of insurance and finance terms* 3.00.24

Clarke, Malcolm *Policies and perceptions of insurance: an introduction to insurance law* 3.10.03

Clarke, Malcolm A. *Law of insurance contracts* 3.10.03

Clarke, William M. *How the City of London works: an introduction to its financial markets* 1.00.03

Cockerell, Hugh *Witherby's dictionary of insurance* 3.00.24

Coggan, Philip *Money machine: how the City works* 1.00.03

Cole, Robert C. *Getting started in unit and investment trusts* 4.00.01

Colinvaux, Raoul *Colinvaux's Law of insurance* 3.10.03

Collins, F. W., ed. *Handbook of motor insurance* 3.86.05

Collins, Fred *Effective techniques for managing and handling insurance claims: a practical guide to handling personal and commercial claims* 3.68.03

Collins, Fred *Public liability insurance: a Hawksmere report* 3.84.03

Collins, Simon *Getting into banking and finance: how to launch a rewarding career* 2.00.02

Collinson, Fiona, Giddings, Michael and Sullivan, Malcolm *Financial products: a survival guide* 1.00.03

Cornell, Tony *Money-saving mortgages: how to take years off a mortgage and save thousands of pounds* 2.78.01

Cornett, Marcia Milton and Saunders, Anthony *Fundamentals of financial institutions management* 2.50.03

Cornick, Timothy C., et al. *Collective investment schemes: the law and practice* 4.72.05

Cotterill, Nigel Morris *How not to be a money launderer* 2.10.03

Couchman, Andy *Facts of life and health insurance* 3.91.05

Courtis, Neil, ed. *How countries supervise their banks, insurers and securities markets* 1.10.21

Crerar, Lorne D. *Banking law in Scotland* 2.10.03

Cresswell, Sir Peter, et al, general editors *Encyclopaedia of banking law* 2.10.21

Essinger, James *Virtual banking revolution: the customer, the bank and the future* 2.33.03

Fawcett, Phillip *Managing information: understanding the impact of IT on the financial services* 2.50.03

Ferguson, Niall *World's banker: the history of the house of Rothschild* 2.37.03

Field, Christopher *Future of marketing retail financial services* 2.56.12

Fitch, Thomas, P. *Dictionary of banking terms* 2.00.24

Fontaine, M., ed. *Insurance contract law* 3.10.05

Ford, Janet, et al. *Mortgage arrears and possessions: perspectives from borrowers, lenders and the court* 2.78.09

Fraser, R. D. A. and Wood, J. R. *Butterworths taxation of offshore trusts and funds* 4.77.03

Fredericq, Simon and Cousy, Herman *International encyclopaedia of laws. [Insurance law]* 3.10.05

Gaines, Robert, ed. *Pensions factbook* 5.00.05

Gamlen, Edwin H. and Francis, Harold *Fire insurance: theory and practice* 3.82.03

Gamlen, Edwin H. and Phillips, John H. P. *Business interruption insurance: theory and practice* 3.83.03

Gandy, Anthony and Chapman, Chris *Information technology and financial services: the new partnership* 2.50.03

Gapper, John and Denton, Nicholas *All that glitters: the fall of Barings* 2.37.03

Gardner, Edward and Molyneux, Philip, eds. *Investment banking: theory and practice* 2.37.03

Gilchrist, Christopher *Sunday Times personal finance guide to tax free savings: how to make your money work harder for you* 1.00.01

Gilmore, Rosalind *Mutuality for the twenty-first century* 2.35.03

Goacher, David *Monetary and financial system* 2.00.03

Goodhart, C. A. E., ed. *Emerging framework of financial regulation* 2.15.03

Green, Andrew K. C. *PMI handbook: the annual review of the private medical insurance market* 3.93.18

Greuning, Hennie van and Bratanovic, Sonja Brajovic *Analyzing banking risk: a framework for assessing corporate governance and financial risk management* 2.02.09

James, Graham *Personal finance on the Internet: a practical guide to savings, banking, investment, loans, insurance, pensions and tax* 2.00.01

Jennings, Marie *Perfect insurance: all you need to get it right first time* 3.00.01

Jess, Digby C. *Insurance of commercial risks: law and practice* 3.71.03

Jones, Steve *Banking operations: UK lending and international business* 2.78.03

Jones, Steve and Palmer, Sally *Customer services: marketing and the competitive environment* 2.56.03

Khoury, Sarkis Joseph, ed. *Advances in international banking and finance. Vol. 3* 2.02.03

King, Mervyn *Back office and beyond: a guide to procedures, settlements and risk in financial markets* 2.50.03

Kinsella, Ray, ed. *Internal controls in banking* 2.50.03

Klein, Gerald *Dictionary of banking* 2.00.24

Knight, Stephen *Art of marketing mortgages* 2.56.03

Koch, Timothy W. and MacDonald, S. Scott *Bank management* 2.50.03

Lake, Ted *Introduction to financial services: the giving of financial advice* 1.43.03

Lamont, Barclay W. *Lamont's glossary: the definitive plain English money and investment dictionary for the finance professional and money-minded consumer* 1.00.24

Largan, Mark *Introduction to law in the financial services* 2.10.03

Largan, Mark and Colley, Alan *Banking operations: regulation, practice and treasury management* 2.50.03

Lascelles, David *Europe's new banks: the "non-bank" phenomenon* 2.33.12

Leadbetter, Charles and Christie, Ian *To our mutual advantage* 2.35.03

Leonard, John D. and Sigee, Jeremy *Tenth annual global banking conference: conference themes, presentation summaries* 2.02.12

Lesobre, Jacques, Sommer, Henri and Cave, Frances J. *Lexicon: risk, insurance, reinsurance: French–English/American, English/American–French: including abbreviations, initials and tables* 3.02.24

Levine, Marshall and Wood, Jeremy *Construction insurance and UK construction contracts* 3.73.03

Lewis, Alfred and Pescetto, Gioia *EU and US banking in the 1990s* 2.02.03

Liaw, Thomas *Business of investment banking* 2.37.03

Susman, Brian, ed. *Insurance manual* 3.00.05

Talwar, Rohit, ed. *Achieving transformation and renewal in financial services* 2.50.03

Thompson, James *Marine insurance megasite: everything on the Net for ocean marine insurance professionals* 3.87.75

Ure, Alec *Tolley's Taxation of pension benefits* 5.17.03

Vaitilingam, Romesh *Financial Times guide to using the financial pages* 1.00.03

Valdez, Stephen *Introduction to global financial markets* 1.00.03

Walford, Janet *Personal pensions* 5.77.18

Walkington, Liz *Daily Telegraph guide to lump sum investment* 1.00.01

Wall, Matthew *Online retail financial services* 2.33.12

Wallis, Virginia *Which? guide to insurance* 3.00.01

Walmsley, R. M. *Business interruption insurance: law and practice* 3.83.03

Walmsley, R. M. *Claims and loss of profits insurance* 3.83.03

Walmsley, R. M. *Claims and standard fire policies, special extensions and special perils* 3.82.03

Walter, Ingo and Smith, Roy C. *Global capital markets and banking* 2.02.03

Watkins, Charley *Introduction to marketing, customer service and sales* 2.56.03

Watkins, Trevor *Marketing strategies in retail banks: current trends and future prospects* 2.56.12

Wayner, Peter *Digital cash: commerce on the net* 2.72.03

Wellings, Fred and Gibb, Alastair *Bibliography of banking histories. Vol. I, Domestic banks* 2.00.26

Wellings, Fred and Gibb, Alastair *Bibliography of banking histories. Vol. II, Savings, merchant and overseas banks* 2.37.26

West, Sally *Your taxes and savings 2000–2001: a guide for older people* 1.00.01

Whitely, John *Saving and investing: how to achieve financial security and make your money grow* 1.00.01

Whittaker, Andrew, ed. *Financial services law and practice* 1.10.07

Wicks, David, ed. *Financial adviser's factbook* 1.00.05

Winfield, R. G. and Curry, S. J. *Success in investment* 1.00.03

Wood, Jeremy, ed. *Butterworths insurance law handbook* 3.10.07

Title index

Banking operations: regulation, practice and treasury management 2.50.03

Banking operations: UK lending and international business 2.78.03

Banking revolution: salvation or slaughter?: how technology is creating winners and losers 2.50.03

Banking soundness and monetary policy: issues and experiences in the global economy 2.02.09

Banking supervisory policy 2.15.05

Banking technology 2.50.31

Banking year ahead 1999/2000: a survey sponsored by the BBA and the Financial Times 2.00.12

Banks and remedies 2.10.03

Be your own financial adviser 1.00.01

Benedict on admiralty 3.87.07

Benefits & compensation international: total remuneration and pension investment 5.02.31

Best's captive directory 3.37.21

Best's guide to Lloyd's market results & prospects 3.25.16

Best's Insight 3.00.72

Best's Insight global 3.02.72

Best's insurance reports 3.02.16

Best's key rating guide international 3.02.72

Best's Marksman 4: the Lloyd's market analysis system 3.25.72

Best's UK insurance security analysis service: ISAS 3.00.16

Bibliography of banking histories. Vol. I, Domestic banks 2.00.26

Bibliography of banking histories. Vol. II, Savings, merchant and over-seas banks 2.37.26

Biennial risk financing and insurance survey 3.64.12

Big four British banks 2.33.03

Blackstone's guide to the Bank of England Act 1998 2.39.03

Blay's Guides savings & finance 1.00.75

Bloomberg.co.uk 1.00.75

Bloomberg money 1.00.31

Micropal workstation 1.00.72

Modern banking in theory and practice 2.00.03

Modern insurance law 3.10.03

Monetary and financial system 2.00.03

Money and payment systems 2.72.75

Money extra 2.00.75

Money laundering: guidance notes for the financial sector 2.10.03

Money machine: how the City works 1.00.03

Money management: the professional's independent adviser 1.00.31

Money marketing: first for the professional financial adviser 1.00.36

Money marketing focus: the professional adviser's guide 1.00.31

Money marketing on-line 1.00.75

Money money money .co.uk 1.00.75

Money observer 1.00.31

Money shop 1.00.75

Moneyextra 1.00.75

Moneyguide: the handbook of personal finance 1.00.05

Moneynet 2.00.75

Money-saving mortgages: how to take years off a mortgage and save thousands of pounds 2.78.01

Moneyweb 1.00.75

Moneywise: Britain's best-selling personal finance magazine 1.00.31

Moneywise personal finance 1.00.75

Moneyworld 1.00.75

Moody's credit opinions. Insurance: insurance holding companies, life & health insurers, property & casualty insurers... 3.02.16

Moody's credit opinions & statistical handbook. UK life insurance 3.91.16

Moody's Investors Service. Insurance 3.02.75

Moody's Lloyd's syndicate rating guide 3.25.16

Morgan Stanley Dean Witter central bank directory 2000 2.02.12